Presence in the Pulpit

PRESENCE IN THE PULPIT

the impact of personality in preaching

HANS VAN DER GEEST

translated by Douglas W. Stott

John Knox Press
ATLANTA

Library of Congress Cataloging in Publication Data

Geest, Hans van der.
    Presence in the pulpit.
    Translation of: Du hast mich angesprochen.
    Includes bibliographical references.
    1. Preaching. 2. Clergy. I. Title.
BV4211.2.G4313   251   81-82352
ISBN 0-8042-1897-8   AACR2

© by Theologischer Verlag Zurich
English translation © copyright John Knox Press 1981

First published in German under the title *Du hast mich angesprochen* by Theologischer Verlag in Zurich in 1978
First English edition by John Knox Press in 1981
10 9 8 7 6 5 4 3 2 1
Printed in the United States of America
John Knox Press
Atlanta, Georgia 30365

Preface

Both preaching and listening in a worship service are risks. Am I as a listener truly engaged, and as a preacher, do I engage others? What do we really mean when we speak of engaging the listener?

I deal in this book with the results of more than 200 analyses of worship services and sermons, most of which took place within the framework of the pastoral counseling training in the Center for Clinical Pastoral Education in Zollikerberg. The question of *effect* stands at the beginning of all reflection within the study, so it is necessary for the participants in the worship services to reveal their reactions. It is not what the preachers intend, nor what they do and say that is decisive for the analysis of effect, but rather only what the listeners hear and register. Such an analysis offers new points of departure and impulses for homiletics, and throws new light on the question of the intention of a worship service and on what preachers should do and say. That is what I want to show in this book.

The results of these analyses make it clear that the institution of the traditional worship service is still a rich treasury. However, it is clear to me that important concerns of the gospel, such as the community of Christians, do not find expression in it. The traditional service has a strong individualizing tendency, yet any person of responsibility in the Christian congregation should remain aware that other church activities are also necessary, activities allowing people to experience deep community with one another. Nonetheless I limit myself in this study to an investigation of the traditional worship service, and even add another limitation. While I discuss both Catholic and Protestant services, the emphasis is primarily on Reformed services. I only take note of the prayers and sermon of the Catholic service. The study is thus concerned not with the traditional Catholic worship service in its entirety, but rather essentially with the Protestant tradition.

This book cannot and does not intend to change the fact that preaching is a risk. In both good and not-so-good efforts we are dependent on the breath and Spirit of God. It is a joy to know that.

I would like to thank all my colleagues who were willing to offer up under my supervision so much personal material from their work and sometimes also from their most inward depths. I especially thank those who have given me permission to publish their personal experiences.

66346

I have found a helpful counterpart in my colleague Kati Huebner, and would like to thank her for all the stimulating suggestions, reactions, and discussions. My venture into the German language was made both possible and easier countless times by another colleague, Susanne Weber-Bollnow.

Hans van der Geest, Zollikerberg/Switzerland

Contents

CHAPTER 1

Effect Analysis of Worship Service and Sermon

Presentation of an Analysis

On Wednesday evening a bell rings with uniform regularity. In the hospital garden, nurses and other employees go to the chapel where they meet others who live or work nearby. The chapel is filled, the organ plays, and the worship service begins. A young minister leads the service, and when he gives his sermon it is very quiet; everyone listens carefully.

After the service is over and the congregation has left, a small group of men and women meet for conversation. Seven of them belong to a training group working for six weeks in the hospital; they are ministers who want to improve their competence in pastoral counseling, and the minister who just delivered the sermon is one of them. Four other people stand alongside somewhat self-consciously, since they have only just been asked by the course leader to take part in this conversation; one is a nurse who works in the hospital, while three others from the town just happened to be in the chapel.

1. First Phase: Reflection

They seat themselves in the conference room in a large circle and the leader explains the purpose of the meeting: They want to discover what effect the worship service had on the listeners. Every participant will have the opportunity to tell what he or she experienced during the service, and every bit of information offered reflecting a genuine experience is welcome. This is not yet to be a discussion about whether or how the preacher might better conduct a worship service. The preacher is to hear and understand what these participants have to say now after the service. The question of their being right or wrong is at this point less important than the reaction the preacher elicited in them and how he elicited that reaction.

They now have ten minutes to reflect on what they will say.

2. Second Phase: Collection of Material

The leader first questions those not theologically trained, then the participants in the course. Each person can speak without being interrupted, and only if something is not clear can the others ask questions. The leader, however, inquires more often and writes the listeners' reactions on the blackboard in short sentences, the positive ones on the left, the negative on the right. Sometimes he speaks for a long time with a participant, and I will report some of this dialogue.

One person says that the second part of the sermon was much too long. (That is not a feeling, but rather a judgment, and the leader must help the participant get back to the feeling.) The leader asks how he felt during that second part.

> Participant: I waited for the "amen."
> Leader: Are you saying you were bored?
> P: Yes, a little bit. (The feeling is now fairly clear: boredom. Now they must discover what led to this feeling, what precipitated it.)
> L: Can you still say when that began? When were you still interested?
> P: I can't really say any more. But when words were used like "exalted Christ" and "renewal of our thinking" or things like that, I just gradually tuned out. I was still interested during the part about the sick young man.
> L: Could that mean you were interested as long as he spoke concretely, and that things changed when he began speaking in all-too-familiar abstractions?
> P: Yes, then it wasn't colorful anymore; it was just words.
> L: Are you always bored by conceptual or abstract words? Would your feeling of time have been different if he had continued speaking more concretely?
> P: Undoubtedly.
> Another participant said she found it encouraging:
> L: What? The sermon?
> P: Yes, the theme, but also the whole thing. And also the way he stood there and spoke. He recalls nice memories for me.
> L: Those are different elements: the theme—by the way, which theme?
> P: Confidence in difficult situations.
> L: But something else as well contributed to the positive effect of it on you, the way he "stood there" and "spoke." How did he stand?
> P: So calmly. He looked dependable. He's convinced of what he's saying. He spoke decisively, and that was good for me.
> L: You mean he inspired confidence by his calm, perhaps fatherly manner?
> P: Exactly. It makes me feel good to hear these things because he says them. It makes me strong, or stronger again.

By "encouraging" this listener means she liked how the preacher said old, familiar things in a persuasive way. By doing this the preacher became for her a benevolent authority.

The next participant also says "I found it encouraging."
> L: What?

P: The sermon, but not the beginning. The second half, especially when he said that God makes what is broken new again, that moved me.

L: So just that promise for what appears hopeless gave you courage.

P: Yes, he didn't paint anything too rosy; I could see my own problems in the sermon. But I wasn't able to look at him; he was too stiff for me.

The content played a more direct role for this listener than for the previous one. The same word "encouraging" now points to quite different aspects of the worship service.

One listener says he gradually became aggravated by the extolling of God. (This statement appears clear, but is still superficial because the reason for the aggravation is formulated in a comical idiom, "extolling of God"; a deeper element is almost always behind such a statement.)

L: You don't like to hear praise?

P: That's not entirely true; you can go ahead and talk about the good things, but . . .

L: When used about God it's unpleasant for you.

P: No, it's more the tone he used. (The leader's misunderstanding forces the participant to express himself more precisely.)

L: It wasn't so much the content that put you off as his tone of voice.

P: He was so deep and serious, it made me uncomfortable.

L: Can you express that more concretely: deep, serious?

P: Let me think; he looked at us so seriously, and never smiled, as if life is only a serious, dramatic affair. And his sentences—he never speaks like that at other times.

L: Can you imitate the sentences, maybe even exaggerate them for us?

P: (He does it, rather slowly and very solemnly.)

Much more was said in this session that I have not reported at length here.

3. Third Phase: Ordering the Material

After all the listeners have spoken we find the following on the blackboard. In the column of negative reactions:

—Does one have to speak so much about oneself? Embarrassing (7)
—Sometimes an almost depressing seriousness
—First prayer was too short, too fast (2)
—Loud, powerful voice was alienating
—At the end I was bored: abstract language, material too familiar (3)
—The weightiness disturbed me: reading too slow, pauses (4)
—The dramatic examples were too dramatic
—Very long
—Too many examples

—Not enough smiling
—Extolling of God was too serious, too deep, aggravated me

In the column of positive reactions:

—Encouraging: calm, dependable. Confirmation of worthy articles of
  faith
—Encouraging: Promise in the face of apparent hopelessness (5)
—Didn't paint things too rosy (2)
—Concrete, vivid examples (2)
—Dealt with the needs of everyday life (3)
—I was able to see myself in Zacchaeus (person used as example)
—Permission to doubt
—Gripping beginning
—Blessing at the end instilled confidence (4)
—Prayer after the sermon, resigned to the will of God

The non-theologically trained participants formulated the first three negative and
the first six positive statements. The number after the statements indicates how
many participants made exactly the same statement.

The leader now asks the whole group if there is a difference between the
reactions of the non-theologians and those of the students in the course. They
find no fundamental differences. The laypersons have already said everything of
importance; the group notes only that the course students gave more negative
reactions.

The leader's next question concerns which reactions were made by all or
almost all the participants. Each person thinks about the statements on the board
for a quarter hour. For various statements the participants remark that they
would not have come up directly with such-and-such a formulation, but that
actually they experienced it exactly the same way. The other person's statement
first made them aware of it; every one of the listeners agreed especially with the
word "weighty."

Either all the listeners (eleven) or almost all (ten) agree with the following
statements as reactions to the worship service:
Negative:

—The excessive use of "I" was embarrassing or disconcerting
—The weightiness was depressing
—The excessive examples were boring

Positive:

—Things weren't painted rosy; one's needs were taken seriously
—Prayer after the sermon: personal, realistic
—Word of blessing at end (recalled the sermon in the word "peace")

The leader emphasizes that not just the common statements deserve attention, but these naturally are very significant. Meanwhile almost an hour and a half has passed since the beginning of the session; they take a short break with refreshment.

4. Fourth Phase: Conversation with the Preacher

The leader then asks the preacher how he felt while listening to the statements. "What struck you, what do you want to talk about?" The preacher remarks that he is very pleased with all these attempts, and he has noticed how the participants sincerely tried to formulate their own reactions. He was pleased with the positive reactions and was especially surprised by the reactions to the concluding blessing. He never knew such simple words as "peace" could have such a great effect.

The negative remarks concern him the most, especially the references to the "weightiness." He understands the excessive use of "I" and will watch out for it; for too long he never said "I" in sermons, but now he sees that his use of it has become excessive.

The leader asks whether the participants understand why this excessive use of "I" and of the preacher's own personal experiences disturbs communication. They all agree that it's embarrassing. What happens when the listeners find the preacher embarrassing or disconcerting in this way? They find the answer: The listeners can then no longer identify with the preacher, and it seems to them he is only talking about himself. The word "exhibitionism" arises. On the other hand, without the word "I" it's often equally impossible for the listener to make that same identification. Obviously one has to find the right balance.

The preacher particularly wants to talk more about the weightiness in his delivery. The leader asks the whole group to state once more what they saw in the preacher in those moments when he seemed too weighty. He interrupts the participants who depict their own feelings ("it seemed to me like a burden pressing down more and more heavily") in order to ascertain their observations. These are collected slowly.

—His voice was unnecessarily loud
—The pauses during the reading
—All the examples he told dealt with dying, accidents, bitter disappointments, and other dramatic moments in life
—There were a lot of examples
—Some sentences progressed with unnecessary slowness; this made them emphatic
—There was never anything to loosen things up
—The sermon seemed to last a long time.

Not every listener experienced negative feelings during every one of these observations, but all the listeners did find the worship service too weighty. For certain listeners this became clear because of certain details, for other listeners because of other details.

The leader now asks to what extent this weightiness had a disturbing effect. Most reply that it wasn't so bad for them. The positive aspects outweighed the negative ones, and they as listeners would gladly go again to this minister's worship service. Others reply that the minister's manner aroused awe instead of agreement, and some even say that they suffered under the pressure of that weightiness; for them the negative recollections outweigh the positive ones. The leader asks whether it's just coincidental that these particular participants tolerated that weightiness so poorly. Laughter erupts in the circle; these are precisely the course participants who have already shown similarities. One non-theologian who also did not take to that weightiness suggests that the sermon was more for deep, serious people than for less serious people like herself. One "serious" participant suggests that just may be true, but even he would have liked a shot of lightness and cheerfulness in the service.

The preacher himself draws the conclusion when he says that his weightiness did not put off all the listeners, but that all of them would be glad for a bit less heavy manner. All the participants confirm this.

Another non-theologian remarked jokingly that she had wondered how this preacher would preach. She had already seen him a few times, and now she had been pleasantly surprised. The leader naturally doesn't let this excellent opportunity go by and finds out that she had apparently expected something bad. After a greal deal of effort they discover what this listener had expected. They find that she had associated the image of a stiff, uninteresting sermon with the serious appearance of the preacher. However, the preacher was not at all stiff and boring. His seriousness is in order and even suits him. He would not be genuine without it.

This appears to be an important observation. The preacher says, however, that it does not make things any easier. He has known for a long time that he comes across so seriously, and as a matter of fact he does not want to come across like this. And he does not want to awaken the impression of a serious, weighty preacher by his appearance. He has already struggled with this problem for some time, and now he finds that this impression disturbs his worship services even more than he suspected.

Two colleagues who have known the preacher for a long time remark that he has already made progress in this direction. His clothes have changed to a more easy-going style and he preaches less theoretically than he did a few years ago. The preacher is glad to hear these remarks and also feels that he is slowly getting away from that weighty manner. But it's all going too slowly for him and he'd like to give himself a push. He was not aware that this characteristic so strongly influences the worship service.

One participant remarks that perhaps the text he chose contributed to the seriousness of the sermon. The leader asks the preacher whether it would be all right to read the biblical passage once more. He agrees, and everyone reads the section—Luke 19:1-10. The whole group, including the preacher, notices the light, cheerful elements: the small deceiver in the tree and especially the joyous meal over against the murmuring of the people. This text in particular emphasizes how festive and joyous Jesus' deeds are. A conversation ensues about the relationship between seriousness and nonchalance in the gospel.

The leader summarizes the discussion of the weightiness. For most of the listeners what was good about the service was the serious treatment of the difficulties of life; nothing was painted too rosy. That was clear both in the sermon and the prayer. The gospel was also well-perceived, and the benediction moved everyone. What everyone missed, however, was the other side of the gospel: the lightness, the cheerfulness, and the carefree aspect. The preacher himself even missed it. Thus now the question remains: How is it possible that he comes across more seriously then he intends? Which factors in him change his conscious intentions so that he does not come across as he intends?

5. Fifth Phase: Personal Background

The leader now hesitates. Does the minister want to speak further about these extremely personal things? Yes, he does. The leader invites the group to fantasize a little: What can it be in a person that leads that person to come across much more weightily or seriously than he or she would like?

Some suggestions are made, but they do not throw much light on the matter. That other negative evaluation is then recalled: the excessive use of the word "I." The leader asks whether the group thought the sermon was really personal, and to their astonishment almost all the participants say no. The examples were, to be sure, all taken from the preacher's own life, but they seemed constructed or artificial. The group basically did not see the preacher himself in the stories.

Now things get clearer. The weightiness and the excessive use of "I" have a negative effect; both are characterized by excess. But does that hide a dearth elsewhere? The excessive use of "I" gives the impression of a personal sermon, but in reality the personal element was hidden. The excessive seriousness conceals a shortcoming. If I fear I am an insignificant person, I will try to make myself important and personal; an unconscious deception occurs. This influences the worship service in that it disturbs communication. The listeners feel uncomfortable with the seriousness and personal element precisely because it's too serious and too personal. What is in reality serious and weighty also has a lighter side, and the truly personal element does not need the constantly repeated "I."

The leader asks the preacher whether all this means anything to him. He is taken aback; it occurs to him, however, how he would really like to *play* in general, but how hard that is for him. He has become aware of a voice in him that almost always—and certainly always in the worship service—says: "Behave or you'll make a fool of yourself."

Together he and the others talk about playing and how it is in the best sense not serious and yet personal. Perhaps it does not belong to theological reflection, but it does belong to faith and to God, who made Leviathan in order to play with him (Ps. 104:26). The discussion ends in an atmosphere of looseness and fun.

6. Sixth Phase: Further Accompaniment

The leader suggests that they speak further on the following day about a reaction of one of the listeners; this listener apparently was speaking more about himself than about the service ("The sermon was good and engaged me until it got to the biblical passage; then it became colorless and boring"). He had already made the same statement about several other sermons.

On the next evening the course group meets for non-verbal encounter. There the preacher has the opportunity to take a decisive position toward his "insignificant identity," and thus to take a small step away from his excessively serious attitude toward a looseness he also needs for his work. (The results of an analysis of worship service and sermon do not always offer the opportunity to help the preacher in this way. Most of the time the preacher later speaks further with his colleague-group or alone with the course leader about the problems which have become visible from the analysis and which bother him. In general it is important that such a personal look at the preacher's problems takes place in a small, confidential group.)

The Treatment of the Material: Worship Service and Sermon as Research Object

Most of the analyses of worship services and sermons which have yielded the material for this book have been made within small groups of participants at training courses for clinical counseling. The participants were not all ministers, but most were, and most had to conduct worship services regularly in their jobs. I will later discuss the possibilities and limitations in the analyses resulting from this particular group of participants. Another problem, however, stands in the foreground for the person wanting to investigate the effect of worship service and sermon on the congregation member: In which form should the analyst or analyzing group seek out the object of research, the worship service and sermon? The previous analyses of sermons work from the printed sermon text;[1] that means a reduction down to the verbal content. This presupposition that the content of a sermon is the most essential aspect is called into question by the listener reactions described in this book.

The optimal situation for the analysis of effect is the analyzing group's personal participation in the entire worship service; then the analysts are themselves in the role of the congregation member before they observe the worship service as a research object. For some participants it takes a bit of training and familiarization in order really to take part in the worship service and not to hold themselves at a distance in the role of observers. However, because most of them regularly attend worship services as congregation members, this role is not new or unfamiliar for them.

Of course, in and for itself it is unusual for a group of theologians to attend a worship service. This possibility is present within the framework of a course, though otherwise it never occurs because most of the participants themselves have to conduct the worship service in their own congregations on Sunday. There are also training groups which only meet together now and then for a day to discuss a sermon, but the sermon has already been given without the participants in the analysis having heard it. A tape recorder or, in rare instances, a video recorder make it possible to experience at first hand a worship service and sermon. (I have personally had almost no good experiences with video recordings. The evaluation group always felt itself to be in the role of an observer. The participation is more intensive in the case of tape recordings.) It is obvious that much is lost when using these media devices; the visual element is lacking with the tape recorder, the true spatial experience with the video recorder. The worship service presentation is in addition a recording which inhibits genuine participation.

If not even a tape recorder is used, the possibilities of analysis are even more limited. The preacher can at most read a manuscript out loud, if such a manuscript even exists. In any case, the sermon is thus taken out of the larger context of the worship service, and even this sermon is offered only in an amended version: The tone of voice is now adapted to the unnaturally small group of colleagues, and thus much is lost which could be of value for the analysis. The intellectual content of the sermon now receives a proportionately larger amount of attention because other elements are suppressed. (I consider the concentration on ''sermon analysis'' already a dangerous overemphasis of the intellectual content of the sermon. The analysis will then show results influenced by the presupposition that the content is the most important element. Listeners' statements are then pre-programmed.)

The least promising situation arises when the participants in the analysis themselves read a duplicated or printed sermon. This is naturally how all previously published sermon analyses have been done, but now even the voice of the preacher is eliminated. An analysis of effect is hardly possible now, and the reduction down to the intellectual content is almost total. "A sermon one hears is 'something entirely different' from a sermon one reads." [2]

The framework of a sermon, the worship service with its various aspects, is determining and often decisive for the effect of the sermon. It is artificial for research to take the sermon out of this context. A sermon also stands in the framework of a certain time and place, and whoever reads a sermon instead of hearing it in a worship service no longer perceives the effect of this framework. Allusions which are only comprehensible at the moment are overlooked later while reading, and also the preacher's intentionally mentioning or not mentioning something can have a positive or negative effect. Later, however, one can no longer perceive that. For example, if a catastrophe has taken place shortly before, and the preacher says nothing about it, that can have a strong negative effect on many listeners. Christian Möller points out that Karl Barth's failure to mention political events in his sermons during the Hilter era was a significant factor.[3] One doesn't notice this while reading the sermons.

Only the listening congregation can optimally reflect on the worship service just experienced, and only from the perspective of concrete participation in the whole event is someone fully justified in contributing to the analysis of effect. Ernst Lerle[4] seeks assistance for the analysis of the effect of sermons in research methods and results developed by psychologists in philosophical, scientific, and medical departments or at technical universities. I find that questionable. The analysts are then not participants in worship services, but rather observers, and from the vestry they look through small window panes into the nave in order to study the faces of the people attending the service. That is voyeur behavior. The observer sees something, to be sure, but perceives only what a voyeur can perceive. The absence of inner participation influences perception; thus, the observer's own criteria determine what is seen as the reaction of congregation members. Lerle also investigates only the intellectual content of the sermon.

The Representative Value of Listeners' Reactions

A worship service and sermon affect each participating listener differently since the listeners cast their perceptions and feelings into a form determined by the reference framework in which they live. Every person has a unique reference system, a system influenced itself by the person's age and position in society, experiences in life, well-being or problems, character and relationships with other people, and by various other factors. Furthermore, the effect on the listeners is only partly a conscious one for them. Hence it is impossible to ascertain the total effect of a worship service, and every description of that effect is only partially valid.

For the preacher, however, it is not really of value to know how the worship service affected every single person there; some reactions are so influenced by the reference system of the listeners that they can have no real interpretive value for the preacher. Nonetheless, the analyses make it clear that the effect of a worship service and sermon is at least in part also representative, that it was experienced by all or nearly all the listeners in the same or a similar way. Thus we must pay attention to the distribution curve for every element in the description of the effect. A generally experienced effect suggests we are dealing with a common reference system; an individually experienced effect suggests a particularized system. That is not to say that only the effect with a large distribution curve is of interpretive value; the preacher has to know the personal background of the listener reaction before deciding whether to be influenced by that reaction. If a listener says she suffered a painful personal loss during the past week and sought consolation in the worship service, and did not find it there, this can prompt the preacher to make an important change even if only one person says this. In the future the preacher will perhaps regularly check during sermon preparation to figure in congregation members who have just suffered some personal loss. If a listener says, however, that he just wasn't always tuned into the worship service because he couldn't stop thinking about personal difficulties, then this reaction should not always be taken too seriously, particularly if staying interested in the service was not a problem for other listeners.

For the evaluation of the analysis it's important to know the distribution of the statements. The reactions with the most concentrated distribution naturally deserve the greatest attention, and here is where one discovers the most instructive surprises for the preacher.

Who should be polled? The analyses of worship service and sermon began in the courses of clinical training for pastoral care, initially without paying attention to the problem of how representative the inquiry could be. However, this question arose very quickly because the analyses yielded dramatic results appearing to be extremely significant. The obvious question was to what extent the congregation would react like the course group did. It is also decisively important to discover how the congregation reacts to the worship service since they, and not the course group, regularly attend the services. But how is one to conceive of "the congregation"?

I know of no way to poll the congregation in its entirety. One finds it extremely difficult if not totally impossible to mobilize a whole congregation or even a representative part of it for an evaluation of the worship service. The post-worship-service discussions attempted in the last few decades have not come across persuasively as having interpretive value. The participants in the discussions are not representative of the congregation without qualification, and the problem of the supervision of such a session is also difficult to solve. If the preacher leads the discussion, openness and frankness are inhibited. Most commonly, however, these discussions take place without supervision and then break down quickly because of endless observations. Extroverted participants talk on and on, while most of the others say little or nothing, and the discussion almost always centers on "themes" instead of genuine evaluation. The positive value of such discussions concerns more the exchange of congregation members' views about what was dealt with in the sermon; the value as an interpretative reaction for the preacher is severely limited.

For an open and frank discussion about the effect of a worship service one needs a great deal of trust, since it must be possible for people to say very positive as well as very negative things. One needs basically a small group for this, while the traditional worship service comprises much larger groups. Under certain circumstances the church advisory council or board can serve as such a group in which this kind of discussion is possible. I tried this when I was the minister of a clinic congregation. There were two of us there as ministers, and my colleague led the discussion of the worship service I had led; I led the discussion of his sermon. The results were valuable but few. We found that the participants hardly knew how to express themselves; this was further complicated by the fact that they scarcely were able to say anything critical.

Groups within clinical counseling training offer several noteworthy advantages as interpretive vehicles. In the first place, the participants are accustomed to articulating feelings; it requires practice to discover and know what one is experiencing, and that cannot be expected of many congregation members. It is one thing to experience something, but quite another to articulate that experience. Psychoanalysis and psychosomatic studies have shown how often people suppress their experiences, and how often they do not know what they experience. There is no reason to assume that this is any different for people attending a worship service. Whoever wants to discover the effect of a worship service must find people with the capacity to articulate their experiences. The experiences of those unable to articulate them remain diffuse and vague. Those attending a worship service do not clearly see, for example, that it's the preacher's theoretical language that has bored them; for them it simply remains a vague feeling that they "did not get much out of the sermon." Such statements are useless for an inquiry because they could refer to so many different things.

In the second place one finds that a large measure of mutual trust develops in the courses permitting a greater degree of openness. As far as I can see, these two advantages make groups within the framework of clinical counseling training—or any group fulfilling these conditions—best suited for the investigations of the effect of a worship service and sermon.

Such a group, however, also has disadvantages. For the most part these are "congregation members" who themselves often give sermons; to what extent does this color their statements? This must be determined, since there is little value in the discovery of how worship services affect theologians. Services are not meant for theologians, but rather for the congregation. The theologians' statements about their own experiences as listeners are of value only if they are representative. Another disadvantage is the non-representative educational level of the group participants in a clinical counseling training program. For the most part they are academicians, and it would be disastrous if their views caused the preacher to gear his sermon more to academicians and thus to remove himself even further from the large number of non-academic congregation members. A final disadvantage is that the evaluation group does not belong to a single congregation; it is together for only a short time (six weeks) and attends a worship service not held specifically for the group's members.

Several times I have investigated to what extent the listener reactions within the counseling group differ from the reactions of other listeners belonging to the congregation in question. The distribution of the reactions was exactly the same for both groups except for one important difference. That is, the reactions came not from just one, but rather in high density from all or almost all counseling group participants as well as from all or almost all the people in the other group. The reactions with a low distribution density were similar for both groups. The only difference was that the counselers made somewhat more negative remarks; these critical remarks, however, always represented a low density. The non-theologians also mentioned aspects of the worship service generally experienced as negative.

My thesis is that it's possible to obtain from such a group of pastoral counselors an evaluation representative of the whole congregation. It's only a matter of proper questioning; then it's possible to eliminate the theological-vocational or educational elements—i.e. that which is not representative. One does this by differentiating between spontaneous and reflected reactions. The spontaneous ones are in principle the same for theologians and laypersons; education and vocation influence only the reflected or carefully thought out reactions. It is the art of supervision that allows one to work back from the reflected statements to the spontaneous feelings. I will describe this path more precisely later.

What has astonished me is the role-playing of congregation members on the one hand and the preacher on the other. The same person in the role of a preacher has other principles, other feelings, other ideas and even another theology than in the role of someone attending a worship service. Hence it is possible to question preachers about the effect of a worship service, since they behave as congregation members themselves much differently than when they themselves preach. To be sure, their behavior as someone attending a worship service is not always conscious and is often glossed over with vocational behavior, but proper

supervision can uncover their real experience, an experience not differing fundamentally from that of other congregation members.

What we have is a situation similar to that of driving a car. A person who
drives has other ideas, other prejudices, and a different behavior than someone
who walks. And yet one can experience both roles on the same day, indeed
within the same hour. The pedestrian complains about the discourtesy of the
driver; the driver is aggravated by the unreasonable behavior of the pedestrian.
We experience the same role problem in the family, since the world appears
different to us as children and as adults; but that too can be controlled within a
single hour. Our role determines our behavior and our perceptions. Whenever
preachers attend a worship service as listeners, they fundamentally let their perceptions be determined by that listening role, just as do the other people attending the service. (This thesis does not exclude the possibility that the listener role
of the theologically trained congregation member might be layered over with
vocational thoughts. In this context many preachers must learn again how to be
a normal congregation member; then they find their way back to their actual
feelings and perceptions. The vocational layers can be separated from the experience of the worship service.) And this is the way it should be; they are then
suitable as research subjects if we wish to investigate the effect of worship service and sermon.

All the analyses of services and sermons described and used in this book
took place fairly soon after the service or its reproduction; thus they analyze
the short-term effect. There is also, however, a long-term effect about which
these analyses say nothing. I have excluded this area not because it's unimportant, but because I have found no employable method for it which promises to yield usable or accurate results. I am also not aware that investigations
have ever been done in this area; the only results we have deal with the capacity to reproduce the content of the sermon after an extended time lapse. I
don't really find it helpful to look into such studies because a sermon is not
supposed to be a transferral of knowledge. It would be equally senseless to
see whether the partners in a marriage are able to recall what they discussed a
few weeks ago. An investigation of the long-term effect of a worship service
and sermon would simply have to proceed in some other way. This is not the
concern of the present study.

Spontaneous and Reflected Reactions

The new element in the effect analyses of worship service and sermon
over against earlier analyses is that feelings, and not opinions, are the point of
departure. In previous analyses the sermons are measured against theoretical
standards. I do not intend to challenge the validity of this procedure, but one

can never find out the *effect* of a sermon in this way. One has to discover what *effect* the worship service has on the participants, especially feelings and perceptions it has elicited in them. That is no easy task. It begins with the questioning of the participants. But do they really know what they have felt or perceived? Are they capable of articulating the effect of a worship service? This is a problem too often overlooked. Between their participation in the worship service and their statements of its effect on them, the listeners unconsciously rework and reflect upon their spontaneous reactions. What they then say is not necessarily trustworthy, and if the leader of the analysis does not take note of these reflected elements, the whole analysis is distorted.

Let's take a closer look at what can happen between the feeling and perception and then the statement. The chart attempts to make this clear, and we have various stages to differentiate. For the sake of simplicity I begin with the worship service reduced to the words of the sermon. This sermon comes to the listeners from an external source; these are not the listeners' own words, and as far as they are concerned they belong to the outside world. Their hearing of the sermon is an *external perception.* Two things can happen then: Either the words affect them directly and immediately, or they are somehow detoured or warded off, and only affect them indirectly. In the first case the communication is simple and undisturbed; in the second it's complicated and disturbed. The thorough, detailed description of a situation bores a listener, but an original exegesis surprises him. Both are direct, simple, undisturbed effects. The first is negative because the preacher makes a mistake; the second is positive. The spontaneous reactions of the listener during the sermon analysis would be the following:

—The extensive description of the historical situation bored me.
—I was surprised by his exegesis.

However, it's not at all certain that the listener communicates this in this way. Now the question is whether the listener is ready and has the capacity for *inner perception.* Is he acquainted with his own interior world, with his spontaneous reactions? Does he want to communicate them? It's possible that he doesn't particularly like the preacher; perhaps his relationship with him is one of rivalry. He would then naturally be prepared to make the first statement about boredom with no hesitation, but that by no means holds true for the second statement. That statement sounds like a compliment, and the question is to what extent the listener is prepared to pay the preacher this compliment. If he is not, then he will vary that statement, perhaps even totally unconsciously:

—The clever exegetical trick appears questionable to me.

The leader of the analysis might be inclined to misunderstand this state-

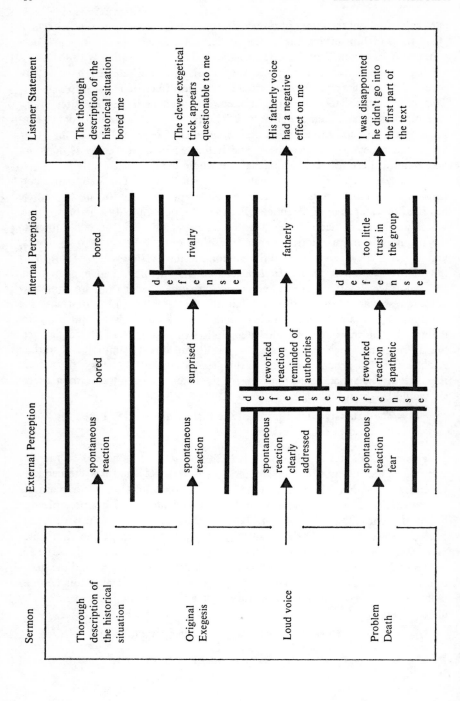

ment. Such an unclear or unusual exegesis may, of course, really have a negative effect on the listener, and it's important for the preacher to determine this. But in the above statement that plays only a minor role; in reality it is a question of group dynamics, namely rivalry. The listener says more about himself and his relationship to the preacher than about his experience of the sermon. It is essential that these things be disentangled and clarified if the analysis is to succeed, otherwise the preacher is confronted with statements which in fact do not at all concern his worship service. In the above instance the listener did not really exercise a true inner perception. His external perception was direct and immediate—one notices this to a certain extent in his statement ("clever trick")—but his internal perception is determined and structured by the rivalry.

Even the external perception can be determined in this way, and then things are even more complicated. Consider the case of a listener with an authority conflict. The preacher has a loud voice. Instead of letting herself be directly affected by it—as do the other listeners—this listener subconsciously associates it with authority. She does not just hear a voice; she senses commands and manipulation; this makes her defensive, and she will say:

—His fatherly voice had a negative effect on me.

For the analysis it is important to discover whether the preacher's voice is indeed too loud, loud enough to arouse feelings of commands or orders in several listeners, or whether only this one listener is allergic to a strong, clear voice. (See also the worship service analysis already given in which an individual participant says the biblical passage ruined the sermon. This remark led to a conversation between the group and this participant about her relationship to the Bible in general. It was clearly the listener's problem, and not the preacher's.) Or do both apply here, more or less? The interpretive material reaching the preacher must be precisely formulated here; or he will try to correct himself in the wrong area.

Things are most complicated when the external as well as the internal perception is disturbed. The statement during the analysis is totally misleading and useless in its given form because the spontaneous feeling and perception has been twice reworked. A listener, for example, has a great fear of the topic of death. As soon as he is confronted with it he becomes so afraid that he closes himself off inwardly. The spontaneous feeling is fear, but since it's too threatening for him to admit that to himself, he suppresses it immediately. He becomes apathetic, loses interest in the sermon and is bored. Let's assume he's vaguely aware that he always loses interest when the topic is death. But now his inner perception is **further** disturbed because he doesn't trust the collective group enough to articulate the unpleasant feelings. He does not say:

> —I became apathetic when the topic was death; that topic is unpleasant for me.

Instead, he reworks his feeling which has already been reworked and restructured during the external perception; he now says:

> —I was disappointed he didn't go into the first part of the text further.

It is a rather common mistake of sermons not to pick up on the expectations aroused by the reading of a text. But in this case it would be totally erroneous to suggest that the preacher pay more attention to the effect of the reading of the text, since the listener—without knowing it himself—means something entirely different.

Thus three of the four possibilities are traps. The participants in an experienced group slowly learn to discover and articulate their real feelings and perceptions, though the possibility of distortion is always there. The analysis makes clear how strongly participants have listened from the perspective of their own particular worlds, and how strongly those personal reference systems determine their perception. For this reason the analysis of the worship service is an exciting procedure for the listeners as well, since they can find out how others experienced the same service partly in agreement, partly in a different manner than they. It becomes emphatically clear how selectively every person experiences, sees, and hears.

What is particularly tedious in the analysis is the tendency of the listeners to give judgments instead of feelings. If the internal perception is disturbed, the listeners often speak of the preacher instead of themselves when they report their reactions. Instead of relating what they personally experienced ("I was bored") they project the difficulty onto the preacher; for example: "She chose an impossible topic." Here we find a problem similar to that in partner conflicts. Most arguments begin with one partner trying to make clear to the other not what is going on inside himself or herself, but rather inside that other partner; this judgmental behavior escalates the difficulties in communication. Recovery of that communication occurs only by means of the "I"-message: telling what is going on inside oneself. This is precisely the situation in an analysis of a worship service and sermon, since here, too, we must sharply differentiate between feeling or perception and evaluating judgment. We can only perceive what we feel ourselves; perceiving does not include judging others. We cannot feel what another person does, says or is; we can have an opinion, a suspicion, or a fantasy about others, but not a direct feeling or perception.

The difference between "I think" and "I feel, I have the feeling" is decisive in this context. We are ourselves responsible for what we think or find to be the case, but not for what we feel *or* perceive as a feeling, since feeling is our spontaneous, natural reaction to stimuli from outside us, a direct perception of the external world. I am only responsible for the extent to which I communicate my feelings, not for the fact that I have them or for how I have them. A familiar trick is for one person to rebuke another by beginning with "I feel"; the tricky part is that a personal opinion for which I am personally responsible is presented as if it were felt (perceived as feeling), thus as necessary and valid. The responsibility is thus shifted from one person to another. No analysis leader should permit such devices:

—I have the feeling he's an authoritarian preacher.
—I feel she has a soft voice.
—I felt it was too short.

"I felt I was treated in an authoritarian manner" is not the manifestation of a feeling. With the word "authoritarian" the listener evaluates the preacher, but says nothing about his or her own experience. This person probably wants to say he or she felt treated like a child, and now one can try to find out what elicited this feeling. Perhaps an authoritarian characteristic of the preacher aroused it, perhaps something else; this is what should be investigated. The situation is similar when we read how someone "felt the address was arrogant." The listener "finds" or "considers" it arrogant! What was felt is not clear.

It is clear one can only with difficulty demand that everyday speech use an exact terminology; we are not concerned, however, with linguistic perfection here. We are concerned with differentiating between evaluations for which one is responsible on the one hand, and feelings one has without being responsible for them on the other. Only the latter are a firm basis for the analysis of effect.

Genuine feelings are always valid because they are genuine. One can, however, discuss evaluations or judgments attached to these feelings, since the real feelings are often hidden behind judgments and evaluations; they must be separated out. Thus the feeling of being swept along by one's own thoughts and diverted from the sermon often appears in statements such as "I found him too drawn out" or "she didn't adequately pick up on the text's possibilities." With theologians the leader often has to fight against attempts to start an exegetical-theoretical or dogmatic discussion, especially at the beginning of a course. Statements such as "the preacher overlooked the synoptic parallels" or "after Moltmann one can't talk about hope like that any more" are worthless for the analysis in this form. The leader must try to get through in the conversation to the particular listener's spontaneous reactions, for example: "I waited for the synoptic parallels and then was disappointed that she didn't go into them" and "I had the impression of being a better theologian than he is; I felt superior."

An analysis of worship service and sermon is thus first of all an analysis of listeners' statements. They must be cleansed of reworking and variation so that the original, spontaneous reactions become clear. The preacher can do the most with these.

But it's not enough simply to ascertain the listener's feelings; one must also know what elicited them. This, too, often requires a tedious search. In the analysis given at the beginning of this chapter we see how different the intentions were of similar statements such as "I found it encouraging." A participant says in an uncleansed statement, "I found him too drawn out"; he then discovers in a discussion with the preacher that a gripping image had led him into his own thoughts, or discovers that the abstract language taxed him too much mentally; the listener's cleansed statement is now: "The gripping image led me into my own thoughts and associations; I didn't find my way back to the sermon any more" or similar. This statement stands clearly in the context of his feeling and is for this reason of use to the preacher.

But even if a listener's feeling is clear, his or her statement may not be. A reaction such as "the vagueness mixed me up" tells us, of course, what the listener experienced. What elicited it, however, is not clear. What is meant by "vague"? What did the listener observe? Listeners have the tendency to hide their observations in images.

—It was like a high-altitude flight; I was dizzy.
—A glass wall was between the preacher and me.

A listener's statement becomes useful for the preacher only when it's clear what behavior or words led to the effect the listener describes. The analysis is fruitful only when one succeeds in exactly identifying the two quantities: *cause* (in the sermon) and *feeling* (in the listener).

The Discovery of Communication and Its Disruptions

The leader has collected and arranged the statements with the other participants before the preacher himself enters the analysis discussions. Two categories of statements emerge, positive and negative, and it is decisively important that the distinction be made clear between ones made only individually and those occurring more commonly.

The value of the positive statements is that they show to what extent and how the communication between sermon and congregation has come about. (How to evaluate that is another question. A successful communication can in and for itself be illegitimate or questionable. False prophets are unfortunately capable of splendid communication. The effect analysis of worship service and sermon described here does not guarantee that this will be discovered, since standards other than direct experience are necessary for that. For this reason the effect analysis can never claim to offer preachers everything they need; every preacher also needs an exegetical and dogmatic self-corrective.) This is instructive for the vocational preachers among the participants. No theory is offered here which still needs to be put into practice; here it becomes clear which behavior reaches and engages the listener.

The negative statements are more exciting. The reactions occurring with a high frequency show where and why the communication between preacher and listeners has not succeeded. Most of the time the summarized negative statements point to effects not intended by the preacher. (If they are intended, for example, as shock effect, then we apparently have a difference of opinion between listeners and preacher about the purpose and meaning of a worship service. A theological discussion is then necessary. "What are the prerequisite conditions under which a preacher should use shock effect? Are they met here? In what way is shock effect appropriate?" Such questions must be discussed; that can happen now in a meaningful way since the objective problem is not a disguise for personal problems. If that were the case, it would have emerged already in the second and third phase of the sermon analysis and would have become the topic of discussion.) Now it becomes clear: Unconscious factors not under the control of the preacher have influenced the structure of the worship service and sermon. Now we must discover these factors. That is a highly personal and sometimes painful procedure. The leader must have a fine sense here for what is appropriate and promising and what is not. Exposure is abominable in an atmosphere without adequate trust, but is beneficial and helpful wherever there is loving trust, understanding, empathy and respect. Some even suggest that a sermon analysis outside a supervised group procedure is irresponsible. If the preacher indicates (sometimes only non-verbally) a desire not to go any further, the leader must concede even if he or she would like to penetrate more deeply.

The preacher is almost always highly motivated to better self-understanding and to discovery of the source of the disruptions exposed in the worship service communication. This attitude is sure to benefit a deeper analysis; the preacher won't defend himself or herself even if there is reason to do so, but will always first try to understand what statements or what manner of presentation elicited certain negative reactions in the listeners. The analysis will threaten to collapse as soon as the preacher defends himself or herself against the listeners as if they had reacted in the wrong way; then a discussion about what should be replaces the conversation about the preacher. It is especially unfortunate if individual listeners perhaps also feel hurt by the statements and then try to come to the support of the preacher. The analysis leader must try to avoid these developments.

Various methods enable the leader and group together with the preacher to get closer to the source of the disruption in communication, but it's always a touchy process. It's helpful if the group already knows the preacher to a certain extent, since it can then see parallels between the behavior ascertained during the sermon and this person's general behavior.

One possible access to the preacher's personal problem is to assume that he or she unconsciously intended the listeners' negative reactions which have shown up in the discussion. This implies that there are unknown but very effective impulses in the preacher which intentionally, if unconsciously, lead to this kind of sermon evaluation given by the group. That means that a positive evaluation would be basically even more threatening for the preacher than the negative one which is in fact received.

Of course that seems like nonsense. Who wants to come across negatively? The impulses of a personality, however, have their own ethic which is often not apparent for our conscious reflection. The analysis given at the beginning of this chapter shows a clear example of this. The preacher comes across too seriously and heavily. He finds that unpleasant because it's a negative response. But he has an even greater, unconscious fear of coming across more loosely since for his experience that is associated with the shame of being banal. Thus he achieves, or rather, the unconscious forces in him achieve exactly what they want: The listeners are greatly impressed and it never occurs to them that the preacher could not be this serious and heavy. But these forces or impulses in the preacher did not figure that the listeners would suffer under this desired weightiness! This negative response now becomes the key to the personal problem of the preacher. Precisely this negative effect yields the means by which the preacher can be helped.

The preacher is invited to think along with the whole group when it searches for the benefits or "fruits of the sickness" from the negatively evaluated effects. The discoveries now made are the most impressive ones of the entire analysis. A personality, a whole, cohesive system of coming to terms with life can become visible. Tears and humor, fear and astonishment, but above all relief because of sudden insight—all this can emerge. It also becomes clear why the preacher had the effect which showed up in the listeners' reactions. The listeners then understand their own reactions better, or they even understand them for the first time. Many sermon analyses repeatedly show how listeners come to understand their own reactions with a certain degree of astonishment as soon as the problems which have hindered the preacher become clear.

God does not always give us the opportunity for this kind of deep, personal conversation. Then the analysis must remain more on the surface. Even if the preacher says nothing, it is still helpful for him or her to listen to the reactions of others to the worship service; the really promising work, however, lies in the depth of the personality. There the great questions of faith in Jesus Christ are unavoidably posed to the preacher.

The listeners can also have important experiences. The remarks about the effect made by a particular individual can become the springboard for a meaningful discussion about faith. It is possible that this listener has disclosed a great deal about some personal problems without being aware of it. The listener's external or internal perception is then probably disrupted as I showed already above. A good group notices this and under certain conditions picks up on it.

The speculative answer to the question of how the preacher could have structured certain parts of the service or sermon differently or better can often show the preacher very clearly what the listeners found missing; it can also show in what direction a corrective might be found. When colleagues offer suggestions for improvement at the end of an analysis, the preacher very often has an "aha" experience.

The Task of the Analysis Leader

All the analyses of worship services and sermons used as the basis for this book took place within the framework of clinical pastoral education. It would be possible to investigate the effect of worship service and sermon with other methods and from other contexts. A few prerequisites, however, which are decisive in any analysis procedure, are associated with this task of discovering the effect. I have described these conditions in the previous sections, but the question remains concerning the function of the analysis leader. In clinical pastoral education the function is already determined to a certain extent by the nature of this training. In the analysis of worship service and sermon, the nature of the leader's role as it normally occurs in this training is adapted in a special way appropriate to the topic.

The analyses of worship services did not emerge because of a homiletical interest, but because of a general interest in the ministers taking part in the course; for this reason I will begin the description of the task of the analysis leader by explaining that function within the framework of clinical pastoral education. Afterwards I will mention which elements of that function are necessary for the homiletical concern and which are still missing.

The leader of a course in Clinical Pastoral Education offers supervision. "Supervision" means a certain kind of vocational training. The supervisor helps the course participants to perform their work competently; the pupils should become specialists. It is not a matter of technical ability, but rather of the development of vocational identity such that they personally invest themselves in the performance of their work. Pupils should acquire access to themselves in their work. A personal development and change is necessary for this kind of learning.

In this kind of training we do not simply teach principles and rules. The course participants learn, but do so with internal understanding and are themselves also responsible for their learning. The goal is for pastors to notice in the training just how they apply themselves to their vocation and what effect that has on others. By means of analysis of and reflection on their work, for example pastoral counseling visits, it becomes clear where their strengths and weaknesses lie. The group of colleagues serves as a response mechanism. The relationship to these colleagues and to the course leader is of decisive significance and forms an important part of the learning material; the vocational problems of course participants recur or are reflected in these group relationships.

The supervisor normally does not tell participants how they should do their work, but tries to help them find their own ways.

This implies the following for the supervision of the worship service analyses:

1. The supervisor must help the preacher discover how he or she really comes across and what effect this produces. The response cannot come from the discussion contributions of a congregation member who was visited, as in a pastoral counseling discussion, since no conversation is conducted in a worship service. The response comes now from listeners who are questioned. As I have already explained, it is essential that the listeners' reactions are cleansed, essential that one ascertain exactly which elements or characteristics of the preacher elicited which reactions. The supervisor must guide the listeners to fulfill these prerequisites to the extent that they do not already do it themselves.

2. The supervisor must see to it that the conversation between preacher and colleagues/listeners progresses in an orderly fashion. Most of the time this means the supervisor must give rather energetic leadership to the discussion. This person must have a sense for where and how to make a move if the group doesn't follow up on important topics or gets away from the focus on this one preacher. He or she will often have to offer unambiguous help so that the discussion participants can understand each other better.

3. The supervisor must notice when the analysis results point to personal problems of the preacher. With or without the group the preacher should be able to find out how technical or theological phenomena (such as speaking too fast) are rooted in an attitude toward life. One must decide according to the capacity of the preacher and the level of trust in the training group what should be discussed in the group, what in a personal conversation, and what should not be discussed at all. It should be clear that the supervisor has a great responsibility here.

4. The supervisor should be sensitive to the group dynamic developments during the analysis. Compliments and criticisms are often directed at the person and not at the subject matter. By the way, that is not unrealistic. Many people in a worship service let their relationship to the preacher influence their experience of the service. Ernst Lerle points to this when he calls the "static contact" the first component of the communicative act. The static contact is "a condition built up over a period of time in community work, pastoral counseling, and in sermons. It influences . . . the listener-resonance." [5] (The actual phenomenon

of contact during a sermon should not be investigated an an entity separate from this group dynamic condition.)

5. The supervisor must be schooled homiletically in order to give the preacher and other course participants insights into the various contexts, and to give them an exact description of the problems as well as references to the current discussion. The supervisor should not, however, explain how the preacher should preach, but should help the preacher find his or her own way.

An important practical problem concerns which questions the supervisor should ask. Questions are in any case one of the most important tools in supervision, so a question's content carries decisive significance. With these questions the supervisor enables the course participants to become conscious of certain problems, attitudes, intentions, and emotions. One thing is the same in all analyses: the beginning. What does the supervisor ask the listener? That is to say: To what does the supervisor direct the listener's attention? It does not appear to me to be very useful to reflect on the questions the supervisor ought to ask during the further progress of the analysis; every analysis necessarily progresses in its own unique way.

I find the least suggestive questions to be the most promising ones if the effect of a worship service is to be investigated. We are investigating the effect of a worship service, so the question will sound like this:

—What effect did the worship service have on you?

The persons questioned now have the freedom to bring out the areas and dimensions of the worship service occurrence which became important for them as they listened. Maybe they will speak about deep feelings aroused or not aroused, maybe about the message which either did or did not engage them, or about a few individual moments still strong in their memories.

Ernst Lerle has done important work in his sermon-resonance research. He correctly points out that the exploratory questions should not suggest to the listeners an improper critical attitude toward the sermon, and I would only add that this condition applies much more broadly. The exploration should even leave the listeners the choice of what part of the service phenomenon they wish to address. Lerle investigates basically only the content of the sermon, but by doing so he imputes to the listeners that the content must be as important to them as to the questioner. Many people attending worship services, however, experience sermons differently. One also sometimes finds similar imputations in circles of clinical pastoral education. Some leaders ask the listeners:

—What kind of message did the sermon convey to me?
—First of all we want to concentrate on what we like in the sermon.

It's clear to me that these questions direct the listeners' attention to important aspects and areas. But the danger is great that these areas then appear more important in the analysis than in the actual experience. What some suggest in the way of questions is nothing less than a subjective homiletical system which is forced on the listener. In this way the analysis falls back into a theoretical content analysis; this is valuable, but it is not an effect analysis.

The intention of discovering the effect of the worship service and sermon is better served by the following question:

—Just tell what happened to you while listening to the sermon.

This question leads the listener to relate in which areas of experience he has been moved. This requires of the analysis leader a flexibility in taking these areas seriously, even if he himself experienced the worship service quite differently or was engaged in other areas.

It can be very instructive if the analysis leader finds it helpful to direct the attention of the questioned listeners to particular areas, for example, to the content of the sermon, the relationships between sermon and text, the language, or the relationship between the preacher and certain listeners (sick people, for example). The leader simply must remain aware that doing this programs the reactions and thus prevents discovery of the spontaneous effect. The significance of an area rises with a question envisioning this area.

The discussion during the further progress of the worship service analysis most of the time demands a very great presence, much caution, and also a bit of dexterity from the analysis leader. The analysis is a success only if the preacher and analysis participants are open and personal. An intensive bond between preacher and colleagues grows especially in longer, six-week courses, and releases an open sharing of joy and temptation in faith in Jesus Christ. It becomes apparent to many participants that the power of the Lord himself, present in the experience of the worship service, also makes possible this common exchange of views on an existential level. It is especially the "communion of saints" which the course participants long remember. For many this kindles the desire to speak regularly with colleagues in this or a similar way, to speak about sermon and worship service, about faith, and about God.

Results of the Analyses

In this book I investigate the results of analyses of more than 200 worship services and sermons. These results encompass many different things: the listener statements, the discussions with the preachers, and the effects on the development of these preachers.

The listener statements are subjective and therefore not a dependable statement about the effect of the worship service. It would be senseless to study the effect of sermons on individual listeners. I will use only those listener statements made by all or nearly all the questioned listeners. In the analysis itself this differentiation between commonly experienced reactions and reactions emerging in only a few or even a single person is decisively important. Although statements made by only one listener can also be significant, I do not consider them here. When I make an exception to this rule I will present the statement *in brackets*.

As already shown in a sample analysis, a double list of statements appears at the end of the questioning of the listeners, a positive one and negative one. In both lists the ubiquitous reactions, i.e., the ones experienced by all or all but one of the participants, are emphasized. I will work in this book on the basis of these reactions set off from the rest, and would like thus to attain a certain degree of universality. One can assume for every statement given without brackets that the service or sermon concerned would elicit that statement in most of the listeners.

The exact formulation of a listener's reaction is, of course, always unique. In a strict sense there are no statements made by listeners in exactly the same way. But the statements are often so similar that I think it permissible to consider them one. Whether I am right on this point cannot be subsequently proven. I always had the course group as a corrective; in every case I let them decide whether a statement in the described sense could be considered generally valid. Often one of several listener statements was then chosen as a summary of similar reactions; often it seemed necessary to formulate a new summary.

I no doubt cannot offer pure objectivity in this undertaking. As far as seemed possible for me, I have tried to register the statements independently of my own feelings and convictions. I gladly recognize as a possible limitation of the value of this investigation the fact that I have not entirely been able to avoid personal influence on my part, even though the attempt to do so succeeded otherwise. I can't get out of my own skin, nor do I wish to. I never expected better results from a more precise registration or greater objectivity. Whoever is interested in my investigations must accept encountering not only the pure effect of worship services, but also me here and there, the analysis leader and author.

I could now list one after the other, chronologically or alphabetically, the listener reactions which were ubiquitous in the described sense. I will forego this. In the next three chapters I will present them in an order I chose myself. Whoever wants a whole list must do this himself. It appears more sensible to me to explain my own ordering of them.

While comparing and ordering these listener reactions with the highest density distribution I noticed the following:

1. The most frequent and strongest statements focus in one way or another on the theme "personal." The strongest wish among the needs of the listeners is for the worship service and sermon to be personal.

2. A second central concern of the people in the worship service is to be offered release or deliverance. A large number of listener statements deal with this topic. The listeners want to be released from pressure. If the sermon makes legal demands, they go on the defensive.

3. The rest of the statements can be summarized under the theme of knowing and understanding. It's important to most listeners that the worship service and especially the sermon guide them to insights into the existential problems of their lives.

This is the order which spontaneously occurred to me. Subsequent reflection led me to differentiate three dimensions in the experience of a worship service corresponding to these three summarizations.

Three Dimensions in the Experience of a Worship Service

Whoever wishes to bring together and systematically discuss the various elements important in a worship service must come up with some kind of order. The myriad divisions in the many homiletical textbooks show just how many variations are available. My own discussion of the problems of sermon and worship service finds its point of departure in the analysis of their effect. This point of departure determines the order for the themes I intend to discuss. There are, of course, several other possibilities of systematization along these lines, and the one I have here chosen simply intends to meet the demand that the experience of the worship service listeners be the point of departure for our reflections.

I have used the word "personal" to point to what surprised me most in the effect analyses of worship service and sermon. It is the discovery that the content of what is said is much less important for the process of engaging the listeners than most of the homiletics textbooks claim, with the exception of Otto Haendler's book. The participants are most deeply moved, most glad and most thankful for the worship service when the preacher has awakened in them a feeling of trust and security. The content of the words spoken is not an unimportant element in the occurrence of this feeling of security, but neither is it the only element, and often not even the most important. The more deeply the listeners feel themselves engaged and spoken to, the more security they experience in the service. This leads me to consider first the dimension of security as deserving attention in our evaluation of the results of the analyses. This dimension of security cannot, however, be considered by itself. No feeling of security arises without the consideration of the other dimensions still to be named. It is only for the sake of a theoretical overview that I present the dimensions separately here.

Security remains primitive and infantile without a second dimension already alluded to by the terms "pressure" and "release." I call it *the dimension of deliverance*. Adults feel truly spoken to or addressed when their daily reality is taken into consideration, when they come to a perspective on it which they just can't see with their own eyes, when new courage arises again to live on even in the face of serious danger. This is where the security experienced in a worship service is different from the intoxication given by things such as alcohol, drugs, or fanaticism. Deliverance shows that it is not only old, familiar things which give peace. It is simultaneously that which is new letting one hope again. Only in the context of the dimension of deliverance does that of security become effective.

A third and final series of analysis results points to the *dimension of understanding*, without which a sermon cannot engage a listener. Those in a worship service do not just come to church with their need for security; they also have their questions, their skepticism, their temptation. If they don't feel those taken seriously, then they don't feel spoken to or addressed and there is no trust or joy. The proclamation is not or is no longer as perfectly clear as (perhaps) for past generations. They want to get to know it anew, really anew, and that includes consideration of their justified and understandable reservations.

These three dimensions cannot be separated; in the worship service event they are a unity. There is admittedly a security without release, but it is an infantile security addressing only immature people; and without understanding, it is naïve. Release without security is irrelevant; release without understanding is not dependable. Understanding without security is impersonal; without release it is sterile. The three dimensions are intimately related. They are variations of the trio of love, hope and faith. The fact that love is first here is probably because I take my cue from the experiences of the listeners, and not from the other side, from the mandate of proclamation. "The greatest of these" is, after all, love; thus it has the greatest effect.

In the analyses of worship services and sermons I have noticed that the engagement and address of the listener only happens when the preacher does justice to all three dimensions discussed. I now intend to investigate these areas more closely on the basis of the results from the analyses.

The three dimensions are not individually identifiable in a worship service or sermon. One dimension may be more clearly recognizable in certain places than the others, but basically they are serviceable only in subsequent reflection; they are theoretical aids for comprehending something of the more complex reality. The individual homiletical areas of concern also cannot always be unequivocally identified with a particular dimension. The boundaries are not sharply drawn. I believe one does justice to reality better in that way than with a compartmentalized categorization.

Is such a method of procedure normative which does not proceed from the mandate of God or from a theological grounding of the proclamation, but rather from the reactions of the congregation? Does it not just describe how a preacher can satisfy the people? Does this book belong in theology or in recruiting technology?

That which becomes visible in the listener statements does not in itself suffice as a basis for homiletics. A worship service is not just supposed to satisfy the needs of its congregation. The listeners' statements have, however, a great value as response. It's not just primitive or, for that matter, illegitimate wishes alive in them, but also expectations awakened by worship services in the past and still alive. At least in part these expectations are a reflection of what a worship service and sermon intend to mean to a congregation. To ascertain this meaning is not so simple. Who may really say what effect a worship service should have? Who has the right to formulate rules here? Two different categories of people come into question as being justified: the preachers and the listeners. Normally homiletics asks only the preacher, or, more precisely, a preacher. Homiletics is normally written by a theologian who preaches. The writer naturally will refer to the Bible and to theology, but the perspective is one-sidedly the pulpit. The significance and thus also the basis and program of the sermon are formulated from the perspective of the mandate of proclamation; this means the theologian also formulates the focus and task of the preacher. The one-sidedness lies in the fact that a homiletics originating in this way—in spite of the use of biblical passages—is subjective and oriented toward the role of the preacher. I seek the other path in this book. The listener should have the opportunity to say how the rules, the program and the bases of the worship service should be.

From the role of the listener the whole then looks somewhat different, though testing is necessary here as well. Just as the sentences of the pulpit homiletics, the expectations of the congregation must be tested for their realization potential and for their legitimacy.

CHAPTER 2

The Dimension of Security

A formulation often used by listeners to indicate what they experienced in the worship service and sermon is the expression: "I felt spoken to," "It spoke to me," or the very personal "You spoke to me." People going to a worship service can naturally mean this statement with various degrees of seriousness. The experience indicated by it can be relatively superficial or intensive; it is at any rate positive. If this experience does not happen during the service, the listeners are disappointed. It is an unquestioned expectation for them that this engagement should happen and that the preacher should carry some of the responsibility for it.

What exactly is meant by "engagement" or "being spoken to"? I believe what is meant here has several levels. I will supplement this general statement with some others bringing to expression either an equally positive experience or disappointment in its absence; what has happened will thus become clearer.

—The sermon really took me along with it.
—I found it interesting, but it didn't hit home with me.
—I remained cold.
—Wherever I was surprised I felt well, elevated, cheerful. The crust of worries and cares fell away; I found my trust in God again.
—[Sometimes a splendid, warm air came: "God is doing it."]
—The closing part awoke trust in me.
—The whole thing settled me down.
—His clear, slow voice gave me the feeling: "It's good like this" (funeral sermon).
—The image of the mountain lake really struck me; I didn't want to get away from it.
—[Mentally I was absent, but it was pleasant to see him (the preacher) and to hear his voice.]
—[I felt encouraged again. It was nice to see that song afterwards; I didn't feel alone anymore. It really picked me up.]

Some of what was said about the preacher's voice also belongs in this context:

—So decisive.
—Warm and guiding.

—Engaging, dependable.
—Convincing.

This collection, which could yet be supplemented even further, shows some noticeable phenomena.

1. The description "warm" or "cold" appears several times.

2. A positive attitude is often expressed diffusely: "really well," "cheerful," "splendid," "good like this," "pleasant."

3. Some words betray a hidden relationship to the feeling: "taken along," "hit home," "elevated," "struck."

4. Qualifiers are listed which normally are used for parents and other intimate authorities: "guide," "engaging," "dependable."

5. The most important feelings aroused are: trust, courage, peace, and the feeling of no longer being alone.

From these statements we can conclude that the listeners let themselves be moved in the deeper levels of their personality. If they do not feel spoken to there, they experience it as a lack, a disappointment. Obviously they hope the worship service will touch them in their depth; even the deepest experiential level becomes visible in the statements presented. The oldest longing of human beings is the yearning for security. Security is the first thing a person must experience in this world in order to survive at all. Even when we experience security later, it always gives us a strong positive feeling. Whenever we expect it but don't get it, it's a painful disappointment. The deepest human perplexity lies in the dynamics of security and insecurity.

The tension between security and insecurity, between primal trust and primal mistrust, first comes to us in the first period of life, in the oral phase. This explains why we have the tendency to indicate experiences of security with words and images pointing back to the first phase of life. The five phenomena presented in the statements above are to be understood in this way. They show that people in a worship service expect to be spoken to in the deepest, oral level of experience. They figure on the religious experience reaching this deepest level of experience. "You spoke to me" means then: "You strengthened, confirmed, renewed my feeling of security, my trust." In this chapter I deal with this deepest level of being engaged or spoken to.

Basic Trust and Its Continual Need for Renewal

Our deepest feelings are also our oldest feelings. The existential questions are the ones we encounter as soon as we see the light of life. There are no problems for us in the womb. We didn't have to decide whether we really wanted to live or not until we had become physiologically independent and had to experience disinclination, hunger, misery, waiting and anxiety for the first time. After we had biologically arrived in the world, the question had to be answered whether or not we now wanted to affirm the life we had received, the "existential birth." The psychiatrist Ronald D. Laing[1] uses this expression. He maintains that the existential birth is the foundation for the feeling of being a real person, a living and continuous personality. The existential birth means the emergence of a fundamental or ontological security. Wherever this is missing, psychotic behavior results.

The existential birth follows upon the biological birth only when the newborn person feels well and secure enough in the alien world. If the person feels only insecurity and discomfort, he or she will become defensive against life and will die. Continuing to live presupposes the fundamental confidence that the future will bring good things. Thus the human will is included in things from the beginning, even if not always completely consciously. This will to life is awakened and strengthened by the warm, dependable behavior of the mother or her representative. The normal course of things is that the child very quickly affirms life because of the positive relationship to its mother and then develops in a healthy fashion. This child has acquired a feeling of primal or basic trust. (The psychoanalyst Erik H. Erikson[2] coined this expression. He calls this primal trust the "cornerstone of the healthy personality." It is a basic feeling diffusely permeating a person's exterior and interior, consciously and unconsciously. There are several dimensions of basic trust: conscious experience, behavior, and unconscious inner conditions. Basic trust is a matter of the positive attitude to oneself and to the world. A healthy measure of basic trust is so natural for most people that it does not have to be conscious. Psychoanalytical research has shown how powerful the existential decision is that we make here at the beginning of our lives. In the middle of an alien world, between danger and promise, we come to a feeling of ontological security, of primal trust stronger than primal mistrust.

Basic trust does not mean, however, that there is not more mistrust. In the first place, we never completely succeed in overcoming primal mistrust; even in the most favorable situation this phase of the soul's life appears to leave behind a vague, yet pervasive yearning toward a lost paradise. In the second place, basic trust is not an acquisition which lasts forever. A power struggle takes place throughout the course of life between the opposing primal feelings. Trust is continually threatened; thus we again and again seek opportunities to strengthen and maintain anew our feeling of security. We seek these opportunities in different realms, both externally and internally. We want to experience everywhere anew that our world is still in order.

In the face of the deepest and final questions of life, people also seek the confirmation of this basic trust in the worship service. Things have changed a great deal since our mothers took care of us, but our need for dependability, affirmation, and love still exists. It is a need for a security which is not easy to define. People ask diffusely rather than clearly, unconsciously rather than consciously:

—Do I have a future?
—Am I lost or supported?
—Do I have ground under my feet?
—Am I left alone by myself or is there help?
—Do I have to defend myself, brace myself, or should I relax and be giving?
—Does it make sense to have courage or should I be resigned?

Our individual situation is always different when we human beings ask these "final questions." It is not here a matter of whether these questions are always justified or mature or adult. What is important to me here is the discovery: People again and again seek confirmation and renewal of their basic trust. This search is in any case understandable. Life is simple only for very few people. Disturbances and dangers are daily bread for most. Indeed, just that simple life of the countless simple people without public significance is a difficult life: having to assert oneself in our society, at work, in the family; trying to find warmth and understanding when we need it; rearing children; living with unsatisfied wants; having to bear missed opportunities, jealousy, sadness, worries about health; and everywhere disappointments and assaults threatening to destroy our basic trust.

The worship service is one opportunity among many to experience the renewal of basic trust. It is different from other such opportunities especially because in it persons are addressed in their relationship to life as a whole. They are considered in their "absolute dependence." But the worship service also has its limitations concerning the renewal of basic trust. Whoever has never experienced a strong basic trust will hardly find it in a worship service. Decisive elements are missing for the awakening and emergence of ontological security. A well-defined partner relationship is necessary for that, but in church a certain anonymity is usually the case. The worship service can, however, make the pains of insecurity often accompanying daily life bearable for people experiencing their basic trust in connection with their faith. These pains are no longer decisive for those who find their support in God. For this reason, people coming to a worship service again and again seek the strengthening of their security from the church. When we ask them what they expect from the worship service, they express this in different ways—and not always theologically correctly:

—I want to forget day-to-day sufferings for a while.
—I am looking for strength for the coming week.
—I would like to get out of the rat-race and find a little quietness.

—No more arguments, I want a little peace now.
—Someone has to talk kindly to us once in a while too, and give us
   courage.

Before we protest here that the gospel is not in fact supposed to settle us down, but rather to get us going, we need to consider that it is not a matter here of affirming or maintaining a status quo. We will later discuss "change" and "renewal" within the framework of a worship service. It is a matter of that deepest trust with which people live both in permanent conditions as well as periods of radical change. For people coming to a worship service this deepest trust is associated with God and the gospel; believers interpret their primal trust as a trust in God. "The participant in a worship service acquired a certain Christian system in his past, a system he uses to interpret the world and to make evaluations. In the worship service he experiences in spoken words and in being with others not belonging to his closest circle of friends, that his reference system holds, that his interpretation of values is correct." [3] One must not always think this "acquisition" of a system is a consciously occurring event. Its roots can possibly lie far back in childhood, where a mother used to sing a prayer out loud to her child. The last support, Christians believe, is the Lord. To find their basic trust strengthened and secure means to discover anew and to believe the support of yesterday. For believers it is the security in God; that is what they want to find anew, to see, experience, believe or feel. Like the manna in the desert, a living faith cannot be maintained for long, but the memory of that faith exists further and leads a person to seek it again. People are disappointed if they find nothing of it in a worship service. "I came out of the church exactly as I came in," they say; and they do not mean they unfortunately didn't get any new ideas, but rather that they are not strengthened in their faith and their security has not been renewed.

A regression takes place in the listeners to the extent that security is awakened in a worship service and in listening, a return to behavior and feelings of the earliest phase of life. There are, of course, destructive regressions, but also constructive ones. Sleep and many common modes of behavior are regressions serving the regeneration of the person and having recreative meaning. Why shouldn't the worship service also have the function of providing people with a beneficial regression? Manfred Josuttis[4] considers the repetitive aspect of the worship service and the entire procedure of repetition of learned behavior a positive confirmation of the continuity and identity of the individual. Without stability, freedom and change are also unthinkable. This is why it is beneficial for a worship service to secure this stability. By means of such regression it's possible to experience again what we did initially at the beginning of our lives.

We experience trust in certain experiential forms, and it is no accident that these forms remind us of childhood. Particular, unique behavioral modes are activated for the first time in the oral phase of life, when primal or basic trust emerges. When we experience renewals of this basic trust in later life, we always do so in experiential forms known and familiar to us from this oral phase. Experiences such as "to be struck," "to become warm" are our access roads to that basic trust.

The word "oral" alludes to the mouth, an important center in this phase for the approach to life. Certain invisible activities correspond to eating, such as "to take into oneself," "to be fulfilled," "receive," "to be satisfied." Receptive behavior characterizes this phase. In that intimate, loving relationship to one's mother one experiences what it means to "be secure," "to feel carried or taken up," "to participate," "to belong"; "we-ness" and "partnership" also become experiences. These things together make all-embracing basic trust possible, the ontological security.

It is obvious that the listener reactions we have seen very often belong in the categories of the oral experiential phase. The five summarizations often agree verbatim with the terminology of this oral phase. And not only listeners' statements do this; the Bible and theology also offer promises which, viewed psychologically, are realized in experiential forms of the oral phase: communion with God, God as "all in all" (1 Cor. 15:28), "Christ lives in me" (Gal. 2:20), "and they were all filled with the Holy Spirit" (Acts 2:4), and many more could be listed here. If we are looking for expressions of oral experience, we will find church hymns to be a veritable storehouse.

With "basic trust" I have taken over an expression from developmental psychology. When I use experiential reactions of listeners to the worship service event as a point of departure, I necessarily submit myself to psychological categories. It is clear that I can encompass only a part of the worship service event in this way, the part accessible to psychological perceptions. I do not wish to maintain that the listeners' trust is only a matter of newly experienced basic trust. I believe much more happens. People come into contact with the living God! That, however, cannot be comprehended in psychological categories; it is an incomprehensible mystery. What is important to me is the fact that in this incomprehensible mystery it is also a matter of the renewal of basic trust. That is the side of things which is comprehensible to our analytical cognition.

The realm I envision with "basic trust" and with the dimension of security can also be indicated with the word edification. I am speaking about edification in this chapter. It is clear from the listeners' reactions that edification belongs to their deepest concerns: security in the old and familiar. In homiletical textbooks little or no attention is given to edification in the sense of renewal of basic trust.

Whenever Karl Barth teaches about edification, he emphasizes that people should hear God's command and become obedient to it. Only within the framework of "obedience" is the second element permitted to come: edification through the grace of God to life. But that is only the "zeros added to the one.'' [5] Not a word about trust or courage. Certainly one must see these statements in the context of their time. Today one says "edification," in contrast to the biblical usage, to mean an individual experience. But things aren't helped by our regarding this individual edification as suspicious. It should be supplemented, not replaced. Security has been sold short recently not only in homiletics, but in all of theology. Even the word is missing for the most part. The atmosphere in our theological world is not very well suited for maintaining what is old and familiar. And it's not only in theology that innovation is more highly valued than tradition. If I see things correctly, a gap exists between the contemporary inclination toward the new felt by us all, and the cultivation and maintenance of tradition; this gap is the prerequisite for the awakening of security. The participants in a worship service hope the preacher will strengthen and confirm their basic trust, that deepest and oldest part of them. This requires a flexibility from the preacher which also permits a conservative posture. (I would have preferred to avoid the word "conservative" because it is used almost exclusively with negative connotations. Most of the time it is a synonym for "limited," "ignorant," "narrow-minded," "backward," and "out of date." The myth of progress does not tolerate conserving. In Western European politics, "conservative" is an insult almost everywhere. But the conservative stance is recognizable and even necessary in every political debate. The characterization of conservative parties is, however, seldom open; they are usually glossed over with expressions such as "Christian Democratic," "People's Party" or similar ones. When I use the word "conservative" in this book, I mean a posture of stability seeking to maintain what is good; a posture not easily giving up tradition for fads; a posture seeking energetically to uphold proven foundations; and a posture open to the new, though always attempting to order it while maintaining as much as possible of what is already there. Other stances are necessary in the church just as in life in general. At this time, however, we are speaking about the traditional worship service and its presuppositions. The old differentiation of emphasis between priestly and prophetic becomes visible here.) Such flexibility is the prerequisite for the possibility of awakening the feeling of security. It is a matter here of a *conditio sine qua non*. The positioning of the conservative stance should not mean that the preacher ought to behave conservatively in all areas or that the challenge of the new in the worship service should have no place at all. However, a basically conservative attitude does appear to me to be essential for a positive effect in a traditional worship service. Participants in a worship service are most sensitive to the variations in the normal, familiar liturgical procedure. Changes in the way the worship service progresses are much more of a reason for aggravation than the contents of the sermon. By trivializing this aggravation one simply overlooks the dimension of security with its search for support in the old and familiar. The ritual reaches the existential depths of the personality more than do concepts and doctrine, and thus offers the preacher only a limited area for variation. The focus and expectations of the people attending a worship service thus call on the preacher to confirm what has been proven by time. This focus will not always be a conscious one for the people in the worship service. It is, however, inextricably connected with their hope for renewal of basic trust. But is this expectation legitimate? Is the preacher here allowed to give what the people demand?

The answer must in my opinion be a cautious yes. Cautious, because only one side of the gospel becomes visible here, and there is also another side. But an affirmation of this listener expectation is basically in agreement with biblical and systematic theology. This is particularly the case in the psalms, which are testimonies to faith experiences and thus also witness to the expectations of the congregation. The association of the familiar with the old is common: "Yet God my King is from old" (Ps. 74:12). The expression "from old" occurs often; (Ps. 143:5; Ps. 93:2). One can also think of the expression "from everlasting to everlasting" (Ps. 41:13). In systematic theology it is called God's immutability or stability. All loyalty presupposes stability, but that does not have to mean that everything remains monotonously with the old. Loyalty proves itself ever anew, and under certain circumstances that can be quite dynamic. What is new in God is the fact that he "confirms Himself anew as the One He has been from all eternity and from the creation of the world." [6] What is new is the fact that the old is still valid, and that is exactly what basic trust is able to confirm for a person.

The persons in a worship service hope for the renewal of their deepest trust, and are thankful when this expectation is fulfilled. A procedure from the theological side catering to this expectation is also unobjectionable. Then what is the problem? The fact that we preachers are not aware enough of this hope. The analyses of sermons and worship services show clearly that we make our worst mistakes in this dimension. I wish to pursue the question of what it means for the structuring of the worship service and sermon to arouse feelings of security and trust in the congregation. The opportunities and dangers for the preacher will then become specifically clear.

Preaching Personally

Feelings of security are aroused only if love is expressed. Whenever people go into a worship service to find feelings of security, they are seeking love, clear signs of love. For love seeks communion, love reaches the existential level of experience where the need for security originates. In the worship service we are not only looking for love among our fellow human beings, but rather—in an all-embracing manner—the love of God. If I have understood the related listener comments correctly, that is the deepest concern in a worship service. People are seeking "our loving God," as the popular expression goes.

Biblical parallels can be found without any trouble for this congregation theology, if I may call it that. Not only does 1 John 4:8, 16 write that "God is love"; the entire biblical message can be summed up as the love of God for his people. Even if the word "love" is absent over long stretches of the Bible, the same thing can be found in other expressions: the covenant, Yahweh's mercy and similar ones. It is easily understandable that the essential concern of the Bible has also become the essential concern of the congregation. The church-goers hope and expect to discover and experience in the worship service that they are safe and secure with God, that the deepest qualification of their lives is to be loved. I am expressing in concepts here what for most people in a worship service is more than likely present only vaguely as a pious yearning.

What does this now mean for preachers? How can and should they contribute to the congregation's finding security and God's love again? Of course, no preacher can produce God's love and present it. God simply cannot be manipulated like that. My question is not: How does one do it? I am asking rather: What should preachers do if their congregations are hoping for this feeling of security? What is the proper behavior?

My first thesis is that they should be personal. Love is fundamentally a personal concern, a matter of the heart, in a unity of feeling and deed. Now, this deep concern of congregations is not a matter of being loved by the preachers. The preachers are to witness to them the love of God. But now we come upon a unique and peculiar discovery in the analyses of worship service and sermon: The more personally the preachers present themselves, the stronger is the experience of security among the listeners.

We must be careful here. I am not talking about intentionally causing something, but rather about suitable behavior. If preachers become the cause of the experience of trust, they slip into a trap, since in that case a neurotic dependency on the preachers develops. You also find this now and then, and not always without meaning and promise. It's just not what I am trying to bring to attention here. It is a matter here of a parallelism between the love of God sought by the congregations and the way the preachers present themselves. Because the first quantity is very personal, the second should be, also. Preachers proclaim God's seeking and supporting love more authentically the more personally they present themselves. Proclamation requires personal confession. The personal speech and presentation of the preacher affects the listeners as a sign of the personally intended love of God. The feeling of security with God becomes accessible to experience through this sign.

Being personal has an individual and social side: sincerity and concern for others.

1. Being Sincere and Genuine

Whenever listeners complain that the preacher is impersonal, they normally mean they have not been moved inwardly. There are several reasons for this, and I will give some of the statements connected with the general evaluation "impersonal":

> —He really tried to proclaim the gospel, especially at the end, but what he said was colorless.
> —The general statements didn't move me at all.
> —His speech was colorless.

A missing component of sincerity is indicated here: clearness, definite contours. If we are genuine we present ourselves clearly and quite visibly; we thus become comprehensible and accessible, and it makes us dependable. We only avoid colorlessness when we confess colors. One's own point of view is unavoidable here. A concrete result of a clear stance is the use of the personal pronoun "I." It is the clear signal that the preacher identifies with the message. But not every "I" in sermons has a positive value. There are different kinds of "I." Manfred Josuttis[7] finds the "verifying I" which intends to support faith with the help of one's own person, to be a questionable use of "I." He further differentiates the "biographical I" which interprets things from the experiential perspective of a person's life; the "confessional I" which goes into the differentiation between God's truth and human reality; the "representative I" which sets up the preacher as a representative of the listeners; the "exemplary I" which shows in one's own person what the gospel means; and the "fictional I" serving to tell a story from a certain perspective. Here we find the problem of relevance. The people in a worship service have not come to church to find out what "I" see and think and believe. The preacher is not *that* important! But that is only one side of things. The other is that feelings of security, including security with God, can only be experienced if the proclamation happens in a personal fashion. But then we also should say "I"! No word in our language is more personal than "I." To be sure, earlier generations did not want this "I." Josuttis sees the roots of this even in politics; to say "I" means one is possibly a spoil-sport, or it signals commotion. "We," on the other hand, implies I adapt and renounce my own individual wishes and needs. More common in sermons are expressions such as "one," "man," "whoever," and especially "we." Rudolf Bohren attacks this homiletical "we"[8] behind which the preacher hides and becomes impersonal. The results of sermon analyses are, however, not quite this strict. "We" does not always give an impersonal impression, and neither is it absolutely necessary to say "I" in order to come across personally. The "we" and "I" are only symptoms of an attitude. If the preacher's attitude is genuine and personal, the sermon will move the listener inwardly. (In a sermon which was generally evaluated positively, personal pronouns and possessives came up 156 times within a half hour. Of those 52 were "I," "to me," "me," or "my," hence 33 percent. "We," "us," and "our" came up 165 times, hence 41 percent.)

Another component of sincerity becomes visible in the next listener reactions:

> —I couldn't see the connection between the actual message and everything else. It was like a foreign body.
> —It became so theological then, it was just empty catch-words for me.
> —He always let Peter speak; I wasn't sure whether he himself also sees and believes that way.

There is always a certain recognition in these statements, but an embarrassment, a lack of being convinced weighs more heavily. Here we come upon a new aspect of being genuine and sincere. It's not clarity that's missing here; it's openness. This aspect can be negatively described even more closely. A facade, a deceptive appearance comes across to the listener, or at least they fear it. They have to guess too much about the person of the preacher. Everything that is said may be right, but if it doesn't come from the preacher, if it's taken over from somewhere else or just tacked on, then it's not believable. And it's not believable because whatever is objectively correct only has power if it's a personal possession of the preacher. Strange to say, the danger of a facade threatens precisely in the decisive statements of the sermon, when one speaks about God, about Jesus Christ. That is perhaps because the preachers say more then than they actually consider important, and they betray themselves through signals warning the listeners. Actually, it's very good that the congregation notices when the preacher piously deceives them, since in this way they are protected against seduction.

Other complaints about impersonal preachers go back to physical presentation:

> —It bothered me that he was so dependent on the paper.
> —His voice is monotonous.
> —She stands there totally motionless.
> —There was no surprise or wonder (the preacher never took a deep breath).

And positively:

> —His gestures, his facial expressions, everything was lively and spontaneous; I liked that.

People in a worship service are as a rule sensitive to what they see. A worship service is also a show, and every regular congregation member knows what an important role a pleasant visual sight plays. This is to be taken seriously, because bodily stance and behavior are also language: breathing, the tone of voice, the movement of the hands, the gaze. Body language is more persuasive than words; it speaks directly to the spectator's subconscious, and thus has a deeper effect than the intellectual word. Paul Watzlawick differentiates between analogous and digital communication. Language is digital because it is based primarily on imitation. Only an accidental connection exists between a word and the thing described. Body language is not accidental; it belongs to analagous communication. A direct connection emerges between the gesture or facial expression and the feeling expressed by it. For this reason non-verbal, analogous communication is more persuasive than digital communication.[9] This means that the good news cannot come across as good if given in a monotonous voice. Isaiah says that even the feet of the bringers of good tidings are beautiful (52:7).

Being genuine embraces the whole person. Whatever I say with words I must also say with my body; otherwise, I will come across impersonally.

A final component of sincerity is missing if preachers come across as cool and distant. This means that they are not putting any of their own emotions into the structure of the sermon and prayer. Being genuine includes just this conveyance of our own feelings. In this way we become a real person for the others around us, and we come closer to them. It is not a matter of simple augmentation or enrichment; it is a matter of all or nothing. The listeners lose their involvement if the preachers repress their own feelings. Preachers can expect the worship service to have a positive effect only if they find access to their own experience. And their own experience is in this context nothing other than their personal belief, their belief experiences—perhaps wonder about God, gratitude for life, for work, resistance to discipleship in Christ, aggravation at God's hiddenness. The effect is a personal one only if preachers are willing to stand consciously in this experience while preaching and praying. Only then are they genuine.

One-sidedness threatens us at this point in our reflections about the effect of worship service and sermon. The problem is that linear logic does not suffice to understand what happens in a worship service. One side is the power of God, the effect of the Spirit, which we cannot grasp in any way, including homiletical theology. Another side is the effect of that person leading the worship service and preaching. The temptation of reflection is to over-generalize the statements about the effect. Then, because God's effect is inaccessible, the preacher is not supposed to introduce technical tricks. Or else it is supposedly in our power to structure a good worship service if we just employ the proper psychological insights. Such hypotheses play off one pole of the effect against the other. But in reality both belong to the effect: God's power and the credibility and personal warmth of the preacher. They are not related as two complementary parts, they are two dimensions of an indivisible event. Discursive thinking is unable to grasp that. Only with humor, and without systematic compulsion, can we understand anything here. In the proclamation God fits together his own part and the person of the proclaimer. For this reason the preacher's emotions and what he or she does with them is of fundamental—not secondary—significance for homiletics.

The book *Predigtanalysen* by Hans-Christoph Piper is a clear example of how the repression or bracketing out of one's own emotions (fear, helplessness, aggression, disappointment) is a major reason that many sermons fail to have a positive effect. This insight leads to a thesis and a question. The thesis suggests that homiletics has to distribute its attention differently than it has in the past. It needs to take a more inclusive perspective on the person of the preacher; preachers can then learn to lend their work that characteristic without which they either have only a slight effect or none at all—their own personal character. The question asks how this can be realized in theological training. Can one expect such strongly personal training from a professor of practical theology? Can a single person do it? Or is this development of the person only possible within the congregation, the mature congregation? Is it, after all, more a spiritual maturation process than an acquisition of vocational authorization? I will take up this question in the final chapter.

We can also find perversion of sincerity, exhibitionism. This danger appears to be less likely than that of too much reserve. Listeners say much more often that preachers were not personal enough for them than too much so. They are too personal if they tell things about themselves which have an embarrassing or discomforting effect on the listeners. A limit of what is private exists, and a speaker is not permitted to go beyond it. Things that are too personal bring the preacher too close to the congregation, and it turns away. The statement: "Fellow congregation members, I am actually very tired, I would rather not have come to church today," was experienced negatively by all. The statement had no connection with the sermon topic, was thus irrelevant and in this form simply was embarrassing. A sermon dealing with the pastor's vacation experiences was experienced as embarrassing or discomforting because it related a great deal of private material of no use to the listeners. Preachers do not make themselves personal by telling about their private lives. Being too personal is basically a disguised form of being impersonal. Only the appearance of sincerity is given.

True communication always exists in the tension between closeness and distance. For this reason sincerity and genuineness have their limits. Whoever disregards proper distance meets with rejection. Relevance for the listeners is the standard preachers should use to determine to what extent they should speak about their own problems.

I have just discussed the characteristics of being genuine. A sermon comes across as "personal" only if the preacher is authentic. But an impersonal sermon also reveals a great deal about the preacher! Personality shows itself more clearly, in fact, in a monologue than in a conversation. Actually, a sermon is always personal, yet listeners nonetheless often complain they found the preacher too impersonal. The word "personal," however, means something quite different in both cases. The congregation hopes the preacher is personal in the sense of "original." Whoever acts originally lives spontaneously from a deeper level, oriented to the true center of the personality. Preachers act genuinely just as they are. Preachers also have an effect if they do not do that. An alternative to a good effect is not that there is no effect, but that a bad one takes place. Every sermon is an expression of the personality, personal in the sense of subjective. Reading, even reading aloud from a page, also cannot be structured objectively; tone of voice, pace, loudness are all subjective elements. The quasi-theological objection that a worship service should not in fact be structured personally, because it is a matter of God and not of the preacher, is unrealistic even aside from the docetic heresy. There is no escaping personal effect. If it is positive, it's praised as being "personal"; if it's negative, it's qualified negatively as "impersonal" or in some other way.

Otto Haendler calls the continually present influence of the preacher's personality the continuum. "Out of everything in a preacher and coming from him, a unified stream emerges affecting those listening as a steady life stream, a stream remaining basically the same for each individual." [10] This stream comes from the deed levels of the personality, and words are not persuasive without a positive stream or continuum. This stream is always active and decisive under the surface, even though a particular moment may cause variations for anyone; thus every preacher can have good and bad days. The continuum is always there, clearly or hidden. It is in reality the driving force to the extent that the preacher structures the worship service.

It seems to me to be a peculiar phenomenon that among public speakers only the preacher is required to be personal. He or she is to offer for greater and greater numbers what otherwise is possible only on a two-on-two basis or in small groups. In difficult times that's also required of political leaders, but then only as an exception and certainly not every Sunday! At most, a personal style in a packed house is required only of an actor, but a preacher can only partly be compared with an actor. Even if the acting is not at all to be considered ungenuine, but rather is a living portrayal as opposed to something like giving a lecture, there is still a difference: The actor "plays" another person, the preacher plays himself or herself! One accepts no "play" from the preacher. The preacher's behavior has a positive effect only when it also comes to light outside the worship service.

But even with all the laborious groans cause by this demand for sincerity and genuineness from the preacher, is it not rather a splendid affair? Being genuine is fundamentally the most simple thing that can be required of us. Being ungenuine is always more complicated and requires more energy. Being genuine presupposes that I open myself up, expose myself and maybe even make a fool of myself. Precisely this risk makes us "personal." In the final analysis it's a question of whether we are willing to make ourselves understandable and vulnerable in this way. Nothing less than giving of oneself is required here. Without this corresponding giving of ourselves we cannot effectively preach Christ, who revealed his Lordship in his own giving.

I have dealt with being genuine, with the individual side of personal effect. The person of the preacher was central, one's self-communication as a component in the worship service event. Being genuine is the point of departure of one's personal effect. I will now turn to the goal, the social side of the occurrence, what is called "preaching personally."

2. Speaking to or Addressing People

Preaching personally does not just mean that preachers reveal important things about themselves; it also includes their taking the people in the worship service seriously. "You have spoken to me" means "you took me into consideration," "you spoke to me by name." Those spoken to also stand in the center of focus, and are the second center in preaching personally. Manfred Metzger describes this aspect of preaching personally when he says of the listeners that they expect "to be sought, found, and brought home by the good news." [11] The analysis of listener statements confirms this. Negative statements concerning this topic can be summarized in two types:

—I didn't feel spoken to. I had more the impression I was hearing a lecture. It wasn't important at all that I was there.
—It bothered me that he was so dependent on the paper.

Among the statements already mentioned I recall here expressions such as "taken up with it," "struck," "moved."

Apparently many people in a worship service—I believe all of them—expect to be personally moved. Only when that happens is praying or preaching personal for them. As a completion of being genuine it is here a matter of the second aspect of a "personal" presentation: seeking the other person. This aspect is the social or external side of a personal style.

Here, too, the congregation theology is fairly orthodox. Proclamation is missionary activity; the proclaimed Lord is soliciting his people, so solicitation and preaching are related. One can even call the sermon a kind of manipulation. An exclusively negative evaluation of the qualification "suggestive" for the way a preacher speaks doesn't take into consideration the soliciting character of the proclamation. This characteristic should also be clear in that way of speaking. These are not objective truths which are being presented in the worship service;

a truth is introduced which aims for and awaits participation. People are spoken to, thus the *spoken* word is indispensable if the preacher wants to have a personal effect in a worship service. Just as in Paul's time, "faith comes from what is heard" (Rom. 10:17). Wolfgang Hammer draws attention to the fact that optical communication media such as television and film are of almost no use for proclamation.[12] This results from the possibility of language calling directly for participation, either explicitly or implicitly. Looking at people or showing them something never attains the degree of personal engagement that speaking to them does, be it one-on-one or in a small group.

Just as the personal pronoun "I" belongs to being genuine, so also does "you" belong to personal address. A few simple examples can make that clear:

—If you already know this story, then perhaps you are no longer surprised by the ending.
—That is the direction the Lord wants to lead you with these words.
—When everything's going wrong for you and you no longer have the courage to go on, then you stand there and ask bitterly where God is now that you need him.

Even if we don't have to be bound here stylistically, we nonetheless see that the frequent or infrequent occurrence—or the complete lack—of this direct form of address is generally a clear sign of whether and to what extent preachers intend to take their listeners personally into consideration. There are some spots in the liturgy where "you" is unavoidable. In baptism, for example, we say "I baptize you," or in a blessing "God bless and keep you" (although "you" is sometimes changed to "us"). God is addressed in prayer: "May your name be made holy." You can find similar passages in hymns. But in a great many worship services the use of the direct form of address is limited to these prescribed passages. It never occurs to countless preachers to address their congregations with "you." And these preachers may even be of the opinion that a sermon should be an address, so this opinion or conviction is not yet a guarantee that they really "address" their congregations.

There are probably preachers who speak personally without ever using the word "you." Language analysis is concerned only with the verbal, and personal style can show itself in non-verbal forms as well. Nonetheless these analyses give important insights when the homiletical "we" is used too frequently. The "we" has the tempting possibility of replacing not only the "I" of the preacher, but the "you" as well. In both cases the preacher may be trying to hide.

—We have trouble because we have to live in faith and never in seeing.

By simply changing the personal pronoun we see how much more direct and personal the sentence sounds:

—I have trouble because I have to live in faith and never in seeing. Do
you have the same trouble?

This new tone, however, presupposes a different attitude. Many participants in
analyses of worship services and sermons discover personal pronouns for the
first time in the analyses; then they try to use "I" and "you" more often.
Without exception they find out what kind of internal change has to correspond
to it; otherwise the "I" and "you" come across as insincere.

A second possible effect of the homiletical "we" is forced inclusion:

—We've lost the childlike joy for Christmas.
—We always push the guilt off on someone else.
—We await death with anxiety.

If the listeners don't really see themselves in such statements, they feel included
illegitimately, taken in, and they resist it. The we-address "tends . . . to coerce
the individual without questioning into a collective, puts subjective and ideolog-
ical one-sidedness in the place of a genuine common sense and thus violates the
person's freedom." [13]

But there is also a suitable form of the we-address, a form without the hiding
game or forced inclusion, and this needs to be brought out against Bohren's
wholesale negative evaluation of the homiletical "we":

—That is an unheard of gift: He gives himself! The question is now
whether we want it. It demands a total turnabout from us. Do we want
to let someone give us this gift? Isn't it the most difficult thing for us?

The "we" here signals a genuine solidarity between the preacher and the
congregation.

It becomes obvious how complicated, or more precisely, how deeply the
problem of address is rooted. It cannot be solved with a mere conscious choice
of words. The inner attitude of the preacher is decisive: Whoever really wants to
approach the congregation will find the forms. Whoever then finds that something is not quite right with the forms, whoever finds a discrepancy between the
intention and the actual effect, must go to work on himself or herself. Only then
will the forms of address change organically from within.

We have taken a look at forms of address. The worship service is not only
a verbal, but also a visible event. Listeners complain almost without exception about being bound to paper. The Bern Preacher Act of 1667 requires of
preachers that they give the sermon extemporaneously; it requires "that they
must not read the same in front of the congregation from notes or paper,
which is a mockery to have to watch and which takes away all fruit and grace
from the preacher in the eyes of the listeners." [14] The Bern church authorities
paid attention to the effect of a sermon and not just to the content, something

which is more the exception than the rule in homiletics. The listener statements are a massive testimony for the correctness of this regulation. There is
much more at stake than those who support the writing down and reading
from notes believe. The personal style, the direct address indispensable for
the awakening of trust, is in general seriously impaired by reading from notes.
This is the case because not only the content, but precisely the presentation—
including the visible—is essential for gaining access to the realm of emotion.
But what does such reading from notes show us, no matter how sophisticated
it's done? The sermon does not *emerge*; it comes from yesterday. The preacher misses the "act of restructuring during the moment of speaking." [15] Ernst
Lerle also sees the connection between the low-intensity act of communication and the boredom in the reception process.[16] At best the sermon read aloud
is written language translated into spoken language, since the spoken word
can only be gotten down approximately on paper. Even if it's possible to find
formulations earlier which sound like speech, the unavoidable process of reproduction disturbs contact because the preacher is basically not there, but is
tarrying in the past. Richard Kliem defends speech-thinking; by this he means
that the preacher thinks during speech just as during a conversation. "Just as
every sentence finds its wording from the preacher's intention which is at first
not yet articulated, so also does the entire speech find its sentences and words
in its overall intention." The sense of words is grasped more clearly and more
quickly while listening to a speaker than while reading a book because the
tone, pace, mimicry, indeed the whole appearance of the speaking is itself a
language not found in reading. But as soon as the preacher reads, the body
language for the most part falls by the wayside.[17]

Extemporaneous speaking—without a manuscript—does not mean that the
preacher prepares any less thoroughly or is just supposed to improvise. The
English preacher Spurgeon used to say to his pupils: "The most difficult and
best way is to collect enough material for the sermon and then give it just as the
words come to you. This is . . . not an improvised sermon; the words are improvised—and I consider this correct, but the content is the result of thorough
preparation."

For Swiss preachers this problem is played out in the struggle between dialect and written language. Since their everyday language is not normally ever
written down, it's clear to them that they are speaking a different language, a
written language, whenever they use a manuscript. This is basically the case
everywhere when speakers read from notes. The problem of dialect in a worship
service is even more complicated than this. As a Dutchman it is not for me to go
into this further. I mention only that the majority of participants in sermon analyses get away from written German or at least want to, and as time goes by
increasingly use more dialect. The problem of the manuscript is directly related
to this change of language.

Marshall McLuhan also emphasizes that dialects are gaining a new significance today because of the influence of television; dialects have an effect at a deeper level than does the standardized language, thus the use of dialect enhances the personal character of speech.[18]

Friedrich Schleiermacher strongly emphasizes the advantages of extemporaneous speech and requires only that the "more provoking and strong" speakers write down their sermons in order to tone themselves down. It's the question, however, of whether a speaker is permitted to sacrifice directness in order to attain moderation. Be that as it may—sermon analyses seldom offer perfect or incontestable principles, including here—it is unmistakable that the listeners generally have less understanding of manuscripts than the many homiletical textbooks. The thorough defense of the sermon without a manuscript, as Eckhard Altmann gives it, is fully supported by people in the worship service.

Learning things by heart is seldom a good alternative for reading aloud. Basically it's nothing more than reading. If the manuscript and a certain memorizing can become a kind of inherent part of the sermon, that is of course a positive factor; but it's dangerous when formulations become rigid.

As soon as the address is missing, the proclamation threatens to change into a treatise. It makes it almost impossible for anyone to be moved directly. A speaking about God takes place instead of a speaking in the name of God, an aimless development of writing. Instead of speaking to the congregation, the preacher is basically just talking with himself. Maybe he's "personal" in his statements, but the listeners lose interest because they don't feel included. They are not spoken to. Whatever the preacher reveals of himself remains without a positive effect. Preaching personally means both things: showing oneself clearly, and directly addressing and speaking to the listeners. The prerequisite is that the preacher is really willing to get involved with the congregation and to take the responsibility for them.

Exaggeration and hence perversion are also threats in this, the social aspect of a personal presentation. Anything that is too strong or too personal puts off the listeners. Listeners often complain about what we may call "pulpit pathos." This kind of distortion is brought up and lamented three times more often than the other form of exaggerated personal communication, the exposure of one's personal life. A pressing and insincere tone of address calls forth a defense because the preacher is getting too close, and the listeners will not let themselves be taken in by force. A preacher is too personal if he or she tries to repress the personal instead of overcoming it. That means that the rejected "pastoral" tone is hiding an inner insecurity and emptiness. That emptiness has an effect, not the personal address that's only feigned.

It's not at all so simple! Personal maturity is required on the one hand to assume responsibility for addressing the listeners, and on the other to maintain the listeners' freedom. Preachers will be able to walk that fine line required of them only if they find a suitable path in the polarity of leading and letting people go their own way which is already a part of their lives. Authoritarian leaders betray themselves by their coercion; leaders who don't want to bother the listeners betray themselves by their non-obligatory speaking style. The forms of address here are only symptoms, and to change only them would be nothing more than an emotionless technical procedure. Listeners notice when correct words and behavior are the natural, commensurate symptoms of an inner attitude.

Accepting Responsibility

It has become clear from the analyses of worship services and sermons that the service reaches the deepest level of experience where it is a matter of a person's deepest trust. From the listener statements it has become clear that this trust is awakened only if the preacher has a personal style as opposed to a distant or cool one. I earlier characterized personal preaching as being genuine and speaking directly to people. Speaking thus to people presupposes that the preacher is willing to carry the responsibility for the congregation. This thesis deserves attention now.

It is a matter of a certain aspect of authority. Having to be an authority figure today is a questionable matter for many older and younger pastors. Only for a very few is it self-evident, and even then it often appears in an authoritarian form causing disgust in countless people. I consider it one of the most important purposes of this book to go into this problem. Here we find the roots of several different distressing problems not only for preaching, but for the execution of the office of pastor in general.

The problem of authority arises in all three dimensions of a worship service: in awakening trust, proclaiming deliverance, and in the breakthrough to understanding. In the dimension of understanding it's always associated with the fact that the preacher represents the congregation and is thus also a questioning listener. The preacher's authority then resides in solidarity, in the capacity to integrate the temptations of the congregation members in the worship service. In the dimension of deliverance the preacher's authority is that of a messenger representing God's matters. The preacher's authority is the full power to say unbelievable things on the basis of the Holy Scriptures. I will direct my attention to these two aspects of authority in the next chapters. Now, however, I am concerned with authority in the dimension of the feeling of security. The suitable behavior or stance of a person who, with a mandate from a church congregation, plays a central role in the worship service, needs to be clarified here. I am speaking of what people have for centuries called the pastorate, not in its entire scope as pastoral counselor and so on, but rather only in relation to the worship service.

All the anxiety, begging off, experimentation, and scolding can't get around it: Conducting a worship service, in a church, and especially preaching, presupposes that a person is willing to be commissioned as an authority. Even the arrangements of chairs and benches, the pulpit or microphone, maybe even the robes all speak a distinct language which can't be covered up by some contrary interpretation: One person will stand in the middle, one person will be the most important one. The congregation members can hardly or only in part see one another. But they all see this one person. In Protestant churches it's still customary to give the name of the preacher beforehand. In addition, everyone knows that this one person—in contrast to almost all the other congregation members—has been commissioned by the church for this work. The boundaries are clearly drawn, whether we like it or not.

Even if we should change all of that—and why couldn't we do that some day?—there would still be the need for an authority in one form or another. Wherever people come together for the purpose of having their deepest trust renewed and strengthened, there has to be one person (or several) willing to assume the role of the one awakening that trust. That happens to be the parent role, an authority. As long as we wish to fulfill the need for renewal of primal trust, this will prompt us to assume the function of a leader.

Is this need for security, and for a person who mediates this security, legitimate in the realm of the church? Isn't the Lord himself this authority? This question can be answered in various ways. Karl Barth expresses it clearly and simply when he says that "the Word of God does . . . claim to be represented within the realm of man's will to obey, (and) does . . . demand a definite function in the church." [19] The "correspondence" is the connecting link between God's authority and humanity. One can see from the listener reactions that any answer which overlooks the decisive influence of the preacher is unrealistic.

One thing in this context is not to be forgotten, though it is in fact often overlooked. It's not the preacher's self-evaluation that's important, but rather how the preacher is evaluated by those participating in the worship service. Even if nowadays one doesn't often find the old hero worship of the pastor, nonetheless the people in a worship service—and it is about them that we are concerned—hold more recognition and respect for the preacher than he or she is often willing to admit. Why is that so? Certain things don't go unnoticed by the congregation: the fact that certain people see their life's task in working in the church; that they for that reason announce openly their positive relationship to the values represented by the church—that is, to God; that they are considered capable and dependable concerning that task of guiding the church. The preachers combine their life's task with the proclamation of values which concern every person at the deepest level and which are existentially significant. This points to a mysterious connection between preachers and listeners which leads many listeners to a deep respect. The following drawing might make this connection clearer than concepts do. Preachers—whether they want to or not—represent, embody, or bring to consciousness what is there in the listeners as the deepest existential concern.

Heije Faber searches in the unconscious archetype for the reason people think so highly of the pastor. He emphasizes in his description of the pastor's identity that the figure of the ecclesiastical office-holder is upholstered with the archetype of the "wise man." Faber refers to Carl Gustav Jung when he maintains that people experience personifications in the representatives of certain vocations, personifications of the help and guidance in life they need for their spiritual development and spiritual peace.[20] More often than not, this experience is vague and unconscious. In primitive immediacy it can become visible, as in the mongoloid girl who always addressed the clinic pastor as "God." Considered only on the surface, the pastor is a normal person as far as the congregation is concerned, a person they can criticize and reject. The experience of the "great helper" is sometimes unconscious and hidden very deeply. Perhaps this is not the case with all people, but it certainly occurs more frequently than we realize. Signals for it are, for example, the normal astonishment at the young age of a pastor; the archetype of the wise man is automatically associated with an older person. It is also expected that the pastor—much more so than the physician and psychotherapist—lead a morally unblemished life. Compare the prerequisites for the office-holders in the apostolic letters: 1 Timothy 3:1-12; Titus 1:6-9. Even greater alienation results if a woman has the role; the archetype is a masculine principle.

The archetypal experience of the congregation members can be understood as an expectation imposed upon the preacher. Many people assume either half-suspectingly, vaguely, or unconsciously, that the preacher has access to secrets

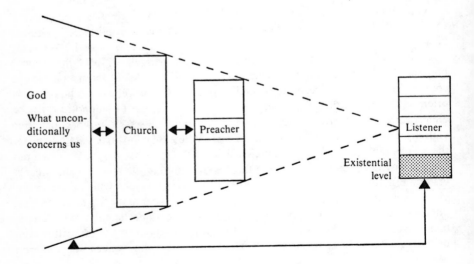

of life or at least can claim to have such access. They expect the preacher to do justice to this claim and to fulfill the expectations thus awakened; otherwise, they are disappointed.

The theory represented by Faber makes it understandable why pastors so often complain that people impose unrealistic expectations on them, since virtually no theologian wants consciously and openly the role of a "wise man." They don't want to be authorities, but they continually find that they are considered authorities. At this point the expectations of the congregation and of the preacher are completely different, and the situation is only made more difficult by the fact that the conflict goes on partially or even entirely on an unconscious level with both parties.

The pastor becomes a preacher in the worship service, and the preacher has the archetypal characteristics of the pastor in general to a greater extent than any other role. The people in a worship service view the preacher as the authority and themselves as the ones to be led by this authority. This situation is a clear expression of the regression necessary for the renewal of primal trust. It is clear that no one can be forced to take part in such a regression. Only inward participation makes it possible, and then it can be meaningful and constructive like many other regressions. Whoever caricatures such a regression shows either an unfamiliarity with the inner feeling or an unwillingness to take notice of it. This is the case with Yorick Spiegel when he writes that the traditional worship service creates "an authoritatively conditioned regression . . . in that it is structured as an interaction between a father and errant children who need to be talked to." The congregation's need to really be the "children of this father" is here considered only as immature behavior.[21] Elmar Maria Lorey's image of the sermon is also a caricature; catch-words abound, such as "the model of absolutistic thinking," "remission," "array," and "to bring in dogmatically secure statements."[22] Spiegel and Lorey's mistake is the one-sided exaggeration of the authoritarian element. There is then no longer any difference between "authoritative" in the sense of "recognized esteem" and "authoritative" in the sense of "external, imposed power." The differentiation between the holder of the clerical office and the congregation can be viewed as a kind of playing rule. Every congregation member knows that the pastor is just one of them, but he or she simultaneously has the dignity of the archetypal leader. This, of course, requires flexibility on the part of the pastor and congregation. In the case of the congregation, it has already been acquired gradually through practice for centuries now.

The great difficulty is that the majority of contemporary pastors have little or no desire to take on a clearly authoritative role. A gap has opened up here between the expectations of the congregation and the actual self-presentation of the pastor. The external marks of dignity are going through difficult times; the robe has already been abdicated in many places, the pulpits have become more modest, and now it's even customary no longer to give the sermon from the pulpit. As far as I know, these changes are never or rarely prompted by the congregation or the people coming to worship services, but rather always by preachers who balk at adapting themselves to the customary forms. So the preacher appears at a lectern under the pulpit with a green tie and says: "Mornin', everybody." His whole appearance wants to make one thing clear: "I make no pretensions; I don't feel important; I'm not an authority."

This resistance against the role of an authority goes even further. The whole institution of the sermon is being attacked. There are several different reasons for this, but one is certainly the rejection of the responsibility assigned to the preacher in the worship service. Wolfgang Steck translates this resistance into the following words: "I feel too closed-in in the pulpit; I stand up there alone, helpless and abandoned, facing the many with their unrealizable expectations, their hidden mistrust, their fear of the double ground of my sermon." [23] The analyses of worship services have not yet given me a single listener statement questioning in and for itself the fact that only one person conducts the worship service and is permitted expression in it. That is clearly the preacher's problem and not the congregation's. They are firmly convinced that all force and manipulation are worthless for genuine human communication. Very often they have suffered too much under school or university coercion, and many have also fought too enthusiastically against authoritarian structures to want a position of authority in their own vocation. To be the carrier of dignity would violate their most holy principles; they would be ashamed before their own consciences, and their spiritual potential would shrivel up if they had to do their work with the help of external power. They believe in partnership, in the true equality of all the people around them. They also want to learn throughout their lives and not just teach. Their attitude is one of modesty and reserve; obtrusiveness and pathos are alien to them.

This mistrust of the role of authority is not explained by calling it an unresolved authority problem. That existed in earlier times as well, but without these results. Perhaps the question is rather why the unresolved authority problem manifests itself as it does today. The crisis appears to me to lie at a deeper level. Even people without authority problems today often want nothing to do with authority. Adults are indeed willing to take responsibility for themselves, but in preaching it is a matter of assuming responsibility for *others*. That's no longer tempting, and an allergy exists against such responsibility. The cause of this can be found in a development which has grown stronger in the last few decades and can be viewed from several different angles.

The firm value systems no longer function persuasively and unequivocally in the ethical and spiritual realms. The need for values is less pronounced, and the decline in the feeling of responsibility stands in connection with this. Value systems give security; when they fall, security also disappears. A person who is no longer secure can no longer lead.

At the organizational level we are on the way to a "fatherless society" in which assuming responsibility for others has a bad reputation and arouses fear. This fear is the so-called manager sickness. Managers are not seeking responsibility in their upward climb, but rather only the benefits.

In the realm of self-experience, people are discovering how strongly they project; they are becoming aware to what extent they often thrash out actively their own problems when dealing with other people. This discovery unfortunately leads easily to the fear that one will do it again, and that prompts a retreat from responsibility. We prefer to let others have their own way than to become guilty of manipulation.

David Riesman has tried to understand the behavior of the people in our culture by means of the concept of external guidance. In an earlier phase people were more often internally guided; people had securely acquired their parents' principles through strict upbringing and were thus capable of finding their way through a complicated life using these principles as a compass. If such people were strong, they gladly assumed responsibility because in this way their principles would have a larger area of effectiveness; this was generally recognized as a good thing. Now, however, we are dealing more and more with people who are externally guided and to whom good relationships with others are more important than fundamental staying power. Their behavior is characterized by a sensitivity for what happens outside themselves, and their need for adaptation and recognition is comparatively greater than before. Here, too, it becomes understandable that people don't want responsibility. At most, externally guided persons might occasionally try to attain autonomy, but not power. They intentionally withdraw from power. They don't want to be president.[24]

I find the modest man with his green tie sympathetic in comparison with the authoritarian preacher. A long-awaited breath of warmth and humanness goes through the church. But it's all in vain if in the final analysis this modesty means detachment. Only an involved preacher can awaken feelings of security. But involvement includes—also in a partnership—taking on responsibility for the other person. The decisive question is how the assuming of responsibility can be separated from authoritarian behavior, with the insight that we are not better and know no more than the congregation listening to us.

Maybe the whole thing can become more comprehensible when it's made clear *what* must concretely be assumed in "assuming responsibility," when the images of official authority are separated from the fear and caricatures and viewed under a sober light. Assuming responsibility refers to the preacher and to the listeners. In reference to preachers, assuming responsibility means that they stand by their work and words. People have to be able to sense that their preachers consider the worship service and sermon important; that their words point to something existentially important for them. In reference to the listeners, taking on responsibility means the preacher's claim that what he or she has to say is also decisively important for these listeners. People must sense that the preacher is thinking: "I know a topic now, a word, and a way of dealing with it that can be a help to you." Or a bit more modestly: "I know something important for you, and I hope I succeed in making it clear." The concrete form of assuming responsibility is an attitude making it clear that one's words deserve the greatest attention.

Two elements are thus necessary. Without a living, personal faith this responsibility is an excessive demand, yet any participation in God's work which is felt to be genuine can serve as one of the bases for assuming this responsibility. It is a guarantee that the preacher is speaking about things which are also important for him or her. But a second element is necessary. The responsibility is also an excessive demand if the conviction is missing that this, one's own concern, is also important for those listening. This conviction does not have to be identical with an enthusiasm for conversions or with an urge to evangelize, but something of this must be present if the preacher wants to awaken feelings of security. Only the words "for we cannot but speak" (Acts 4:20) can make the preacher dependable. The risk of an enthusiasm for conversions is unavoidable for anyone who would speak a word of involvement. The decisive factor for a non-authoritarian effect is the way in which this involvement and responsibility are structured. (I will say something more specific about this below.) There is a responsibility which frees the other person, or at least leaves the person some freedom. Responsibility which overpowers and subjects the other person—for example with the coercive "we" sentences—is a perverted form. If the preacher speaks to the congregation in an authentic way and with the presupposition that the concern of the preacher is also important for the congregation, then precisely this presupposition can make the preacher recognizable as that dependable authority the listeners need for the renewal of their primal trust.

Expecting God

The first prerequisite for preaching personally is the willingness to assume responsibility. The second is that the preacher can expect the miracle of the Lord himself to have an effect among the listeners. One might certainly formulate this thesis differently, according to other theological traditions, but this is not the place to determine the dogmatic correctness of this way of expressing it. From the perspective of this chapter it might even be possible to formulate the thesis less theistically, or even atheistically. Otto Haendler puts the same concern into somewhat looser words when he calls the congregation's deepest expectation "the existential longing for eternal truth." [25] C. Aalders is even more cautious when he says that people seek an encounter with the improbable, the strange, the surprising.[26] The true concern of persons in the worship service is crystallized in this encounter. If they later say they felt spoken to, they are pointing in this direction, and the congregation is only satisfied if this depth experience becomes a reality. It becomes quickly dissatisfied if it doesn't occur at all. It hopes and expects to experience contact with God in prayer, in the text reading, or in the sermon. Martin Kriener[27] maintains that a "general consensus" exists concerning the uselessness of the Sunday sermon; this is, however, very likely not the case for the regular participant in worship services.

What the congregation—according to its own words—expects and finds again and again corresponds with the words of the New Testament—among others Luke 10:16; 1 Thessalonians 2:13; the words "lo, I am with you always" (Matt. 28:20) also stand in direct connection with the previous commissioning for proclamation, with the confession, and with theology, especially the Reformed. The mystery has never been expressed more clearly and simply than in the Confessio Helvetica Posterior: "Praedicatio verbi dei est verbum dei." That is a statement of confession; it is believed, not proven. It says that the congregation believes it encounters God himself in the preacher's words. The proclaimed Lord is himself the moving force. That is the precondition for the possibility of the experience of having come into contact with God himself. Through the activity of God the worship service and sermon acquire a sacramental quality; the "true presence of the Lord" resides in the word. Expecially Rudolf Bultmann has strongly emphasized this. This event occurs anew repeatedly in the "mediation" of the event of the revelation of the grace of God in Jesus Christ.

Karl Barth resisted the view that the sermon thus becomes a salvation event. Barth differentiates between the unconditional and absolute proclamation of Jesus and the speaking about Jesus, but he must also say that the sermon participates in the proclamation of Jesus. Whoever accepts the statement from the Confession Helvetica (as does Karl Barth) thus characterizes the sermon as a salvation event. What else should the encounter with God be but a salvation event? I suspect that Barth argues too one-sidedly christologically and not pneumatically enough in this dispute with Bultmann. Just as in the sacraments, something is "dispensed" in the proclamation: God gives of himself. The theological questions needing to be answered here do not belong in this work. I only want to suggest how easily one can find parallels to this congregation theology in the Bible and in theology, a congregation theology manifesting itself in the expectations and experiences of the listeners.

What is happening in worshipers when they claim to encounter God? What is the nature of the occurrence which is incomprehensible for psychological observation and interpretation? The dialectical theologians have come close to a description with some of their formulations. With reference to Karl Barth, Hermann Diem says, for example, that the proclaimed truth is never a truth in and for itself, but is rather only true in an event, and this means in the event of the encounter between Lord and congregation.[28] The experience is described even more clearly when C. Aalders uses Karl Jaspers' differentiation between objective and subjective truth to show what the participant experiences in the worship serivce.[29] No one feels moved or engaged by objective, rational truth. Engagement occurs when we come into contact with subjective, existential truth. It is not universally valid in its objective formulation, but it is uncondi- tional. In the worship service the participants can encounter subjective, existen- tial truth, and when that happens they have a primal experience which touches them existentially. They are more deeply persuaded in this occurrence than ra- tional arguments could ever accomplish. They have an experience of evidence in which rational insight and emotional engagement come together. What brings the participants in a worship service to church is the expectation that they will experience an encounter with God in praying, singing, or listening.

To the extent that he or she can influence it at all, the preacher must try to create the space for this experience, or at least try not to hinder it. In various parts of the worship service it becomes clear whether the pastor has figured on this occurrence of an encounter between God and congregation. Isn't solemnity, intended positively, the characteristic of the attitude and mood corresponding to the expectation of this occurrence? "But the LORD is in his holy temple; let all the earth keep silence before him" (Hab. 2:20). Only through reverence can the preacher make it believable that God is expected. The analyses of worship ser- vice and sermon show that the majority of listeners are very sensitive in this respect. They will not put up with something trivial. Humor is sometimes taken well, even very well, but is also sometimes rejected. In the latter case the limit of reverence has been violated. Examples or jokes which play with the Lord or the Bible are quickly taken as tasteless and slovenly. (Nicknames for Jesus al- most always have a negative effect: "The great traffic cop," "he's a miner.")

The preacher cannot hope to have a good effect without some clear expres- sion of this expectation of the mystery. This assumes, of course, that the preach- er is believing and is expecting the living God. One highly expressive moment is prayer. It will be a tremendous obstacle to the congregation's experience of encounter if the tone of the prayer does not show clearly that the pastor is trying to speak with God. The structure and character of the sermon is a final testimo- nial to whether the preacher is expecting God or not. A religious lecture, a speaking *about* God, differs from a sermon, a speaking in the name of God, precisely in this lack of expectation. If this expectation is missing, all the preacher can do is offer up "general truths" which the listeners can find for themselves.

Kornelis Heiko Miskotte has suggested that a sermon in this sense occurs only in the Christian church. In other religions the sermon is either an illumina- tion of the world's riddle or an admonition to proper living. Christian preaching, however, means pointing to values which "are not" (in the sense of general truths), but rather which "are coming" and become real only in the actual encounter with them.[30]

A preacher who is only modest will thus end up being too modest in the face of this encounter with the improbable. A person in expectation is a person who is not always and not so quickly satisfied.

A final problem in this context is the preacher's own attendance of worship services. This question is circumvented in homiletics. Is it too bourgeois or unpleasant? "Du sublême au ridicule il n'y a qu'un pas." ("From the sublime to the ridiculous is only one step.") The question needing to be answered is, however, whether preachers can have a persuasive effect if they themselves do not regularly attend worship services like other people. This is not a matter of the healthy experience of putting oneself into the situation of the congregation members. It is first and foremost a matter of expecting God. If this expectation is the prerequisite for conducting worship services in which people are seeking to renew and confirm their deepest trust, then the question is the following: How significant does it have to be to the preachers themselves if they are to come across persuasively? If its significance is only that of meeting the requirement of one's own sermons, then that's not enough. The suspicion of falseness arises without fail. Isn't the truth quite simple? The preachers who expect God in their own worship services naturally go to church when others conduct the services, because if it's true that the congregation can expect God's coming in word and Spirit, then they will not want to miss the opportunity to be there, too. The Letter to the Hebrews encourages a faithful attendance of gatherings (Heb. 10:25). Simply pushing aside this demand would be just as superficial as legalistic obedience to it. The stakes are nothing less than contact with the God known to the church. Where else do we find his presence than "through his word and Spirit"? The assumption heard so often today that one experiences God simply through contact with fellow human beings is at any rate not supported by the New Testament. Isn't this a mix-up?

The Relationship Between Preacher and Listener

The analyses of worship services and sermons have shown that participants experience the traditional worship service in a strongly emotional manner. Either they are thankful and enthusiastic because their deepest feelings, their courage, and their trust have been strengthened, or they are frustrated because this did not happen. This dimension of the worship service is more important for experience than the others. For example, enthusiasm for a new insight occurs less often and less strongly. The dimension of security and of trust stands clearly in the foreground for participation and experience. Those attending a worship service are much more concerned with the effectiveness and power of faith than with clear and correct concepts. Experiencing, sensing, and feeling are more important to them than insights and being persuaded. They are more concerned with the effect of what is said than with its meaning. They want to experience something.

I can see that this constitutes a fundamental challenge to traditional homiletics. The customary importance of the content, of the meaning of the spoken words, is called into question. Leonhard Fendt has most clearly spoken the way the entire field of homiletics basically thinks: "In the Protestant sermon of today everything depends on the content." [31] Karl Barth could also be mentioned here; in the discussion about whether a sermon should be read aloud or not he simply says: "The most important thing is that what comes should be correct and responsible." [32] No less than precisely that is thrown overboard if the listeners are permitted to say what's most important to them. They are more concerned about the experience of trust. Quite aside from the question of who is right or wrong, it's extremely unsettling to find such a large gap between sermon theory and sermon effect. It means either that the congregation does not at all understand what their preachers want to offer them, or that homiletics is looking past the congregation at a crucial point. Let's have a look at the formidable army of textbooks. They concentrate either for the most part or entirely on the content of the sermon. Otto Haendler is an exception. For example, he maintains that identical words can have a different effect coming from a different person. [33] This means that something other than the content determines the effect. This is even the case in reading. A written devotion is variously judged according to whether the reader thinks the author is sympathetic or not. I don't want to doubt the good intentions and not even the great value of homiletical publications, but an unrealistic perspective limits their value. The most essential element, as far as the congregation is concerned, cannot be found where the sermon theorists think it can.

Where can it then be found? The contact with the improbable, the encounter with God: Where else could it be besides in the meaning of what is said, in the content? If anywhere, isn't God's word experienced in the meaning of the human word? Not at all! But then where?

In the investigation into listener experiences made in this chapter, I have determined which elements make a renewal of primal trust possible for a congregation: the personal self-presentation of the preacher, genuine attitude, speaking directly, willingness to assume responsibility, an attitude of expectation. The integration of these various elements is the prerequisite for a renewal of primal trust. In the worship service the participants are seeking this renewal in the encounter with God, and are seeking it in the face of the final, existential questions of life.

I draw the conclusion: The real mystery of encounter occurs for the experience of the congregation in the relationship between the preacher and the listeners. The communication between pastor and congregation is the place where "it" takes place, if it takes place at all. "It" is the communion of Lord and people in faith; that's how one expresses it theologically. It cannot be grasped in psychological terminology. An ascertainable experience like the renewal of primal trust is only one aspect of a larger event.

I believe the congregation is right, and not homiletics. Homiletics has given itself over intellectually to the content, the meaning of the spoken words. But the content is not the essential element. The essential element occurs in the relationship between preacher and congregation; the content of the words has its significance only within this framework. The effect of a textual explanation is inextricably associated with the effect of the preacher. The listener statements speak clearly: There are sermons which have a strong, positive effect without the listeners' being able to say exactly what the content was. But they rejoice because their joy and trust are awakened; they praise God without being able to reproduce the sermon. I get the impression that this is always or almost always the case with a large majority of uneducated people in worship services. Just because it's sometimes different for educated people, just because they can now and then reproduce a sermon, this does not mean that they've listened more closely. The relationship essential in a worship service is more important than anything spoken. Christ doesn't offer himself in the cognitive meaning of the spoken word; his promise is meant for the two or three gathered in his name. There he is "in the midst of them" (Matt. 18:20). The truth is not cognitive, but rather communicative. Adolf Sommerauer expresses something of this: "Christ

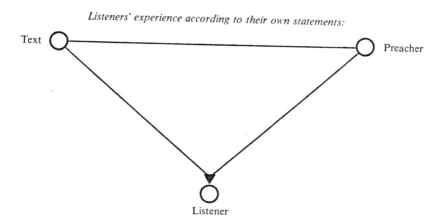

Listeners' experience according to their own statements:

Text

Preacher

Listener

For the listener the effect of the text is inseparably connected with the effect of the preacher.

is not only proclaimed by the calling of His name, not only by the description of His offices, but rather also and certainly no less by the behavior of the preacher." [34] In the collection of essays "Didaktik der Predigt" edited by Peter Düsterfelt and Hans-Bernhard Kaufmann, the same insight is sometimes found, especially in Günter Rohkämper and Dieter Seiler: "We believe that the 'gospel' manifests itself not only in the content, but also in the manner of communication of this content." [35] In the same collection, Hans-Werner Dannowski supports this attention given the dimension of relationship in a sermon, though he limits this to the so-called "acts of speaking" (assertion, warning, challenge and similar aspects). But that touches only a part of the problem of relationship. This limitation of attention to acts of speaking—thus only to the structures of speech—eliminates decisive aspects of the preacher's self-presentation: credibility, warmth, and so on. The effect of the preacher's personality does not come fully enough into view. Just as in love, the relationship itself is the most important thing. In his theory of communication Paul Watzlawick finds that language loses in meaning to the extent that it is purely a matter of the speaker. This is most clear in love relationships and in hostility. The same thing suggested for homiletics also holds true from pastoral care. The essential element is not to be found in the statements themselves, but rather in the dimension of depth, in the non-verbal encounter.

The mystery of the worship service occurs between the listeners, the preacher, and what the preacher represents and what qualifies him or her for the listeners. The text (in the sermon and liturgy) is an allusion to the Lord himself, just as is the preacher. What characterizes the text over against the preacher is its

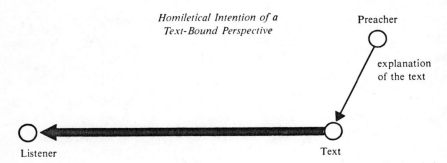

For the listener only the effect of the text is important. The preacher only offers it up. The mystery of the worship service lies hidden in the text.

Hans Urner verbalizes precisely what I am calling into question: "In reality the proper sermon comes only from God, who reveals Himself in His word. Thus everything depends on the text, and nothing on the preacher. God causes the text to speak and the preacher as well as the listeners to hear" (Gottes Wort und unsere Predigt, p. 93).

unlimited dependability and objectivity. But by the same token, the preacher has what the text lacks: the capacity to speak, to present oneself visibly, to be there live. The actual mystery of the encounter with God is perhaps more directly connected with the text than with the preacher, but the *place* the text comes to the congregation is the relationship to the preacher.

It would be senseless to conclude that only the preacher is important and not the text, or that it's only a matter of feelings of relationship and not of the content of the words, and this conclusion should not be drawn. It is possible I am offering the occasion to do this in this section where I am emphasizing the decisive importance of the relationship between preacher and listeners and am trying to justify it theologically. The next two chapters, however, will make it clear that the sermon's text and content should by no means complain about not getting enough of my attention.

Something very important from biblical and Hebrew life has been preserved in the occurrence of the worship service and sermon. This becomes clear when we look at the difference between the Hebraic term "davar," which we normally translate into English as "word," and what the term "word" actually means. "Davar" describes what goes on in communication, while our term "word" describes a meaning hidden in the word. "Davar" points toward the activity in the relationship as that which is most important, while our "word" points more toward whatever lies behind the word. For us a word is only an unimportant husk, what is essential is actually behind the word. When we look for the most important element behind, under, or over a word, I see this as a parallel to western anthropology's underestimation of the body in comparison to the soul. The word's form—for example the way it's pronounced—is then naturally much less important, since the main thing is the content. This is not the case with "davar." Here the form—the way a word is pronounced—is decisive, and there is no differentiation between content and form. The decisive factor is then what happens between speaker and listener. A word happens, it is not just spoken. Consider the customary introductory words to the prophets: "And the word of the Lord came."

In Luke 2:15 the shepherds in the Christmas story say: "The word (thing, deed) that has happened." Not only does the content meaning reside in this occurrence, but also in the act and manner of speaking. Word and action cannot be cleanly separated. The personalities of the speaker and of the listener play a central role in the Hebraic understanding of "word," while for our "word" the speaker's personality is unimportant. It's more a matter of meaning, and when we have grasped the meaning, the word itself is no longer important; this leads us to disregard the speaker's personality. But now we find that people experience a worship service and proclamation of the word more in the biblical-Hebraic than in the western fashion. The explanation for this phenomenon may be that a powerful biblical structural element is asserting itself here which is

64

otherwise a foreign body in its cultural environment. But the explanation may also be that it becomes clear in the behavior of the person attending a worship service that the western separation between word form and content meaning is just not experienced by the person hearing the word. The biblical way of speaking thus uncovers a generally human experience. Gerhard von Rad views these differences between our "word" in its almost exclusive function as bearer of meaning on the one hand, and the creative, powerful function of the biblical word on the other, against the background of the entire world of antiquity; there a word generally represented a force or power. He, too, agrees that various functions of words have been lost in late cultures. What is suspected of being magic may well be a lost treasure.[36]

The place of the actual worship service event is the communication between preacher and listener. Feeling oneself spoken to by God and feeling oneself spoken to by the preacher are interdependent facts, and this requires that homiletics take the preacher's personality more seriously than before. The campaigns for an improvement in the content of sermons only treat the symptoms and are not very promising. The preacher's entire education should take into consideration that the contentual element, valued so highly, only has meaning if the preacher's personality is capable of communication within the realm of Christian faith. The elements discussed in this chapter—being genuine, speaking directly to the congregation, assuming responsibility, expecting God—all deserve not only intellectual consideration, but also thorough application in the training and continuing education of preachers. To be sure, homileticians have known for a long time that the proclamation of the word has a human component: human words. Both homiletics must take a significant further step toward discovering the *humanitas Christi:* proclamation includes not only the content and meaning of human language, but also the preacher's whole capacity for communication or for disturbing communication. Homiletics is still too idealistic here and thus even a bit docetic. The human element is even more human.

The corrective in the 19th century's understanding of faith and sermons, brought about by Karl Barth and dialectical theology, encompasses two main elements. The first is the rehabilitation of God's independent activity which awakens faith, and which is the real preacher. This insight threatened to go under in Schleiermacher and Ritschl's emphasis of the Christian personality. But Barth's corrective has a second element, an intellectual one. Because of the concentration on God and his word, the understanding of the word has become so important that experience is threatening to disappear from view. Here it's a matter of emphasis. As little as one can really accuse the theologians of the 19th century of seeing only the individual Christian, likewise one cannot really accuse Barth and Brunner of total intellectualism. The shift of emphasis is nonetheless great enough to misunderstand what happens during the worship service and sermon. Barth tried several times to define what the sermon is. I will present the definition given by his "Homiletics" (1932/33) because I get the impression one cannot say of this definition—as one can of so much else in this book—that it has been superceded by something fundamentally different in Barth's later publications. The definition embraces two parts:

1. The sermon is God's word, spoken by him using the medium of the explanation of a biblical text directed to contemporary people, given in extemporaneous speech by a person called by a church obedient to its commission.

2. The sermon is the attempt required of the church to serve the word of God by one called to that service, to serve in such a way that a biblical text is explained to contemporary people as something concerning them directly and as the proclamation of what they are supposed to hear from God himself.

It's clear how strongly God's independent activity is emphasized. This was necessary as a corrective for the understanding of the sermon expressed by Carl Immanuel Nitsch, Johannes Baur and others, an understanding in which the Christian personality and individuality of the preacher had authoritative value. But the other element becomes clear unintentionally: The only thing remaining of the preacher's activity is the "explanation in extemporaneous speech." Barth's definition overlooks the fact that the whole personality has an effect: Only the "explanation" counts. Of course, one can "explain" in a thoroughly played-out fashion, and Karl Barth probably did this himself, as listeners of his sermons attest. But a person can also "explain" in an intellectual fashion, excluding the experiential aspect, and the reduction of the preacher's activity to an explanation opens the door wide for an intellectualistic proceeding. This intellectualistic danger is not just an imaginary one for Barth, either. "Only that sermon is a sacramental act in which every word can be fully and completely answered for." He presses for a "painfully exact working out of every word," and this demand is an absolute rule for everyone. The sermon must be "ready for the press" before it is given.[37] The forced language of these homileticians becomes apparent in even a general reading. Again and again there is talk of "danger." (This overemphasis probably belongs to the period in Barth's work in which these lectures originated; I am not aware that it can be found in the *Church Dogmatics*.) Have preachers done what they are supposed to if the text is correctly explained? That's just not the case. They are to *witness* to the gospel, and for that they need something more than just the ingenuity of explanation. "Witnessing" brings to expression the involvement in the relationship between preacher and listeners.

If we take seriously the results of the analyses of worship services and sermons, we contribute to a partial rehabilitation of the theologians of the 19th century. We will especially want to hear Friedrich Schleiermacher again with his emphasis of feeling as the locus of faith, though this feeling can never be the *basis* of either systematic theology or faith. Precisely this is what Schleiermacher asserted. For him dogmatics consist of statements of faith which are the verbal expression of "religious affections or emotions." [38] At this juncture Barth and Brunner correctly put him aside. God himself always takes the initiative. However, in theology we also have to appreciate human feelings, the faith experience, and general religious experience. But here the dialectical theologians abandon us. The new person "needs only to believe, never to perceive in an empirical, inward fashion." [39] This may be true, but there is another side as well, though Brunner has no interest in it. The differentiation of which Schleiermacher spoke concerning the faith experience disappears with this condemnation of experience as a basis of dogmatics. For Schleiermacher there are several words for the experience of faith: feeling, perception, being affected or stimulated, seeing, disposition, instinct, being moved. The interest in the individual element is also lost for the most part in dialectical theology and the theology influenced by it. In homiletics this manifests itself in the fact that the preacher's personality receives only peripheral attention or none at all.

The model for the preacher is, I suspect, most of the time that of a teacher or even a university professor. "I think I was better prepared to be a professor of theology than a preacher to businessmen." [40] The unfortunate part is that this overemphasis of the content already begins with the focus or identification of the preacher. We need to find a more suitable model for the preacher. Rudolf Bohren calls homiletics the "teaching of the language of love." [41] However, his homiletics are still no exception to the rule that the content is considered the most important element. Willem Berger compares the worship service to certain situations in a marriage. Just as marriage partners speak, eat, and play, so also do participants in a worship service do different things. Just as it would be inadequate for a married couple to measure the value of a weekend spent together by whether or not they acquired clear insights, better understanding, or new information, so also the evaluation of a worship service based only on its content is simply unrealistic.[42] The image of the person in love appears to me best suited for the preacher, especially for the dimension of security. It contains all the elements I have listed except the expectation of God. That's where the preacher differs from the courting lover who only intends to offer himself. But the emotional disposition of the person in love better corresponds to the preacher's commission than does the objective, informative one of the teacher. Whoever accepts the model of the person in love can also see the difference between that and the manipulation and authoritarian arbitrariness so often falsely attributed to the pulpit preacher.

This also characterizes much of the criticisms of sermons in general: the false conception that the conceptual-content meaning of what is communicated is the most important aspect of the sermon. Serious structural criticisms have been leveled at the institutions of the Sunday sermon and traditional worship service in the past few years. Almost all these attacks are closely bound up to the content, and falsely believe that the worship service is or should be a matter of the communication of cognitive knowledge. This is the way Hans-Dieter Bastian ascertains the almost total lack of effect of the sermon, but he views it from the perspective of the communication of information.[43] That is where his error lies. By doing this he brings the sermon into a context where it doesn't belong and is not even experienced. It's no accident that Bastian opposes the word "sermon" and prefers to speak of a "pulpit discourse." With the word "sermon" he fears the excess baggage of so many prejudices that the important aspects are distorted before one even gets to the analysis. He overlooks the fact that with this shift in the direction of a "pulpit discourse" he himself has already distorted the most important aspect. The essential element in a sermon lies deeper than information; it intends to guide one to an encounter and to trust. And when Hans-Eckehard Bahr accuses the traditional worship service of backwardness, he betrays how he himself misunderstands the institution with his characterization of the gospel as a "public opinion and as information within the process of other understandings of the world."[44] I basically agree with Wolfgang Hammer's criticism of the word "information" in relationship to the proclamation.[45] Truth, witness, and confession are more than information. However, Hammer does not interpret Bahr correctly when he maintains that "information" is totally neutral or not necessary for life. "Information" means something communicated which sets people in motion and makes decisions possible. The expression is of no use to the proclamation not because it might be uninvolved or non-obligatory, but because it overestimates the value of the content. "Opinion" and "explanation" are typical words for the contentual element. The use of cybernetic laws is only justified if one views the sermon as information.

Occasional sociological-psychological observations and test studies also make the mistake of viewing the sermon as a discourse in which the communication of knowledge takes place. These studies find that the learning process requires a dialogue situation, that the listeners of a sermon are able to retain only very little, and that things stand very poorly with the cognitive learning process in our worship services. Memory work is required of the listeners, and the sermon itself is supposed to strive for a communication of knowledge; this knowledge is then to become reproducible memory-content for those listeners.

The customary sermon analyses are also always firmly oriented toward the content of what is said. Even the custom of having sermons published probably hearkens back to this preoccupation with content. The fact that a sermon is also a visible event, that it's also determined by the presence of a group of people, and that it stands in the context of a worship service—all this is bracketed out. The value of these analyses cannot be much greater than if one wrote down and analyzed the words of two friends during an intensive encounter, unless one investigated a certain topic, some content of knowledge. A sermon is, however, as we have seen, essentially more than that.

The fact that the experience, renewal, and confirmation of the fundamental feeling of life plays such an overwhelmingly important role in the traditional worship service is commensurate with a modern need Marshall McLuhan has called the concern for depth. He maintains that the modern person of the age of electronics wants to experience something more than to understand it. Our comprehension of what is happening is particularly changed by television. We no longer comprehend part by part as in reading a newspaper, word for word, but rather inclusively as in television, which immediately shows us the whole. By means of the simultaneity made possible by the electronic communications media such as telephone and television, people are able to participate much more deeply than while reading. This heightens our capacity for participation and engagement. The improvising television actor lets the spectators participate in his or her inner life. In connection with this development people today demand above all inner participation, intimacy, and an experience of depth. The content is no longer the important element, the effect is what counts. Content is only the communication of information; the effect embraces the whole situation. The experience of basic trust felt by those participating in a worship service as the deepest dimension is precisely this concern for depth as McLuhan describes it. If we are seeking forms in which the worship service today can speak to people, the traditional worship service—by making possible the experience of trust and joy—is more promising than the experiments in which the content element is more pronounced; these include the discussion and so-called information worship services.

For preachers who regularly conduct worship services, the discovery of this dimension's importance means that they ought with a good conscience to try to awaken feelings. The choice of songs, especially of melodies, is an initial step. Of course, the large majority of church hymnals are extremely reserved in their capacity for emotional expression; more value is placed on the historical correctness of a trill than on the opportunity to carry along the average church-goer inwardly. One need only consider here the century-old preference for baroque music in worship services—with its tendency to hold back feeling—and the avoidance of the organ works of the romantic period. Historicism is often the dominating factor concerning the organ. An open acceptance of the significance of emotional experience would lead to important correctives in church music.

I do not mean to argue for a general admission of emotions into the worship service. The limit of what is possible is quickly reached in the traditional service, and coercion only drives the participants away. A healthy acceptance of the fact that the people in a worship service are justifiably hoping for a deep experience will lead the preacher to pull the emotional side of communion with others out of the watered-down state in which it is all too often found.

CHAPTER 3

The Dimension of Deliverance

In this chapter I will continue the consideration of listener reactions to worship services and sermons by summarizing and offering up for discussion those statements witnessing to a consciousness of the concrete, visible reality around us. People in a worship service feel spoken to only if this second dimension is also taken into consideration. The first dimension—that of security—encompasses the deepest feelings, indeed human life in general, primary existence. "Faith" at this level is characterized by trust or security in God. The second dimension is not as deep, but it makes up for that in scope. It deals with life in the concrete world, the process of living together, problems of family and work, of justice and guilt, the opportunities as well as the impossibilities of life. This second dimension is like a large concentric circle around the first, and encompasses the area that comes into view after the deepest feelings of security are there. People in a worship service are generally not truly engaged or spoken to if the preacher does not expressly include this broader dimension.

It is almost exclusively negative statements that make this dimension visible:

—I thought it was good that he didn't avoid the pain.
—This beautiful, sound world . . . I just don't believe it.
—The idyllic part aggravated me.
—I thought it was rather harmless. I don't experience God that way.
—It was too nice. What happened to the guilt?
—I missed the sadness, and I missed Mrs. R. (funeral sermon).

These statements make it clear that the listeners resist when the preacher doesn't expressly take seriously the dirty, painful life of reality. This complaint occurs frequently in the case of funeral sermons; the listeners just don't accept it when the preacher paints a picture that's too pretty. They want to see real life taken into consideration with the hard facts not bracketed out.

From another angle this dimension becomes clear in the following statements:

—I found statements of faith were missing.
—She only barely mentioned the message of the resurrection; it was just much too far away from her whole sermon.

—I found the "vertical" dimension missing.

—His voice and the whole atmosphere was soothing, but there was just no hope in it (funeral sermon).

These reactions show how the congregation is waiting for the gospel. Whether or not they accept it is another question, but they consider it self-evident that an exhortation will come. As we have seen, they resist if the dark side of life is not taken seriously or is rendered harmless; but they also resist if that dark side is all there is, if no word of release is offered as well.

—I was able to listen closely, but I waited for something that never came. That disappointed me.

—I was surprised when it was over. Already?

—I'm not satisfied. Is that all I get from such a powerful story?

Several times here we see the listeners disappointed because they got too little. They are waiting for something, for a word of release. If it doesn't come they feel they haven't really been spoken to:

—"I have to," "I have to!"; that makes me sick.

—Too strong an exhortation and too little chance of doing it.

—The failure wasn't accepted. That's pressure.

—I'm told that it doesn't depend on us, that Jesus is active in us; that made me glad.

Even if a real attempt is made to address this need, that doesn't yet mean the listeners are really spoken to. They resist any pressure, and that is one of my findings that has most astonished me: that the listeners have a fine sense for the difference between gospel and legality. Such legality has a pronounced negative effect on most of them, peculiarly enough also on those who themselves preach about such legality!

—The consolation was vague; I found it depressing.

—The releasing or liberating element was unclear.

—No perspective became visible.

I have already written about such lack of clarity. If it has anything to do with the gospel exhortation—and that's frequently the case—the listeners are understandably even more disappointed than if some image or other part was not clear. They demand clarity concerning the central concern of the sermon because this central element is apparently truly central for them.

I have chosen the word *deliverance* to characterize the dimension which has appeared in the statements presented. The people in a worship service want to have light offered to them in the darkness of their lives; they want to see the hopelessness of day to day life, of life in this world, surpassed by a perspective which can't be found in that day to day life itself. They yearn for a deliverance from the misfortune, oppression, and the misery which are, after all, a part of life. In this dimension the key is the encounter with that aspect of the message which awakens hope, the words about the beyond. This is the message the worshipers are waiting for, the language of release.

Dimensions are theoretical divisions; they are not separated in the reality of the worship service and sermon. Thus the dimension of trust, as it is experienced by those in a worship service, should not disappear from view. What someone says and how they say it are a unity. In spite of this, the dimensions can be taken one at a time for reflection, as long as we remember that we are reflecting on preaching as a totality and are not discussing different parts of the sermon one after the other. Our reflecting attention is now directed toward an aspect manifesting itself primarily in the content, thus also primarily in the sermon. The first dimension lies at a deeper level and is less differentiated; it is visible primarily in the non-verbal components of the way the preacher conducts the worship service.

It would be incorrect to presume that one dimension is more essential than the other. Just as with our bodies and all independent organs, various parts and aspects are essential. There are, however, differences in weight. The dimension of security carries the most import. Whoever makes mistakes there will disappoint the worship service participants the most, and will disappoint them most deeply. The congregation, however, is not satisfied with just the security alone, and awakening trust is not enough. Its effect is lost if it is not associated with a message of deliverance; the preacher will not achieve a positive effect without effectively taking this dimension of deliverance into consideration. However, even the best treatment of this second dimension is ruined if the preacher falls short in the dimension of security. The purest doctrine, the most striking formulation of the good news, has no effect at all if the preacher's appearance does not awaken feelings of trust. Just because two preachers say the same thing does not mean it's really the same. The congregation accepts it from one, but not from the other. Words alone are not strong enough.

The Yearning for Deliverance

I will now take a closer look at the conclusions from the listener statements mentioned earlier in which the dimension of deliverance became visible. The worship service participants yearn for such release; that's the background for all these statements. This yearning constitutes a movement contrary to the need for a renewal of primal trust discussed in the previous chapter. Apparently the worshipers are seeking not only the old and familiar; they are also expecting something entirely new. They seek not only what has already proven itself in their past; they also seek the future. Their expectations are focused both backward and forward. These two movements, which basically are at odds with one another, form a polar tension. The listeners are expecting something old and something new, confirmation and change. If they fail to get their money's worth concerning the one or the other, they are disappointed. They obviously expect that both force fields will be fully taken into consideration.

In connection with the desire for security, I said that a regression takes place in the worship service participant, a return to childlike perception and behavior. This assertion is not judgmental. There are constructive as well as unrealistic regressions. It now becomes clear that the worship service participants are not satisfied simply when they experience a regression, not even when the regression in and for itself is experienced positively. One statement makes this explicitly clear: "His voice and the whole atmosphere were soothing, but there was just no hope in it." This is referring to a funeral sermon in which the pastor aroused a strong feeling of trust through his warm involvement (a child had died). But his words were bland and lacked force; there was no exhortation. It becomes clear here that on the one hand a constructive regression could take place because the pastor showed genuine empathy and was thus able to be a support for the speechless, upset mourners. On the other hand, however, he disappointed everyone because they were waiting for him to speak a word of hope, to offer a perspective into the future. It didn't come. In the worship service people not only expect a return to the protective womb of the loving God; they also want to hear that there will soon be changes, that things won't just remain the same. The people hearing a sermon don't want merely protection against evil, they also yearn for evil itself to be overcome. This world here, this life, should become new, better, whole.

There are probably two reasons for the listeners' strong, constantly recurring expectation. Just as was the case with feelings of security, a universally human and an ecclesiastical, Christian layer can be distinguished. The "utopian spirit," the yearning for a better world, belongs perhaps to all humanity; it most certainly belongs to the view of life in the culture of the west. Ernst Bloch says that this hope originates in the schism in human beings between their present appearance and their absent essence.[1] This yearning can fashion itself optimistically or pessimistically, but it is there in any case. It's this vague, general aspect of the yearning for release which becomes visible in the statements of worship service participants. The Christian proclamation picks up this desire, indeed it puts wind into its sails. For thousands of years the Christian congregation has heard that the Lord is coming, that he will make things anew, and that we are awaiting a new heaven and earth. The proclamation of coming release and deliverance baptized the undefined, universally human yearning and thus gave it a profile, corrected it, confirmed and strengthened it. The two levels of yearning for release or deliverance are named in Romans 8. The creation waits in *apokaradokia*, "with eager long-ing" (8:19), while "we" stand in *elpis*, "in this hope" (8:24). Directed hope stands next to an indeterminate waiting. The participants in a worship service thus expect that this strong yearning—which has even been strengthened more by the tradition of the church's proclamation—be picked up and satisfied or at least taken seriously. The previous listener reactions show what happens to the sermon if this dimension is neglected.

Can what the congregation wants and expects—according to the previous statements—now be considered legitimate and capable of realization? How does this yearning for deliverance look in the light of theology? How can we legiti-mately meet this need? Do the listener statements help discover new theological structures? On a theoretical, cognitive level it might only be a matter of recol-lection, an "aha" insight describing a structure based on the preaching commis-sion and not at all in the listeners' expectations. In that case one would expect the outlines to be less clear in the listeners' expectations than in the theological formulation of the meaning of the worship service and the purpose of the ser-mon. The congregation would only be giving a response; it would only reflect back what it had received.

The yearning for deliverance and redemption is fundamentally a two-sided feeling of life. One side is suffering; the other is hope. A strong awareness of a condition of misery goes hand in hand with the expectation of relief. A knowl-edge of insoluble problems unites with the suspicion of miraculous help. I think it's easy to recognize in this feeling an echo of the proclamation of cross and resurrection. The people in a worship service know that life's incomprehensible, omnipresent misery is taken totally seriously by the church, but they also know that the church has a feeling for something beyond misery and hopelessness. Just as theology always summarizes the proclamation with two concepts—cross and resurrection, judgment and grace, law and gospel—so also does the congre-gation expect to be spoken to in its need as well as its hope. It makes me glad to find this out, and I'm astonished at how purely the gospel's inner constitution is reflected in the listeners' expectations. Even if the contours are not particularly sharp, the basic idea is theologically reliable. How late will we have to discover this! Haven't we always thought—or has it only been I?—that theologians know it all better? But now the people in the pews are teaching us, and perhaps it's even those scoffed-at chancery swallows.

The proclamation of grace and judgment guards against the worshipers stay-ing in unrealistic regressions. Law and gospel make a claim on day-to-day life and awaken hope for life in its entire scope. This claim is inherent in the Chris-tian proclamation, and our institution of the sermon is unthinkable without it. The congregation counts on being spoken to concerning release and deliverance, and this in turn requires that the preacher take both sides of the proclamation seriously. Just because I now call them law and gospel does not mean there are

not other adequate, perhaps even better possibilities for characterizing the proclamation's two aspects. I am not concerned with the words; they are simply
familiar to me and appear to be useful as catch-words.

What is necessary for preachers to take the worshipers' yearning for deliverance seriously? How can they do justice to the dimension of release or deliverance from misery? How can they indeed show or announce a solution for
something insoluble; what does release look like anyway? The same thing holds
true for this second dimension: Only God himself can deliver and release; only
he can truly awaken hope. The homiletical question is, then: How should
preachers behave in order not to place unnecessary obstacles in the way of this
inaccessible mystery?

Awakening Wonder

A yearning for release or deliverance presupposes that the problems are insoluble, that there is no reason for hope within the framework of what is normal
and accessible. Anyone delivering a message of deliverance to such yearning
will arouse either skepticism or astonishment; the listeners will either not find
the message believable or they will be astonished in the face of the unbelievable. A balanced interest or tame attentiveness would be incommensurate with
the import of the matter, with the intense yearning. A person suffering in a
hopeless situation of insoluble misery will take notice when someone speaks of
real deliverance.

Genuine wonder or a new feeling of surprise is unavoidable if a promise is to
be made to the slumbering or aggressive yearning for release. The question remains open whether the listener will joyfully greet the deliverance or will let it
go by untouched. The preacher is not the one to decide this, nor is the listener
always the one. At any rate, however, the discrepancy between the insoluble
nature of the problems and the message of deliverance causes the proclamation
to arouse wonder. It's not possible any other way. This awakening of wonder
thus becomes a sign showing whether a preacher is really preaching such release. Without wonder there is not the slightest suspicion of deliverance. I will
now present some listener statements making that clear:

—I've heard that so often it didn't affect me.
—I wasn't stimulated enough.
—What she said was so joyless and cock-sure.
—I was surprised by the explanation, "Jesus' miracle went through
   Peter's hands"; that made me start thinking.

The listeners can experience something of new hope and possibilities only when
they're surprised with something unknown, with a fresh textual explanation,

with an image, with a striking sentence. Their astonishment means they are seeing beyond their previous limitations, are discovering something new. It means the old is being seen in a new light. Even if it's only a brief moment of astonishment, it's nonetheless the beginning of hope belonging to the promised deliverance. The listeners are happy when it comes to that, as the last statement shows. The others refer to sermons in which there were no surprises.

The problem surfacing here is how to make such astonishment possible in each weekly worship service. The message of deliverance itself should be so unbelievable that it continually arouses astonishment. Well, it is. It's nothing other than a matter of "what no eye has seen, nor ear heard, nor the heart of man conceived" (1 Cor. 2:9). "For the element of otherness that encounters us in the hope of the Old and New Testaments—the thing we cannot already think out and picture for ourselves on the basis of the given world and of the experiences we already have of that world—is one that confronts us with a promise of something new and with the hope of a future given by God." [2] The weekly sermon lives because the message of deliverance is incredible and will always be incredible. This theological assertion requires, however, a quite specific attitude on the part of preachers. They should deliver their messages in such a way that the listeners really can be astonished and can wonder. What does this presuppose?

The preachers' own astonishment is itself fundamental. Speakers don't have to be astonished themselves every time they are to lead others to astonishment. Teachers can amaze their classes with information about geology or history, but in the sermon it's a matter of another kind of astonishment. The congregation yearns for an improbability, for deliverance from insoluble problems. They aren't looking for information available to everyone anyway, but rather for the miraculous. For the mediation of this improbable thing preachers must themselves be struck by the miraculous; otherwise even the most miraculous thing comes across as "already heard it so many times." It then belongs to the realm of the familiar, while the listeners are yearning precisely for something they can't find. Only by their own astonishment can preachers help their miraculous message to have a contagious effect. Franz Rosenzweig describes in his letters why he felt spoken to by a preacher: ". . . There is something extra there, something final, a carrying away of the entire person." [3] This being carried away shows the fascination of preachers themselves. A "shock effect" will go out to the listeners from the preachers' own surprise, something which belongs to the theological criteria by which sermons should be measured.

But what if preachers just don't happen to be really astonished? I believe there are some important things to be said concerning this question, and I will speak of them later; but there is no all-inclusive answer. What preachers can live in perpetual astonishment? It's a difficult insight: In such situations they will fall short in the dimension of release described here; or, more precisely, they will have to survive by filling in the gaps from some other source. The question of how they can continually experience wonder does not seem meaningful to me. One should ask rather how they can come to terms with the unavoidable frustration associated with a task they can optimally fulfill only if they themselves feel existentially engaged. Here we simply encounter the limitations of experiential possibilities.

Preachers can try, however, to recover that astonishment or wonder. This is an important, if not the most important element of sermon preparation. Wonder emerges along with the *idea for a sermon*. A discovery is made, a core idea is found; it leads either to the choice of texts or, if the text is already determined, to the conception of the sermon. Ernst Lange does not call this sudden idea for a sermon a revelation, but rather a "breakthrough in understanding itself leading to the possibility of making something understandable." [4] Preachers make these discoveries alone if they are creative, but one cannot determine for all people just how this receptivity or receptive capacity can be enhanced. A certain peace and quiet, an undisturbed free space appears to me to be indispensable for this inspiration. Without peace and quiet the restless, creative calm, that seeking and yearning preceding a discovery, cannot emerge. However, the sermon idea can certainly also originate with lightning speed, right in the middle of work and schedule. I think it's important that the congregation and other people can guide one to sermon ideas in this sense—not just the quiet study room.[5] Discussions with others about faith, existential questions, or about a biblical text give a different stimulus than meditation. Someone else's misunderstanding—according to one's own judgment—can be especially stimulating.

Hans Adolf Oelker has pointed out a tendency in many sermons which deserves attention here. He finds a discrepancy between the listeners and many preachers. The worship service is for the listeners a step out of the familiar world into a special one. They expect something special, something they don't find in normal day-to-day life. But what do many preachers do? The path to the worship service is for them a normal occurrence. They hardly have a sense any more for the extraordinary element in it. And then they also try to take away that special element by means of contemporaneity and modern speech. The listeners are then disappointed because they simply encounter their same old world again. That special element they were looking for, the holy, is not offered.[6] Although Oelker does not support his assertion with listener statements, I believe he is right. The problem of the distance between the extraordinary, for example, the biblical terminology, and the day-to-day cannot be solved by an accommodation to that day-to-day world. The listeners are waiting for something which will awaken their wonder. An abstruse terminology does not, of course, do the job, but just as little does a sermon arouse wonder in which the extraordinary has been displaced into the day-to-day.

Some important instruction concerning the fashioning of a sermon's content can be found in this context. It is a matter of *alienation*. Whoever makes use of this in the right way will awaken wonder. What is meant here is already very old; Bertolt Brecht gave it a new theoretical formulation. It is the attempt to say something old in a new way so that it awakens wonder anew. Habit and self-evidence undermine attention, alienation arouses interest by showing something known in an unknown dimension and by making something neglected into something important. Bastian bases the necessity of alienation in a sermon on the findings of the science of communication: that information cannot be preserved.[7] It loses its effective power. Only through alienation does one make people get the impression they're hearing something new and thus gain their interest anew. It's clear that it's often a case of something old, as in television commercials. In the sermon—even if things seem most new—it's always a matter of what is old, of the tradition of the gospel. Alienation figures precisely on this polarity of familiarity and strangeness so that a new experience of the old and familiar finally emerges. A clear example of alienation is a sermon about Jesus' appearance in the synagogue, where at the beginning one speaks only about "a young worker." Only during the course of the sermon does it become clear that Jesus is meant. Alienation conveys a discovery to the listener, an astonished recollection. The actual astonishment at the promised deliverance can thus possibly be reawakened.

The effective power of alienation has two clear limitations. First of all, alienation is not understood if it makes excessive demands on the listener's flexibility. Instead of awakening wonder, it provokes an aggravation which cannot be essentially identified with the aggravation or scandal of the gospel. Ernst Lerle warns of an estrangement between the congregation and preacher, particularly if the alienation contains value statements.[8] The process of alienation happens to offer the possibility of a sophisticated use of the gospel for self-seeking reasons, for example for political purposes. The previously presented sermon with "Jesus as a young worker" also arouses suspicions about the preacher's political preferences.

In the second place, alienation contains the inherent danger of making something unimportant seem important. It's tempting to surprise the listeners, but if only this element of surprise is the goal, as a feeling, then the alienation degenerates into a game. Various listener reactions expressing boredom and aggravation were precipitated by a deteriorated alienation. Then the relationship with one's own genuine wonder also disappears. The whole technique of alienation presupposes precisely a real astonishment in preachers themselves. Without this it's a trick which will at best have a deceptive effect. What then emerges is basically a tacky falseness. A covered-up emptiness is hiding behind the sensational words or image.

The preacher's own astonishment at the gospel's strangeness remains the determining factor here. Efforts at renewing astonishment and bringing the congregation to astonishment can succeed only within this framework, and then the strangeness of the gospel will become clear to the listeners even without the technique of alienation. Technique can only give sharper contours to something already existing. If it wants to do more than that, it degenerates and meets with rejection.

The Discrepancy Between Full Power of Authority and Modesty

In the strict sense, the dimension of deliverance requires a miracle. Those in a worship service are expecting something impossible, and they get it in spite of everything if the service goes as they expect. They yearn for deliverance because life's problems are insoluble, and at the end they're happy that this insolubility is called into question. Unbelievable. This does not now mean for preachers that miracles are expected of them personally. Surely no worship service participants see them as magicians. Those listening to the sermons don't need to be convinced that preachers are just as limited and helpless as they are. Nonetheless, they expect the improbable, and that means preachers stand in the middle position. They are to call forth the miracle, the incomprehensible, not out of themselves, to be sure, but from somewhere else. The gospel tradition and the institution of the church stand behind the preacher, and as far as the listeners' perspective is concerned, the preacher and church are as one. The church, of course, has commissioned the preacher, and the assumption is probably easy to make that someone commissioned by an institution can be identified with that institution.

There are some customs in the church exemplifying this. As far as I can see, they seem self-evident and justified to the congregation, but increasingly questionable and even disgusting to pastors. The identification with the church in general is difficult precisely for many of those preachers commissioned by the church. On the whole, this goes without saying for the congregation, so that they don't always notice the signals of this stance. The whole worship service would be truly unthinkable without the preacher's commissioning by the church. If just anyone would conduct the service, then the preliminary trust, the advance agreement with which most church-goers come into church, would disappear.

As far as I know, only a few pastors don't really comprehend that the preacher is ordained and installed, thus officially recognized and commissioned; or only a few accept it with a mixture of disinclination and good humor. Deacons and other representatives of church administrations could write novels about the struggles which go on during installation preparations with those who are to be put into office. This is not always visible or clear to the people in a worship service. They don't have to get in the pulpit; they don't have to speak in an assembly in which all but one person is silent. The problem and the burden go only to this one person.

There is still more making the preacher seem important. The church steeple, the building's architecture, the singing, reverence and ceremony all suggest that extraordinary things happen in a worship service. The whole structure obviously is counting on the coming of the incomprehensible, and now this one man or this one woman is supposed to make an appearance!

The word *authority* comes up again, but now no longer in the form of assuming responsibility, as in the dimension of security. In this dimension it is a matter of the authority of the representative, of the mediator. The preacher represents the official channel from which the congregation is expecting the miraculous. Even if preachers would rather just be themselves, their congregations still experience them as middle persons. After all, the preacher is conducting the worship service in which they are all silent. The preacher speaks and gives the sermon.

The New Testament figure of the messenger or witness corresponds to the customary conception the congregation has. Messengers are not personally responsible for what they say, but they are nonetheless the ones saying it. Witnesses do not speak about themselves, rather about what they have seen or heard or discovered; but they are nonetheless the ones witnessing to it. A messenger or witness is just as important or unimportant; a final, primary authority only becomes visible behind them. Among the many words used in the New Testament to characterize the gospel's direction, *Kerussein* plays an important role. Preachers do not proclaim what they themselves have thought up, but rather what they have been commissioned to say. "A preacher is not a reporter telling about his own experiences, but rather the authorized agent of someone higher." Without a commissioning there can be no preachers. The proximity to *apostellein* also brings this to expression.

There is a great problem inherent in the fact that preachers, in their role opposite the listeners, represent the official channels of the gospel and of the Lord in some way; the problem is that they allegedly are supposed to stand in a positive relationship to these things. They must assume responsibility for representing the gospel's truth to the people in the worship service. This distribution of roles immediately throws up the question for preachers of whether they are themselves convinced of this truth. And if they are, is this conviction then strong enough to take on the role of the representative?

As a simple participant, one can go to a worship service without this personal conviction. I can go to church as someone who is questioning, seeking, and yearning; indeed that is probably the stance most suitable for people today. But questioning and yearning is not enough for the service of a witness or messenger. Am I still at one with the congregation if I separate myself from them and go up to the pulpit? I not only separate myself from them spatially and externally, but I am also taking an inner step: I presume to speak the gospel to them, I presume to be something more than merely someone questioning and yearning. Even if what I bring doesn't have to come ultimately from me, I nonetheless am confessing to having a fundamentally positive relationship to this message. The correct assertion that the preacher's responsibility is only conditional and supplementary is still no real appeasement. Even the assumption of this conditional responsibility presupposes precisely a positive attitude toward the gospel. Isn't this presumptuous? Doesn't that require too much? These nagging questions assail preachers, and they can hate the institution of the sermon because it wants to force them to transform their modesty into presumptuousness or insincerity.

Not even the shock prompted by a respectless exegesis can explain the modern fear of the pulpit. Even without a familiarity with the introductory questions of Christian tradition, the younger age groups stand there insecurely, and even their children already as well. Who can take on the task of holding the tradition high; who dares speak publicly about God? The temptations of sermon work in general are different than in earlier times, and are more obstinate. The fear of presumptuousness also hinders the preachers from feeling called inwardly to their work. To be sure, in pastoral care contacts with preachers it has become clear to me that the conviction of being called to be a pastor usually resides deep in the heart. Difficulties only arise later in reflection. This means that there are hardly any conditions in the environment making it possible for the preacher to take a positive stand toward this inner calling. Doubts come up immediately: "I'm not at all so sure" and "I'm no different from the others." This experience is typical for externally guided people. With this insecurity it's then difficult to conduct the traditional worship service. No wonder those listening to the sermon complain so often. They are expecting the gospel and get instead observations about the complicated nature of life. Yearning for deliverance is proclaimed, but no deliverance. Irritation and aggravation grow in the congregation; things are made increasingly more difficult for the preacher, who doesn't know how to carry on in this impossible situation. He or she is suffering from precisely what we found at the beginning of the incapacity—namely, the fact that there is no longer any authority of the office. The preacher, who has never had much trust in such externalities as ordination, biblical authority, and ecclesiastical tradition, now discovers that the congregation does not simply accept him or her for the mere fact of being a pastor. Even if this generalized description seldom occurs in the extreme, I believe many young pastors are working more or less in this situation. It encompasses more than just the worship service, but I will limit myself to this aspect.

The conclusion from all this seems clear: The discrepancy between the congregation's expectations and the preacher's attitude must be eliminated. On the one side stands the full authority expected by the congregation and presupposed by the institutions of the worship service and sermon. On the other side stands the preachers' deeply rooted reluctance in speaking about God and the proclamation. We must find an effective balance between these opposing forces if the institution of the sermon is to have any future.

I would like to argue for this effective balance. The development of the relationship between preacher and listeners also shows many promising aspects and offers new opportunities giving pastors a dependable foundation for a realistic identification with the mandate of the proclamation. The message of deliverance—as far as it depends at all on people—can be brought without presumptuousness and without the preacher's having to assume an outdated position or stance.

What makes the exercise of authority in our time so difficult—namely, that strong, universally recognized value systems are no longer determinative—is at the same time a good omen. The intelligibility of the messenger's voice is basically all that's important; the messenger himself has nothing to say. If this reduction to the impersonal has seldom or never been the case for the Christian sermon, then today it is even less than ever! Only the preacher's commissioning can be compared with that of the messenger, not the measure of personal involvement. Authority without the power of conviction is either brutal force or—and this is the variation for the sermon—impotency. The preliminary recognition granted to the preacher by the church with its ordination, and by the congregation with its advanced credit of attentiveness and willingness, should in our time more than ever be established personally. But what does "establishing personally" mean for the proclamation? It cannot mean that preachers themselves are the guarantee for the truth of the proclamation; that would be presumptuous and would indeed separate them from solidarity with their listeners. Ernst Lange has pointed out that preachers assume responsibility when they hold the listeners to a certain text or topic, and they're to be held accountable if they decide the tradition is relevant in a certain sense for themselves and their listeners. A preacher cannot push the personal accountability off on the text because "what he says in the here and now about the relevance of the transmitted tradition cannot be found in the text." [9] It is to the credit of Ernst Lange and his associates that they have systematically dealt seriously with the correspondence of the listeners' needs and situation on the one hand, and the relevance of the biblical tradition on the other. An attitude is required here on the part of preachers which exhibits a certain distance toward the authoritative tradition. They are not just supposed to witness to what stands in the Bible, and not just to subjugate themselves along with their personal opinions to the text in order to grant this text a new authority. They should, so to speak, as listeners, look at the transmitted biblical tradition as something different from themselves and take out of it what they consider important and helpful for their listeners and for themselves now. They are accountable for this choice, but not for the credibility of the Bible or the church doctrine; neither do the people in a worship service demand that of them.

In the authoritarian preaching style preachers identify with the text, and the distance between text and preacher is thus missing. The text's primary authority coincides with the preachers' derived authority. Such preachers only feel responsible for preaching the text correctly, while modern preachers limit themselves expressly to what appears relevant to them in the text. The difference is, by the way, smaller than it appears, since previous preachers also considered their sermons relevant. They, too, made selections and in those selections left out some definite and some indefinite elements. It's just that they did not stand openly accountable for it. It is completely possible and even probable that this one-sided emphasis of textual authority in dialectical theology had a healing effect on many preachers and still could have, but the personal accountability came up too short in the process. Although they simultaneously emphasized the qualitative difference between man and God, the dialectical theologians in particular chased preachers into a fearful proximity to the biblical text, so that precisely no more distance between preacher and transmitted tradition seemed to remain. Young theologians are reacting against this drawing together of preacher and divine authority. In the work of Ernst Lange a certain distance is becoming visible again, and preachers are standing openly accountable for wanting to find and preach what is relevant—only what is relevant; then they can establish or support it personally since they consider it relevant. Perhaps they even also tell what they don't consider relevant for our present situation.

The question comes up whether subjective preference does not then take the place of the tradition's objective claim of validity. This danger appears unavoidable to me, but the proclamation can be personally established only under this threat. Without this danger only authority without the power of conviction can exist. The preacher's own discovery of where the Bible's relevance can be found is the only promising access at all to this book, since without this discovering, without this subjectivity the word is robbed of its humanity. Again, in the final analysis it is a matter here of the *humanitas Christi*. Precisely that primary authority—that means nothing other than the divinity of the Lord himself—can only be witnessed to by the fully valid and affirmed humanity of the preacher; and his or her personal opinion about the tradition's relevance also belongs in this context. The preacher's opinion is not that miraculous thing the people in the service are awaiting, but it is the only access to the essentials, to the power of the transmitted tradition, to the authority of the gospel itself. The tradition shows its power first in that opinion.

The liberating aspect of this understanding, which can be seen especially in Ernst Lange's work, resides for preachers in the fact that they don't have to identify with the text. They need only stand accountable for their opinion of what is relevant; they can then pass on what is relevant, and they can do it enthusiastically because it's their own discovery. The demand for a personal establishment of the preachers' authority frees them from having to guarantee the validity or worth of the transmitted tradition. They are not robbed of their modesty because they are expressly granted room for their own insight, and this in turn yields a clearly delineated stance toward the biblical word. The only prerequisite is that they really discover what is relevant; otherwise, they have no foundation for a personal establishment of the proclamation. This leads us back again to the problem of wonder. How can preachers be astonished again if they are not astonished to begin with? How can they discover what is relevant if they don't see it? Ernst Lange's sermon aids attempt to help while remaining aware that this help is not always enough, since the discovery of what is relevant is a very personal discovery. There are no universal aids for that; creativity cannot be organized. Even access to the Bible is basically a charismatic process. What Gerhard von Rad asserts about the Old Testament holds true for the whole Bible: "There is in fact no normative interpretation of the Old Testament. Every age has the task of hearing what the old book has to say to it, in the light of its own insight and its own needs. Any age which loses this charismatic approach will find no help from either Paul or Matthew or the Epistle to the Hebrews." [10]

We must be a bit more precise at this point. Ernst Lange argues for one's own insight into the relevance of the transmitted tradition, of the biblical word. That is something different from an individual opinion. It's not a matter of preachers simply preaching what they consider or have experienced as important, since in that case the primary authority would be excluded. Then only the preachers would be left standing there without a representative larger quantity behind them. No one in a worship service expects the preacher's own experiences to be the source of the gospel. Just as in dialectical theology, humility threatens to turn into its opposite. If preachers want to be so modest that they only speak about their own experiences, then the worship services are turned into assemblies where many people are supposed to be interested in the experiences of a single individual. Listeners frequently react negatively when that happens. Perhaps there are rare exceptions where an individual experience stands in close proximity to the listeners' experiential possibilities, but I have not yet encountered this. Preachers cannot be allowed to relinquish this middle position; they stand between the listeners and the biblical tradition. They should take the listeners seriously, but at the same time, they should offer this tradition and not just themselves. To do otherwise would be a perversion of personal style.

There are other forms of encounter in the church besides the sermon. If a congregation is lively, then conversations, group discussions, and non-verbal gatherings all have their place. I am limiting myself here to the situation in the traditional worship service and especially to the sermon. This kerygmatic communication presupposes the dichotomy between the official representative and the congregation. The preacher's basic stance in the authoritative position of proclaimer is now to be the topic of my defense of the traditional worship service. What does a contemporary stance of leadership look like?

The differentiations Eric Berne makes in transactional analysis between the various ego states are helpful in defining the correct form of proclamation authority here.[11] In every person three ego states can be differentiated:

1. The parent ego (exteropsyche). In this state the basic stance of identification with authorities and their values determines our behavior. In a word: We behave like our parents or their representatives. No one can live without this ego state, though there are of course differences in its integration. There's a big difference between automatic imitation and consent resulting from mature reflection. If out of fear of being out of place I carry on exactly the same religious ideas as my parents, that's not the same as when I now affirm in relative independence what I earlier saw as a model. But in both cases I am identifying with values which have come to me from an external source. That is the realm of the parent ego.

2. The adult ego (neopsyche) is characterized by the examination of reality. In this state I am open to the situation without any prejudices. All of us have the capacity to observe for ourselves and to evaluate the situation, and thus to examine reality. In this ego state it's not determinatively important to me what my parents or other people think and judge concerning the situation and possibilities I perceive. I decide for myself, and what others think is simply one given among many. I myself collect observations, I work through them and evaluate them, and I try to solve the problems myself. If the tradition offers something to me— a behavioral possibility, an idea, a value judgment, even a threat, I will examine it as impartially as possible and then decide if I agree with the tradition or not.

3. The child ego (archaeopsyche) preserves the childlike behavior in every person from the earliest years throughout one's whole life. Spontaneous joy and creativity, giving of oneself, astonishment at the miraculous, aggravation over injury, sadness about great disappointments can all be reactivated by it. Fixations also live in the child, the ground in neurotic behavioral patterns, and they can also be reactivated until they are perhaps overcome by the maturation process.

All three ego states have their rightful place in human life. Each state is a coherent whole of gestures, feelings, words, actions, pace and so on. What is important is only that we choose the proper ego state at the proper time, since different moments, encounters, and situations require different stances, and thus an acting and reacting out of different ego states. The parent ego is necessary for the rearing of children, the adult ego for the solving of problems, and the child ego for singing and playing. This choice of ego states, which normally occurs spontaneously and unconsciously, is decisive for the effect we have on others. An inadequate choice leads to disturbances in communication. Eric Berne views the whole realm of interaction problems from the perspective of the ego states. In every relationship one can pose the question of who is dealing with whom, of which ego states the various participants in a relationship are reacting from. Berne maintains that the insight into this interaction can lead to changes or improvements in a relationship. If, for example, a teacher sees that he or she unnecessarily always appears in the parent ego and that the pupils always react to that with their child egos, or are subservient or rebellious, that teacher will probably not have any trouble finding opportunities for the adult ego to manifest itself. This also makes possible a reaction out of the adult ego for the pupils.

Back to the problems of the proclamation. It's clear that the traditional image of the preacher corresponds to the parent ego, since for general sentiment he or she represents the values of tradition. One must behave properly in the presence of a preacher, since preachers always seem ready to pass judgment. This hackneyed image is more deeply rooted than pastors themselves would like to believe, since it's associated with the archetype of the spiritual leader. The role distribution in the worship service points unmistakably in the same direction: The preacher speaks; the others listen. This can mean—and has for a long time—that the preacher knows while the others are taught. He or she has an elevated, even parental position. As long as this image holds, there is no problem with authority. They arise only when it is found that the preacher no longer has any right at all to be considered as above the listeners in some way. That is now the case, and has basically been the case for a long time already. Academic knowledge no longer distinguishes the preacher; the relationships of authority have fundamentally changed so that the dignity of the office no longer implies some superiority. Only a theoretical knowledge about exegesis and church history remains, but that's not enough for the preacher's parent ego position. Dialectical theology made possible for a while a newly founded elevated position for the preacher, but by pushing aside the preacher's whole personality as unimportant, the preacher was forced completely into the dignity and authority of the text, of the word of God. Human abilities and shortcomings counted for nothing theologically, only explanations remained. An identification with the importance of the text had to grow precisely because of the preacher's own unimportance.

In young theologians an extremely sensitive and decisive intuition is resisting the traditional authoritative stance in the pulpit. They sense that this stance holds no promise, but the conclusion most of them draw from that—namely that the entire institution of the sermon is obsolete—is premature. That intuition, however, is in any case important because it has extremely deep roots, and I intend to take it quite seriously. Hence the thesis: The institution of the sermon can only be meaningfully carried on if preachers relinquish the parent ego position and take up an adult ego one. That's a rather revolutionary change, and has already taken place in some preachers. It must now be theoretically supported and illuminated. I will try to do this by using the scheme of transactional analysis.

What does the change from parent ego to adult ego mean? Surely that the sermon is no longer basically education or the transmission of values. Value judgments will disappear and make room for an examination of reality. Concretely this means what Ernst Lange has already alluded to: The main task of the sermon is not to pass on the text, but rather to consider the biblical word, to question it and present what is relevant. The transmission of values does not have to disappear, though these values are already there independently of the preacher, symbolized in the biblical word and in the worship service as a whole. The worshipers appreciate these values and are seeking them together. The preacher's function is not to convince the participants of the worth of the biblical and ecclesiastical tradition, but rather to examine the tradition as the listeners' advocate. Wherever the preacher rejoices and calls special attention to the tradition, the biblical text as a treasure, there he or she becomes the text's advocate as far as the listeners are concerned. Thus the preacher becomes the text's advocate over against the listeners because the preacher is also the listeners' advocate over against the text. A new kind of power of authority emerges, but without the pedantic stress as if everyone had to see it like the preacher does. The pastoral authority is defenseless and thus credible.

Two examples of sermon beginnings might make clear what distinctions are meant here. First a beginning in the parental style:

> We live today in a world which forces us to achieve. People everywhere expect salvation from their own endeavors. Today is Sunday. Thank God the machines are silent at least for a few hours. People can rest. God gives us this day so we can find our way to him again. And thus we find the words: Therefore do not be anxious about tomorrow.

A beginning in the adult style concerning the same topic:

> Therefore do not be anxious about tomorrow. I think you react no differently than I when I hear these words. The invitation to let our worries go and to concentrate on life's essential things does sound tempting. But it doesn't seem very realistic.

These simple examples make clear that it's not just a matter of the content of words. The tone of voice, the gaze, indeed the entire self-presentation is also determined by either the parental ego or the adult ego. The parental ego style hardly knows of the pronoun "I"; it's not modest and thus forcefully includes the listeners with "we" and "people." It would certainly be worth the trouble to present the pulpit's entire parent ego vocabulary. We'll still have something to say later about the little word "must."

The stance of the adult ego dismantles the unnecessary clutter between the preacher and listeners, though the distinction of roles naturally remains. That disappears only in communication forms in which no one is the leader, something impossible in a traditional worship service; it's not necessary, however, to combine this role with an authoritative appearance and the power of authority assigned to oneself.

There is, by the way, room for play also in the transactional analysis scheme of the adult ego. A non-authoritative partner can also assume responsibility and have an involved concern for others. That's something different from parental ego behavior, in which case the partner would take care of things because he or she thinks it appropriate. From the perspective of the adult ego a person feels responsible for feelings and behavior. In caring for others, then, the person is not doing it from above them. Kurt Marti points out that preachers with the courage to be subjective—who are willing to discuss their statements—come across all the more credibly when they must speak prophetically, when they must formulate something which cannot be discussed.[12] The stance of assuming responsibility I discussed in the previous chapter can be structured entirely from the perspective of the adult ego; in fact, that's the single most promising way. It associates partnership with involvement, modesty with full power of authority, and precisely these two elements together form the only contemporary leadership stance. A certain element of the parent ego is then integrated into the adult ego, and is what Berne calls ethical accountability in the adult.[13] One can view the listeners as mature people and nonetheless assume responsibility for them. A person avoiding responsibility gives a bad example of maturity.

I haven't said anything else about the child ego, since I am primarily concerned with the displacement within the sermon stance from the parent ego condition into that of the adult ego. However, the child ego is also important for a sermon. Here we should recall what was said in the previous chapter about being genuine and bringing in one's own emotions. I don't want to detail the system of transactional analysis any further, though it would be tempting to show how the integration of the child ego into the sermon can turn it into a splendid sermon.

In the preacher's role as proclaimer there is an opportunity corresponding to the yearning of many young people for participation, for a meaningful role instead of just a "job." If it's not necessary to be pedantic in the pulpit; if the best stance happens to be that the preacher speaks authentically and modestly without presumptuousness; and if it's also certain that the people in the worship service are spoken to by such a stance, if they recognize in the preacher's stance a full power of authority: If all this can hold true, then the institution of the sermon is energetically alive. The question is then no longer: "What can I do in the impossible role of authoritative know-it-all if I don't know any better," but rather: "How do I speak authentically about what seems relevant to me in the biblical tradition?'' This question is hard enough itself, but is basically manageable.

No matter how much difficulty is involved in the shift from the parent ego to the adult ego stance, a gospel structure can be seen in it, since the proclaimer's authority in the adult ego style is a non-violent authority. No coercive conscience and no universally accepted value system can help persuade the listeners. The preacher personally can have an effect and have success only with a modest, authentic demeanor and involvement. This kind of authority is an echo of the authority lived by Jesus Christ.

The Monologue Text Sermon

The preacher addresses the yearning for deliverance only by proclaiming. The listeners expect and hope the preacher will have something to say to them which they basically cannot say to themselves. Only a miracle can solve the insoluble and deliver someone from hopelessness, and this miracle happens when a sermon becomes proclamation for the listeners. I have tried to show clearly that it's possible to represent this improbable element within the framework of a traditional worship service without being immodest.

The question remains now concerning how this proclamation looks concretely, both in its form and content. I will take up the question of content in the next section, but for now I am interested in the external form. The proclamation's usual form today in most traditional worship services, Catholic as well as Protestant, is a monologue text sermon. Various remarks can be made concerning this topic, including its relationship to the listener reactions already collected.

1. The Monologue

Much has been written lately—most of it uncomplimentary—about the phenomenon of the monologue in the worship service. The attacks come from two directions: On the one hand, people complain that the church's proclamation always or almost always occurs in monologue form. On the other hand, it's pointed out that absolutely nothing more can be expected from the monologue form. This is not the place to argue the necessity of additional, different forms of communication for the church's proclamation. That subject requires an independent presentation. However, I do want to take the second complaint seriously since it fundamentally doubts that the sermon can have a positive effect. The positive impression given by the sermon analyses contradicts this negative evaluation, though that is not to say the proclamation absolutely must occur only in monologue form. The proclamation is certainly possible in other forms of communication as well. And it has been occurring in other forms for ages. To be sure, the anti-sermon publications of theologians with formal communication training are very impressive with their terminology and blinding generalizations, but they always overlook the church's proclamation which takes place when a mother speaks with her children about God and prays with them, or when a volunteer tells the biblical stories in Sunday school. Those are forms of proclamation which are less noticeable, though their effect may be significantly greater than that of the Sunday sermon; for that reason a correctly applied science of communication will deal with them. Or are these forms not supposed to be church proclamation? Here I am only investigating whether and to what extent the monologue comes into question as one of the possible forms. No rejection of it is clearly discernible in the listener reactions, though naturally the people who are speaking in these reactions regularly go to church and thus have a positive attitude toward the institution of the sermon. To that extent they are prejudiced, and it is possible that worship services would reach many more people if there were no monologue sermon. I doubt it, but it's possible. One cannot at any rate assert that those in the worship service are suffering under the monologue form. Because of the way our inquiries were carried out, it would certainly have become clear if a fundamental dissatisfaction existed in this regard among the listeners, a dissatisfaction to be taken seriously.

Sometimes, as an exception, the following is said:

—I would like to have spoken with the preacher about that.
—That statement made me want to say something in opposition.

These statements concern totally concrete situations, most of the time of a political nature. A few listeners will want to say something themselves concerning *controversial topics*, and whoever treats such questions in a sermon must figure on that. There are experiments which try to do justice to this with a discussion after the sermon.

The great suspicion the monologue stands under is, of course, that it's authoritarian. Anyone who sees the worship service and sermon as an attempt to lead the listeners to specifically determined changes and behavior patterns must no doubt think the monologue sermon is a demagogical affair. At the bottom of such a view, however, is an intellectualistic understanding of the sermon which is completely given over to the content and overlooks, among other things, the deeper process of the awakening of trust. Proclamation presupposes authority; that's clear. I have tried to show that it's completely possible to structure this authority as a partnership; the accusation of authoritarian manipulation cannot apply to the monologue in and for itself.

The monologue has in fact pronounced advantages, and that's probably why the varietal experiments have been able to change little or nothing in the worship service process. When only a small group meets for a worship service assembly, then other forms such as dialogue can prove themselves; but with the large number of participants in a traditional service the advantages to the monologue cannot be eclipsed. Here are the advantages:

1. The distribution of roles in which one speaks and the others listen most clearly represents the fact that God is speaking to his community, that people are spoken to by something inaccessible. One person represents this unheard-of factor the listeners will hear. Just as in the psalms sometimes roles are determined in order to make God's voice audible, (for example Pss. 32, 82 and 89) so also does the monologue convey the promise which comes to us from beyond the human realm. I have the impression the monologue is for this reason not a problem for the worship service participants in general. They are unconsciously persuaded that this distribution of roles is a suitable representation which does not imply a fundamental difference between preachers and listeners.

One may ask whether there is a basically more suitable form for the representation of this subject matter. In a group, for example, does "the voice of the good news become vibrantly audible?" Rudolf Bohren asks this question. He asserts: "The giving of this word by a single individual corresponds to the authority of the word of God."[14] Helmut Gollwitzer insists that the authority of the word can come just as adequately to expression in discussions between equal partners as in the traditional worship service, and can do this without one person's assuming the role of the proclaimer.[15] The discussion form is just much more difficult to institutionalize than the worship service. Gollwitzer's assertion seems unrealistic to me. The one man or one woman in the pulpit illustrates most clearly and most graphically the fact that the message does not come from human beings, but rather from beyond.

The small variations in the monologue character attained by including others in the text reading or prayers have been exclusively judged negatively in the reactions available to me. The complaint was always that there was no unity, though it is no doubt possible for proper direction to preserve that unity.

2. The monologue makes it possible to have listeners. The advantage of this is that the worship service participants are spoken to directly, thus realizing the proclamation's characteristic of encounter. The persons in the service are not just registering everything with a distant interest; they are directly addressed. In this way they are more likely to feel engaged and spoken to. This advantage is naturally lost if the sermon degenerates into a treatise without this element of address.

Hearing is of fundamental significance in the communication of the gospel. Both Jews and Christians agree that hearing is the deepest activity in biblical faith. The *Schema'h* Israel (Deut. 6:4: "Hear, O Israel: The LORD our God is one LORD") is the first sentence the Jewish child is supposed to learn, and the last spoken over a Jewish person. In both the Old and New Testament hearing is the access to faith: not seeing or thinking. Faith is from hearing, Romans 10:17. "This prevalence of hearing points to an essential feature of biblical religion. It is a religion of the Word, because it is a religion of action, of obedience to the

Word.'' [16] The sermon is also grounded in this hearing, especially according to the understanding of the Reformation. "Who hears you hears me" (Luke 10:16). The believers encounter God in hearing. The thinking is that one hears God but does not possess him, that one can have him in hearing as a listener and in no other way.

There is no question such a hearing is also a miracle, as is the proclamation, since hearing is indeed more than merely acoustic perception; it is an encounter. The yearning for deliverance and the proclamation converge in hearing; it is the place of encounter. In hearing, a process not dependent personally on the preacher takes place in the listeners. When those listeners let themselves be addressed by the proclamation, they are opening up their deepest interiors; a spiritual giving of themselves or—in the negative case—a closing off and resistance takes place. They are engaged in a way the preacher perhaps does not even notice. The proclaimed word vies for contact with the listeners; it knocks on the door. To let oneself be spoken to is an intensive affair, since it concentrates the entire person on what is proclaimed; a communion is established between what is proclaimed and the listener. This hearing is made possible by the monologue form, and one can only ask whether the same intensity of address and hearing is also possible in other forms of communication. The intimacy of communion between the listener and God requires a protective shield; if many people are listening at the same time, this shield is guaranteed by the relative anonymity of the assembly. If the preacher were to speak only to a single person, then the limits of discretion would be reached much more quickly. There are, of course, such encounters, for example in pastoral care, but they are rather the exception. Precisely the monologue makes possible an intensive, active hearing.

The prerequisite for active hearing is for the preacher to be aware of this process in the listener. That will determine the preacher's speaking style. The prayers and the sermon will then have the external form of a monologue, but they will exhibit the characteristics of dialogue because the listeners' concerns are taken up into the monologue. Reuel Howe points out that the fundamental character of the sermon is determinative for the effect of communication, not whether it is a monologue or dialogue. "A communication which in terms of method is monologue (one speaker) may at the same time be governed by the principle of dialogue." [17] The listeners will basically be ready to listen if they have seen that the preacher has a sympathetic understanding of their concerns. I will later speak of which possibilities and difficulties have to be considered here.

2. The Biblical Text

Otto Haendler, in the middle of the argument about text or topic sermons, has already said that the question whether a sermon should be text-bound or not is not a question of life or death for the church.[18] Listener statements support him: Only the fewest listeners are concerned about whether a sermon should be bound to the text. This is all the more noticeable because many of those questioned happen to be theologians who themselves sometimes preach. Or has the cry for a text sermon also disappeared because most sermons today do use a text as their point of departure?

Some things can nonetheless be said on this topic from the perspective of the listener remarks. The choice of text and its reading sometimes has a strong effect, and if the preacher does not take this into consideration, he disappoints his listeners. A text causes definite or indefinite ideas, perhaps consternation, aggravation, or even rejection. If the sermon does not immediately and expressly take these feelings seriously, the listeners turn away even more. The reading of Matthew 5:43-48 was followed by a sermon about love of one's enemy. Not one word of the preacher dealt with the statement in verse 48: "You, therefore, must be perfect," though precisely these words had aroused consternation and curiosity in several listeners. Their attention suffered because their expectation went unfulfilled. The preacher must figure on this effect of text choice and reading especially on holidays. If the text does not clearly correspond to holiday expectations, there will be insecurity among the listeners. This can be made fruitful, but whoever does not pay attention to it will lose listeners.

—For a long time I asked myself: What do these words have to do with New Year's Eve?

—[Is ascension being psychologized? I asked myself after the text reading. I was really glad then that the sermon began with just this question.]

In funeral sermons the choice of text can cause vehement indignation. A pastor read the parable of the rich grain farmer—with the warning against wealth—at the burial of a small retail merchant. The suddenness of death was the pastor's reason for the choice of text; the merchant had died of a heart attack. He spoke about being rich in God and did not mention the person's wealth at all. Some of the listeners were nonetheless indignant because for them the choice of that text suggested a reproach to the deceased. The family also complained to the pastor afterwards. It became clear to the pastor in a discussion with colleagues how little his intention, and how much his unintentional effect had been determinative.

Concerning the problem of text from the perspective of the listeners, one can thus say the following: There is a toleration level in the choice of text; the listener is made to feel insecure if the text does not clearly fit the situation. That listener is picked up if the preacher latches onto the effect the text has already precipitated. If I let the statements stand, the listener does not really make any higher demands in this respect. (Let it be formally said that most text readings are felt to be too long. The attention is quickly used up, and this is probably because the reading is a reading out loud.)

It's important for the pastor to ascertain beforehand the presumed effect of the text reading. Sermon aids need to pay attention to this aspect. Many texts do not have a strong effect, and the preacher must be aware of this as well.

In Karl Barth's work and in dialectical theology a tremendous emphasis is put on the sermon's dependence on the text; the sermon's entire function is exhausted in explanation. Barth vigorously resisted the use of a topic or a so-called scope and defined the topical sermon as the great presumption, as if the preacher had something independent to say in addition to the text exegesis. A text sermon means "no private comments are given." [19] The great theologians asserting such things are original enough not to be unnecessarily hemmed in by it, but their students cling to these statements as if they were divine laws. The dialectical theologians' one-sided statements indeed gave rise to such fanaticism. The elimination of the preacher's personal contributions comes from a questionable ideal of purity that would sooner yield sterility than space for the miracle.

The demand that only the text come to expression is unrealistic as well. The choice of text is already personally determined, and all preachers stamp the exegesis with their own personalities whether they want to or not. It's thus theologically more correct and more helpful for preachers if this demand for textual consistency in sermons is formulated more mildly. Gollwitzer lists as the criterion: "The story and reality of Jesus Christ." [20] He means the biblical text can be missing if only this story and reality is not. Otto Haendler says a sermon ought to be "commensurate with the gospel." [21] A sermon without a text is possible because the tradition is experienced not only indirectly, but directly as well. These criteria sound milder and more realistic, and are for that reason also less precise. They offer the preacher enough flexibility to employ fully spontaneity and creative fantasy, but they also contain the possibility of bad blunders. But without this risk there can be no chance of success. These milder criteria do not meet with any resistance from listeners, and people in a worship service at least subjectively sometimes find they have perceived real deliverance in a sermon even if it wasn't bound to a text.

A text sermon has in general better prerequisites for fulfilling the conditions imposed on a sermon by listeners. The text very often protects the preacher from abstract generalizations, sometimes also from abrupt intellectualism, and it frequently offers a natural access to the proclamation. The topical sermon contains more risks and thus puts greater demands on the preacher.

The Proclamation in Its Inner Content

I have mentioned the analysis of listener statements in which the dimension of deliverance becomes visible as an essential dimension of preaching; this analysis exhibits a unique tension. Helplessness and hope stand next to each other: The impossibility of solving life's great problems makes people helpless, yet on the other hand, they expect and hope for deliverance or a sign of deliverance in the worship service and sermon. Argued logically, the one should exclude the other; if solutions are an impossibility, then there is no reason to expect something good. If, on the other hand, one can hope for deliverance, the situation cannot be so bad. Such logic, however, is not able to assess properly what happens in this tension field. The deliverance, the promised release is indeed always grasped, but it cannot be held. The worship service is repeated each week; that characterizes the situation. That deliverance is basically always unbelievable, no matter how firmly it was believed in the past, and though it is always totally in effect, so is the situation of not being free. The yearning for deliverance, as I have called the fundamental feeling of the worshiper in this dimension, embraces a perpetual tension. Those worshipers want to experience again and again how they are surprised by the miraculous and improbable. Deliverance and anxiety stand in a polar relationship of tension; they are both in full effect and contradict one another, thus causing that tension.

1. The Polarity of Law and Gospel

The polarity in the listeners reflects the polarity of judgment and grace, of law and gospel, cross and resurrection. The preacher does justice to the listeners' expectations only if these two poles in the proclamation are in full effect and come fully to expression. As soon as the preacher disturbs the balance of tension between the opposing force fields, the listeners react with disappointment. It doesn't seem easy to integrate the whole gospel as well as the whole law into the proclamation. But what is meant here by the catch-words law and gospel? I will try to formulate them in such a way that the listener statements will be comprehensible later.

I will not deal with the question of what comes first, the gospel or the law. A polarity has no beginning; like every relationship it is there only when both elements exist. If I now reflect first on the law, that is not because of anything inherent in the subject matter.

The law, also the Bible's "Torah," is an expression of a legal order. Legislation decrees that the world be determined for good and not for evil; it qualifies life's forces and the powers in the world and brings evil to light. Justice and guilt are created only by law, and only through the law is there accountability. "Law" does not have to be a written codex; what is meant is orders, or the establishment of an order. The problem of fixing it in written form is a problem unto itself.

If the law is not kept, that threatens the entire order. Was the law an unrealistic fantasy? The biblical proclamation counts on God's maintaining or asserting his law even if people do not adhere to it. He doesn't give up on humanity's fundamental determination for a life in righteousness. This is not to be understood as being without love; it is precisely God's love which becomes recognizable here, since he does not want to permit injustice. His righteousness is a saving righteousness, and in that sense a punitive God is more loving, because he's more dependable than one who does not watch things so exactly. The constancy of his love leads God to maintain the law which makes life possible.

For humanity, of course, this involves a condemnation. The law maintained by God judges and kills human beings. (Dogmatics calls this function of the law the *usus elenchticus.*) Whenever God upholds his law, that encompasses his wrath against the sinner. The biblical proclamation takes this wrath of God into consideration: it is an indispensable element in the message.

Through the law, life and the world—with its dark side, its suffering and its cruelty—are set into a certain framework. There is a connection between misery and disregard for the law. Misery is not blind fate; it is associated with violation. Misery is also seen as punishment; God's wrath comes to expression in the curse laid upon the world, in the isolation in which it is abandoned by God, and in its having been given over to the prince of this world. Neither are the believers spared from this judgment—in fact, it rather begins with them.

This judgment of God is not necessarily described as a visible one, though that can also be the case. On the level of the individual it is often an inward struggle; the psalms especially depict it. (See Ps. 38:1-2: "O LORD, rebuke me not in thy anger, nor chasten me in thy wrath! For thy arrows have sunk into me, and thy hand has come down on me." Ps. 88:16: "Thy wrath has swept over me; thy dread assaults destroy me.") The worshiper's feeling of guilt goes hand in hand with a knowledge of God's wrath. The worshiper cries and laments. The Bible never sees this as depressing, but rather as liberating. In their laments people express what consumes them inwardly, and we find this kind of relationship to God also in the New Testament. Jesus shows his indignation over the lack of fruits of faith and love. With the quote from Psalm 22:1 about being abandoned by God, Jesus himself takes on the suffering under God's wrath (Matt. 27:46 and parallels).

The law has an uncovering and thus condemning effect. It brings to light which idols are determining human affairs. In this way it leads the believing person to Christ. The law is our custodian until Christ comes (Gal. 3:24), who fulfills the law and brings about a renewal of the relationship through his obedience.

The law's original instructing function also remains in effect. The instruction, *paraenesis,* is an essential element of biblical faith. The commandments are there to be performed, not just as a reflection of failure. The imitation of Christ is organically connected with faith in him; that belonging to him leads to a new obedience. The law shows the way into the future.

This short summary does not do justice to the distinctions made in the various biblical books. It gives rather the church doctrine of many centuries, in which an attempt was made to comprehend and grasp the most important structures of biblical faith. Individual theologians have sometimes seen things differently. For Albrecht Ritschl, for example, there was only "pure love" in God; he attributed God's wrath to more primitive generations. In antinomianism there is the attempt to get rid of the law entirely. Did listener reactions in earlier times hinder the continuation of such views?

In its killing function, the proclamation of the law addresses the hopelessness and insolubility of life's problems. The accusation qualifies humanity's undifferentiated suffering; the law prevents our seeing life basically as only dark fate.

This statement about life and suffering cannot, of course, be proven; it is never presented in the Bible as the product of human investigation, but rather always as a decree of God coming from beyond the human ability to comprehend. The question concerning proof or probability does not even arise. The statement requires faith, not rational insight.

The law, however, is only one force field in the polarity; without the gospel it remains incomprehensible. The law's innermost core is not killing and condemning, but rather life-creating. This deepest concern comes to expression independently and anew in the other force field, the gospel.

According to its effect, the gospel is opposed to the law. It does not kill; it liberates and makes alive. It proclaims that *God* in his mercy makes everything new; that Jesus Christ saves the world, and that the Spirit of the Lord leads people to new, healing paths. Decisive are not the guilt and condemnation, but rather the Lord's merciful actions which forgive and renew. The life, death, and resurrection of Jesus Christ are proclaimed as the path into the world, through the torments of life and also through the curse, the abandonment, and the state of having been given over to the prince of this world. They are proclaimed as liberating for persons, though this deliverance is still hidden. What is now in effect will become revealed in the future. The entire gospel is thus nothing more and nothing less than a promise. (The gospel's fundamental character of promise has probably helped determine the fact that "praedicare" has become such an important—perhaps the most important term for the proclamation. In Tertullian's time it was already a preferred term. It combines two processes, that of predicting or promising, and that of teaching, conveying, though the first meaning has slowly stepped into the background. In the German word "predigen" one no longer hears the element of promise, but it's important for preachers not to forget the profound double meaning of "praedicare," since preaching is basically associated with the future. All preaching would be deception without the fulfillment of what is preached. Preaching is also promise.) It does not claim to explain the world and its riddles, nor does it call for realizing a certain program. It promises that all has become different in Christ and that the revelation of this renewal is at hand. It calls fundamentally for hope in the future, not for insight or activity. It gives promises instead of truths. "For in this hope we were saved." (Rom. 8:24). The Heidelberg Catechism expresses the decisive significance of the gospel's character of promise very appropriately when it answers the question of what a Christian should believe thus: "Everything promised us in the gospel." Not "taught"! In this pointing to the future there inheres in the gospel a "breath of unreality and a spirit of 'not yet.' " [22] But the "connection with reality" is still missing from the word of promise. It belongs to the gospel of promise that a new obedience, in acts of love, will grow in the believers like fruits on the vine of Christ. (The frequent use of the future tense is probably connected with this element of promise. It's a Hebraism occurring very often in the New Testament.) Faith will have its own experiences; the imperative and summons to life according to the gospel are only one side of an event guided by the Spirit of the Lord himself. If there is a summons to obedience, it is also promised. Gospel and law are identical in the final analysis, and only penultimately do they stand in tension.

The listener statements make it clear that only a distinct proclamation of law and gospel can awaken genuine hope. Not only theological purity, but the congregation's justified demands point out a clear path: Only if the darkest darkness of the law and the brightest light of the gospel are proclaimed together do people feel spoken to and engaged. Through the seriousness of the sermon on the law they feel spoken to in their distressing reality, and through the unbroken joy of the gospel a perspective becomes visible to them which is simultaneously unbelievable and liberating. The question remains open whether the listeners then let themselves be addressed by this, and it cannot be answered by the preacher. The preacher's task is to present clearly the polarity in the proclamation.

This will certainly not happen in the conceptual words of doctrine as I have just formulated them. I consider the following to be a good example of a sermon on the law:

> . . . Paul is perturbed by the Christians who do not believe in the resurrection. Paul does not say we can know a great deal about the resurrection. He only reminds us that all our illusions will fall apart. We will die. And he shows us that we betray God if we believe only in the reality of death. We all live between faith and superstition. Between the superstition about the omnipotence of death and the faith in the superiority of God. [23]

The uncovering and judging law manifests itself especially in the statement that we betray God if we only believe in the reality of death, because the listener can see himself in that identification with the betrayers. Who of us does not figure on a superiority of death, again and again and in spite of love for the gospel?

What follows is a clear proclamation of the gospel (sermon conclusion):

... Still a chance? If we really try once more. There is no hope in that. "I have called you by your name; you are mine." There it is. He calls my name! Do you also find it hard sometimes to call aloud the name of a loved one? It embarrasses me. The Lord is calling your name. He gives of himself, to you. Certainly it cost him a great deal; from the story of Jesus Christ we can sense how high the price was. But he is calling! Your name! That's new, and it shines over your entire life. "I come and save you," it says. No obstacle will be too great. Let us be glad! He is calling. And what do you do? You are being called! And all your hope lies with him.

In the conclusion this sermon concentrates one's entire attention on God's initiative. With probably intentional one-sidedness all human action is pushed aside as unessential. It is a matter of what is decisive, and that is the deliverance from beyond, something not capable of being made, something only miraculous.

As soon as the balance between law and gospel is disturbed, the people hearing the sermon no longer experience deliverance. Their yearning for release is disappointed. The balance can be disturbed on both sides. Law without gospel becomes legality, and does not take up the joy and freedom of the proclamation. Gospel without law becomes non-obligatory, and is unsuited for daily life because it is unrealistic.

2. Suppressed Gospel: Legalism

It's not gaps in theological training, although they too can be significant, which lead preachers to eliminate the liberating and joyous element of the gospel. The reasons people who basically want to believe the gospel forget or pay no attention to its most important characteristics reside in emotional resistance. The gospel is not a system of thought; it embraces experience. To believe the gospel means a relaxation of tensions for experience, a giving of oneself and rejoicing, a release from care and a trust and hope. But there is much capable of resisting such internal and external attitudes. People are not prepared to give up control over themselves without further ado. Rigidity is a frequently occurring disposition which must be understood as a defense against fear.

What happens in the proclamation if the preacher, probably without being conscious of it, no longer experiences the joy and freedom of the gospel and no longer gives it adequate expression? The other pole will predominate; the law will be overemphasized. But because of this the law also changes. Everything exaggerated becomes perverted. The law then becomes a duty. Instead of being instruction and judgment, it degenerates into legality. The excess of law must compensate for the suppressed gospel. At the root there is always fear; fear of the liberating, joyous gospel. People will want to suppress that because it is a threat.

To be sure, the gospel is still mentioned in a purely formal manner, but listener statements show clearly what effect that has:

—I thought the gospel message was impersonal; do *you* believe it yourself?

—The phrases about Jesus seemed empty to me.

—I noticed that the conclusion (with the exhortation) was formulated in completely general terms.

—The christological passage puzzled me; I couldn't see the relationship with what came before.

Further negative qualifications of the actual proclamation are: bland, too brief, too little, unclear, indirect, too isolated, no real solution, "dogmatic," theoretical, incomprehensible, complicated, confused, confusing. The isolated reference to biblical passages or hymn verses in this context is also often criticized.

As far as preachers are correctly characterized by these listener comments, one must conclude that although they have meant to preach the gospel, they have actually suppressed it. This is a painful insight, since no preacher really intends that.

At the same time we see the law has, so to speak, been multiplied. It must be made so strong that it can push the gospel aside. The law alone, as judgment and instruction, could not manage this task, but when it's multiplied and thus perverted it becomes a sinister power. It suppresses the gospel so that the gospel joy and freedom no longer have a chance. What threatens the preacher is thus warded off unconsciously; the gospel is suppressed.

The accusing function of the law, the *usus elenchticus,* becomes ineffective in such a proclamation. Only a person who experiences the gospel's liberation will dare give expression to the condemnation residing in the law. Otherwise he or she will unconsciously try to alleviate the harshness of various biblical passages in the sermon. There is an excellent example of this in the sermon analyses of Hans-Christoph Piper. A preacher, because of his own aggressiveness, does not feel accepted by Christ; to his way of thinking the liberation of the gospel apparently does not embrace his aggressive resistance. He does not dare relate Jesus' own harsh words in a harsh manner; thus the accusing function of the word to a large extent disappears.[24] An accusatory sermon on the law wants to show from what misery people are delivered and are being delivered; it peers into the chasm from which we are saved. In the sermons heard and analyzed by me and most of the course participants there were only a few in which the *usus elenchticus* appeared. What now and then shows up is a critique of our age, and here a proclaiming of the law is mixed up with moral indignation. In such instances the preachers are calling on reason more than on the word of the Bible. In the listeners they then arouse either the urge to contradict, agreement in the spirit of "I told you so," or aggravated boredom. Such sermons directed against the spirit of the age are rarely original, but rather only repeat what many others are also saying (example: pollution). That is not the accusation of the law directed to everyone which comes not from reason, but from God's decree. Rarely is an explicitly accusatory biblical passage chosen as a text, but here is an area we preachers must learn to traverse anew. No one can evaluate and appreciate the gospel's deliverance and liberation without a clear awareness of guilt. Only while suffering God's wrath do we realize the misery from which the gospel delivers us. I believe we have to discover this wrath of God anew.

The instructing function of the law, the *tertius usus legis,* is devastated in the legalistic sermon, and this is without doubt the worst blunder concerning the proclamation in our day. It's bad in two ways: It consumes the proclamation and it disappoints or aggravates those in the worship service. An astonishing finding from the sermon analyses is that even preachers who themselves preach legalistically are aggravated if they are spoken to legalistically as listeners! (This is however, an instance where the analyses do not always offer a dependable theology. There are listeners who complain that in non-legalistic sermons they get no stimulus for their work. However, it always became clear to me in the discussions that the mistake here is on the side of the listeners. They had grown so accustomed to legalistic sermons that they didn't even demand anything different, and they accordingly reacted negatively to non-legalistic sermons. This interpretation is, however, a personal one and was not always shared by the other participants.) The aggravation concerning legalism in sermons is so disproportionately great that we preachers should without hesitation work on this point. Manfred Josuttis has devoted an excellent book to this problem: *Gesetzlichkeit in der Predigt der Gegenwart.* His warnings are fully supported by sermon analyses. I will here present only a few of the many complaints:

—"I have to, I have to!" That makes me sick.
—Too strong an exhortation, and too little chance of doing it.
—[These demands make me feel helpless, though I can see it would be good to live like that.]
—I won't have someone morally instructing me. Life's too complicated for that.

The most important emotional reactions I've encountered are aggravation and helplessness; aggravation often exhibits a bitter tone, helplessness a resigned one. Without the gospel the law elicits resistance and condemnation, and is legalistic. Something is demanded of the listeners—most of the time the impossible—and they're simply left alone with it. They should take care of it now. The sermon is thus not at all an encounter with the Lord which delivers them. Manfred Josuttis[25] repeatedly emphasizes that the listener is left alone; this gives expression to the fact that the gospel has been suppressed, since the gospel is supposed to be communion with God, deliverance from being alone. People listening to sermons are very sensitive about legalism, and one indication of this is the large number of negative remarks, of which I have presented only a selection. A demand apparently draws a great deal of attention to itself. Ernst Lerle also maintains on the basis of listener inquiries that demands remain longer in the listener's memory than expressions of feelings or cognitive material.[26]

The basic posture of the suppression of gospel and the perversion of law into legalism manifests itself theologically in the reduction of Christ's work to a model. The believer is taken seriously only as an acting person. People forget that the gospel is a promise, that a tension exists in it between the completed work of Christ and the eschatological future. Instead, many preachers view the gospel, often without being conscious of it, as an unalterable system with which we must now work: "Jesus is finished, now it's our turn." It's no accident that eschatology has almost disappeared from sermons; hope is not directed to Christ's future, but rather to human action. The indicative of reconciliation is God's work, and the imperative of the commandments, they insist, is now our work instead of God's guidance. Josuttis rightly emphasizes that the imperative as well as the indicative in the New Testament is God's work, who is leading us to a new life. The call to obedience is not a demand.[27] This primitive theology is not rooted in an inadequate education, but rather in unconscious resistance against the liberating gospel, and this resistance posture leads to recognizable dogmatic and exegetical falsifications. Rudolf Bohren points out how the optative in Paul is often changed in sermons into a legal obligation. The expectation in Paul's work which is directed toward God is postponed. Now we must do it.[28] A conspicuous and typical symptom is the use of the word "must." It never occurs in the Old Testament commandments or the New Testament. Hebrew has no equivalent for it, and although we encounter *dei* in the New Testament, we do so almost always outside of the *paraenesis*. (Walter Grundmann shows how the Septuagint translation already deviates from the Hebraic concept of God when it translates the Hebrew imperfect *nifal* with *dei*. *Dei* then occurs in the New Testament especially in Luke, but most of the time it expresses the necessity of the eschatological event, not a demand. In dogmatic terminology: *dei* means rather *voluntas abscondita* as *voluntas revelata*.) The imperative or future tense is used for the exhortation, and the difference in tone is immense because a completely different attitude is manifested:

—Listen to him! (Matt. 17:5)
—We must listen to him!
—Love your enemies! (Matt. 5:44)
—We must love our enemies!
—Therefore, be perfect! (Matt. 5:48)
—You, therefore, must be perfect!
—Love God and your neighbor! (Matt. 22:37 and 39)
—We must love God and our neighbor!

The intimate guidance, the invitation, and the self-understood quality are all pushed aside and replaced by demand and pressure. It's assumed you want to act differently; behind a "must" sentence lurks an unspoken "if you don't . . ." This threat is missing in the imperative. The "must" presupposes a conscience which is accessible to the reason of faith; the imperatives make the responsibility much more clear: Christ or the apostle himself stands accountable to the imperative. The person inviting or calling forth thus gives himself as well.

If the verb "must" were prohibited, it would get quiet indeed in our churches. In this unbiblical word it becomes clear how much we *must* learn the ABC's of the gospel again! Bible translations also carry part of the blame here. Instead of "will," Luther and many others after him used the verb "ought" as a rendering of the future tense. Instead of "You will love your neighbor" we hear "you ought"; this "ought" has so entrenched itself that translaters only unwillingly relinquish it in favor of "will."

Things are also done in the other way. Martin Buber translates Leviticus 19:18 as: "Love your neighbor as yourself" instead of "You should love your neighbor as yourself; and he translates the Ten Commandments as: "do not kill," "do not covet" and so on (Exod. 20:13-14). To be sure, the character of promise is missing here from the commandments. The problem of translation is too large to treat here, but it's important for the preacher at this point to know and understand the original languages. It is catastrophic for the proclamation if a freely given promise is exchanged for a demanded obligation; this turns the gospel upside down, but it is unfortunately the case when the words "ought" and "must" are overused. But here these words are only symptoms.

There are other symptoms as well. Subjunctive sentences betray that preachers themselves do not believe in the realization of their pious wishes. "That could lead us to a fulfilled life." Manfred Josuttis shows how legalism manifests itself in the structure and content of a sermon, and he considers the legalistic concluding part to be especially stereotyped.[29] The interrogative appears to be particularly popular for giving expression to the legalistic perspective. Sermons without a practical application are often scoffed at. It takes courage to proclaim the gospel without making demands, and it can only succeed if preachers understand the gospel as a promise and are thus willing to be open to God's work in the future. Otherwise only legalistic talk is possible unless the preachers don't want to close their eyes to reality.

How can we fight this distortion? Certainly not by indignation. Josuttis, with all his valuable insights, and also the present chapter of this book, will not help any preachers unless they perhaps already have an idea of what should be done. The difficulty is that legalism is rooted personally at a very deep level, most of the time unconsciously. Theologians who struggle against legalism are astonished when their sermons are evaluated and they hear that they themselves have used legalistic pressure. Unconscious, unresolved problems in preachers themselves prevent them from letting the gospel's joy and freedom have its say. Salvation in Christ pales to a mere possibility which we, through our own power, must realize. They fail to recognize that this immeasurably overestimates human action.

The so-called political sermon is a particular type of legalistic proclamation.

3. The Political Sermon

The renewal of the participants' primal trust is decisively significant for the positive effect of a worship service. An indispensable prerequisite in this context is the discovery that the old and familiar can also be of value today. Stabilization is thus an essential characteristic of a worship service, an assertion I made in the chapter about the dimension of security. Within the context of the second dimension (deliverance), fundamental significance is attributed to surprise, astonishment, and wonder caused by the new thing that is promised. The listening congregation yearns for a change in the sense of deliverance or release. The question now arises whether the listener is prepared for a change. Can the sermon cause a change in opinion or behavior? The answer is simple: It cannot, or only barely can. The sermon is technically a variation of mass communication, and this is best suited for strengthening the listener's present standpoint. A person wanting to influence behavior in a different direction normally has only limited success with mass communication. A genuine, collective search is possible in the monologue situation of the sermon only to the extent that the preacher succeeds in lending expression to a seeking or insecurity already present in the listeners. It is certainly possible for the sermon to effect deepening insights in the listeners, but these insights must fit into what is already universally recognized by the worship service participants. As soon as an opinion is expressed exceeding the limits of this framework, the preacher enters the realm of controversy. The monologue sermon is no longer adequate here, since communication about controversial topics also demands externally a dialogue in order to be effective.

A political sermon is normally understood to be a sermon is which the preacher expressly takes a certain stand on a controversial matter. Listeners generally do not appreciate this. Since this phenomenon has already been studied extensively, I will only summarize the most important listener reactions to political sermons.

> —I was moved by her description of the hungry children. But what am I to do with it? I can't do anything.
> —The guilt feelings he arouses aggravate me.
> —[I don't agree at all, and I found it frustrating that I was not able to say anything.]
> —[I don't go to church to hear *that* (a sermon on draft resistance).]

Positive reactions came only in isolated spots, while most political sermons were generally evaluated negatively. It's probable, however, that the choice of listeners (generally participants in clinical pastoral education courses) shows itself in the evaluation here.

The two feelings aroused by political sermons are helplessness and aggravation. The helplessness comes from the impossibility of overcoming or effectively combating misery caused or partly caused by human guilt. The aggravation is caused by several things. Some of those in the worship service are aggravated that a controversial political topic is dealt with in the sermon at all. Others end up wanting to join in a discussion, and the monologue is suddenly no longer adequate for them. Finally, aggravation is directed toward the legalism inherent in a political sermon. I believe the worship service participants again have three legitimate points.

—The worship service is unsuitable for the solicitation of political ideas.
—Dialogue is necessary as a communicative method for influencing political opinions, not monologue.
—The demand for a certain political behavior takes on legalistic overtones within the framework of a church sermon.

These three theses require explanation.

The view that the gospel and politics are inseparable needs no further proof today. Nonetheless, one must differentiate between the two quantities. The political decision comes only after the encounter with the word of the Lord; preachers should bring their listeners to a hearing of the word of God, but they cannot determine which decisions the people will then make. As soon as preachers bring their own decisions into the pulpit, the sermon degenerates into propaganda. The people in a worship service are not coming to hear *that*.

Another question is where, within the realm of the church, one can then speak about political decisions. There is almost no opportunity at all for that, and perhaps that's the reason the problem "sermon and politics" is always identified in discussion with the problem "church and politics." The church, however, is larger than the institution of the sermon. If one finds the traditional worship service unsuitable for political discussion, then an active church congregation ought to create additional opportunities beyond that. There the politically involved members can put forth and exchange opinions.

It's clear, however, that such discussions will bring together only a small percentage of the normal worshipers. Of all the people I recall from the congregation and from the clinics, only a very few would be interested in such church politics. Perhaps that's regrettable, but it's the reality. The church as a political forum would naturally have strong competition. Daily papers and television no doubt bring together more interesting and important politicians and arguments than a church congregation, and the politically involved people know that. Otherwise they would have found workable ways within the realm of the church long ago. I would even assert that democratic institutions already offer adequate opportunities for open political discussion: television, the press, party meetings, and party boards.

The worship service, with its relatively high attendance, must be a propaganda temptation for every politically involved pastor. The misuse of power is quickly justified when the purpose is good. The insight is obvious that a strong word backed by the pulpit's authority could persuade those in a worship service of a particular political opinion; that's nothing but the centuries-old attempt to legitimize political convictions religiously. Listeners today resist this, for the most part including those who are themselves of the same political conviction.

The content of political sermons is, as far as I have heard, either reactionary, with generalized accusations toward the communists, or, more frequently, revolutionary or progressive, often even socialistic. Martin Kriener formally differentiates the political atonement sermon which calls people to action without being concrete, from the so-called political theology ("political evening prayer") which calls people to specific action. The second kind wants to pass on information to the listeners which has been suppressed or neglected by the press, and, on the basis of that, to precipitate certain actions. Kriener must, however, agree with the critic Schmitthals that this information is undifferentiated, one-sided, and frequently more suggestive than informative. The concern of all political sermons is not to leave political decisions up to the individual, but rather as a Christian community to take the right path. The problem, however, which is so difficult to solve, is who ought to determine which way the Christian community and church should go. In reality it's usually again a single individual, the pastor, who decides. The authoritarian coloring which his expression of opinion then acquires from the pulpit arouses and strengthens the listeners' resistance rather than their agreement. The question arises concerning how political preachers can legitimize themselves. Their opinions are controversial in society at large, so what gives them the right to take positions in the pulpit? It requires sobriety and distance to differentiate here between their own political positions and preferences, and what is important for their congregations. In the pulpit such positions acquire the claim of religious sanction in their effect if not in their intention. For that reason preachers should be reserved in their position-taking on controversial topics in the pulpit. The framework for position-taking is there only where discussion is possible. The prophets went out among the people; in the worship service the preachers have rather a priestly function.

The protest of legalism which has to be made concerning political sermons is of a theological nature. Everything said already about the suppression of the gospel and the perversion of the law must also be said against the political demands made in a sermon. The political sermon is a variation of the legalistic proclamation; it demands literal fulfillment of a demand and this eliminates the listener's mature decisions.

The characteristic of legalism also applies here, namely, that people are left alone. The demands are made from the pulpit, and now the listeners must themselves see what they are to do with them. The "action worship services" have tried to avoid this mistake by giving the listeners the possibility for action, but they have accomplished little or nothing. Rather than pointing to the coming promise, political preachers prefer to form the future with reforms which change society. That means, however, that the promise's "unrealistic" element is replaced by the "unrealistic" political illusion that everything can be made better through changes. Of course not all political sermons are unrealistic. The argument for having a voice in things or for a certain foreign policy aims at something that can be realized. But within the framework of a worship service the impression is invariably awakened: It is a matter of God's will here; it is a matter of his kingdom. The intended political steps are, however, too small and too questionable for such excessive expectations, which would apply only in exceptional situations. If Christian hope is based on human action instead of on God's promise, then one claims political action has potential which only God has, and exorbitant demands are made on human beings. The proclamation degenerates into advice followed by resignation as soon as it becomes clear the political measures are either impossible or bring on a whole new set of problems.

Leaving politics completely out of the worship service would also be an unrealistic solution. Such a decision would be an implicit protective device for conservative politics, and it's usually political conservatives who argue for it. Someone satisfied with the current political developments will tend not to mention politically controversial topics in the sermon or intercessions. People who speak about it want changes. The question is how a preacher can do justice to the congregation. How can the preacher make it clear that the proclamation also guides us to political action without identifying this action with party politics?

Martin Kriener tries to sketch this path.[30] He maintains it's possible to make listeners sensitive to political problems which need to be solved without publicly favoring a particular solution.

By speaking openly about political questions, the preacher escapes identification with that conservatism necessarily attributed to the "theology of the word" which only in a general way points to individual political responsibility. By attempting to do justice to the various attempts at solving political problems, the preacher escapes the propaganda style which must be attributed to the socialistic political sermon. Kriener remarks, however, that on this path of political plurality the question arises concerning what function Christian ethics actually still has, since no clear path is shown. This is a type of insecurity a preacher must live with in attempting to do justice to the complexity of political problems as well as to the maturity of the listeners.

4. Suppressed Law: Lack of Involvement

Without a claim to validity a law would be no law, though precisely this claim makes a law unsympathetic under certain conditions. An agreement is an agreement even in moments when it hurts or takes a great deal of effort to stand by it. Living in a legally ordered society requires that the participants assume responsibility. Their goal must be the "right" life, their aspiration to keep the law. This second aspect of the legal order requires that the lawgiver react with preventative measures, punishment, or other effective means in the case of encroachment with guilt and atonement. Even if the language of the justice department does not quite fit the order of law and gospel, the legal structure in and for itself is given with the establishment of this order, with the determination of human life and the world for love and justice.

The gospel becomes realistic through the law, though naturally God's reality and human reality do not fit together. The world resists and the gospel is a stumbling block and foolishness for them. The law brings together the gospel and human reality. In the first place, it exposes the resistance against the gospel; in the second, it shows ways in which the gospel changes human reality. These two functions of the law, the exposing (*usus elenchticus*) and the guiding (*tertius usus legis*) are indispensable for a good sermon. They contribute to its positive effect because now the listeners are shown that there is much in them resisting the proclamation. Not only is the liberating gospel proclaimed, but the totally natural human reactions are also named and shown: the fact that we do have trouble believing in a hidden God; that we do have trouble living on promises, trusting ourselves to someone other than ourselves; that the sheer quantity of misery and injustice sooner leads us to the fear of fate than to trust in Christ. On the other hand, in addition to the resistance, a proper sermon also shows the traversable paths for life with the gospel, just as the Old Testament commandments and the New Testament paraenesis variously bring them to expression. It then becomes clear to the listeners where in their daily life they encounter God's nearness and activity. Experiences of understanding, forgiveness, and encouragement, and also experiences of challenge and change become transparent to believers as the Lord's activity.

A proper sermon of law will show to the listeners the binding force of life with God. Feelings essential for faith are aroused, and the listeners will be impressed by the powerful resistance both in and around them—resistance against the liberating word of the gospel. They will become aware again to what extent they are given over to other powers, and they will be sad about their failings, humble in the face of what they have accomplished in life. They will lament their lost chances and a life of blindness and unrighteousness, but the hearty will to new obedience, the clear readiness for loyalty will also grow in them anew, with gratitude for all that has been set into motion in small steps and all that is coming. And they will want God to complete his work and will want the resistance to be done away with.

The unsympathetic aspects of the law, including its validity in general, its absolute necessity, its strictness, and also its consequences for humanity, the responsibility, accountability, the guilt, the punishment, the atonement, can scare preachers away. And what about their own responsibilities? Are they willing and able to see and perceive clearly their duties in life in general and in their vocation? How do they themselves react to demands made of them? Have they brought these fundamental problems of life under control to a certain extent, or will they also have reasons leading them to resist the law? Consciously or unconsciously they will then tell themselves they do not want to preach the law, and they thus break up the balance between law and gospel. Those listening to their sermons react in the following way:

> —It was all so beautiful and untroubled. That's not my life.
> —Why didn't he say one word about guilt? Was I the only one who thought of it?
> —[I'm almost envious of this preacher—she seems to have such an unshakable faith.]

These complaints can be summed up in a word: The gospel's binding force of involvement is missing, and with it everything which a proper sermon of law is able to effect falls away—humility, will to obedience, the desire for God to complete his work. An unrealistic gospel is left, a gospel the Christian congregation, as the statements show, will not accept.

Without the law, the gospel becomes so spread out that it is really no longer a gospel, and in the final analysis it becomes an optimism which renders reality harmless. Those in the worship service find nothing addressing their yearning for deliverance, since if everything is in order that yearning loses its basis and is no longer recognized. They feel abandoned in their yearning; that unreal optimism does not speak to them.

It appears complicated. Legalism generally meets with rejection, but if it's missing, the listeners complain as well. Here the importance of that balance between gospel and law becomes visible—the polarity of grace and judgment. Law and legalism are different quantities. The congregation wants law in a proper relationship of tension with gospel, but they do not want legalism. They also resist if the preachers make it too easy for them. The gospel alone is no longer the gospel, but rather non-binding involvement, and there is no consolation and no dependability in that.

There are thus basically two distortions of the proclamation. If the gospel no

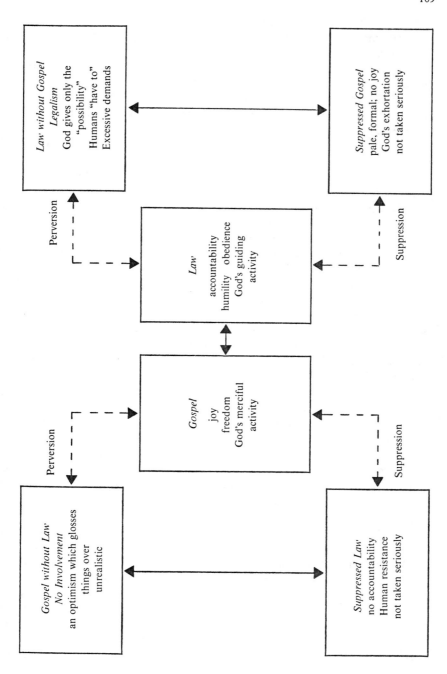

longer balances the law, the proclamation degenerates into legalism; if that tension with the law is missing in the gospel, then the gospel degenerates into non-binding involvement.

The problem concerning to what extent we human beings are responsible for our own lives is more complicated than can be treated in this book. Within the framework of this study, it's important to me that I show how strongly the sermon reactions betray a certain expectation on the part of the people in a worship service. They expect to be spoken to concerning their own responsibility, whether that's painful or not, and the preacher who wants to spare them this will only disappoint them.

Our present generation, however, has problems precisely with this responsibility, something I dealt with at length above. Psychoanalysis has also influenced the problems of human responsibility by showing how strongly people are affected by their earliest experiences. This has led to the vague assumption that these experiences are not only influential, but even determinative. I think it's less well known that psychoanalytical therapy aims at ego-strengthening and thus at the enhancement of the feeling of responsibility, rather than the excusing which the psychoanalytical perspective has so often meant for forensic psychiatry. Childhood experiences then take on the significance of an all-determining cause. This detracts significantly from the person's judgmental capacity. The scientific causal principle has without further ado been applied to the understanding of spiritual processes, and I suspect this vague, generalized disregard for human responsibility in the church has led to a suppression of the proclamation of the law.

The Gestalt therapy of Fritz Perls attempts to call this responsibility strongly back into people's memory. Even if this therapy has grown out of psychoanalysis, it has nonetheless broken with its fundamental principles. Whereas psychoanalysis is seeking the complicated reasons for inadequate or disturbed behavior, Gestalt therapy seeks not the reasons, but rather the *kinds* of resistance in people against acceptable behavior.[31] The new emphasis on human responsibility in psychotherapy seems to me a great help for theology. It can open preachers' eyes to aspects of the proclamation which have too long been neglected, namely to the law. Not a single worshiper is helped by the preachers' ignoring their guilt and with it their binding involvement with God and humanity. Grace is indeed basically cheap, but it is by no means non-binding.

We find an access to people's real sufferings only when their responsibility for their own behavior is taken seriously. Gestalt therapy and similar modes of treatment reach those deeper feelings much more easily than do the analytical methods based on understanding. People are led to *perceive* or *feel* their negative feelings instead of understanding them. The surprising thing is that such feelings then sometimes disappear or make room for others. I have increasingly seen the importance of how the so-called primitive feelings—aggravation, lament, accusation, revenge, envy, but also joy—help people and bind them together. The psalms now gain a new perspective, since here the Israelites also expressed these feelings. How "cleanly" have the authors of hymnals cut back and reworked the psalms! There's a reason for that. As soon as human responsibility is no longer taken seriously, these feelings no longer come to expression and are suppressed. They are, of course, incomprehensible if people are no longer accountable for their actions, if there is no longer a consciousness of living in a legal order. Without the law these primally human feelings are no longer addressed.

The fear of proclaiming the law is usually rooted in the misunderstanding that a sermon on the law is equal to moralistic preaching. This is precisely what a sermon on the law is *not*. The sermon of the law is exactly what the sermon of the gospel is: the proclamation of God's deeds. There is no coercive demand, not in the Sermon on the Mount and not in the paraenesis statements in the apostolic letters. The association of the law with the gospel is too strong for that. I have the impression that it's difficult for all of us to see the fundamental difference between moralistic demands and the gospel's admonition, and to tune our proclamation to the balance between gospel and law.

Preachers who are willing and able to accept responsibility and who simultaneously know the joy and freedom of the gospel will succeed in seeing the incongruity in human life and in dealing with it in their sermons without moralizing. They will fathom some of the darkness in the human heart and expose the tricks and devices by which people deceive God, themselves, and each other. They will dare to peer openly into the abysses from which God saves us, and in this way they are serious about preventing the gospel from floating above life, serious about having it descend into the dark world.

CHAPTER 4

The Dimension of Understanding

When people in a worship service say they have felt spoken to or engaged, we must understand this in yet a third dimension. If in the service justice is done only to the first two dimensions, if trust is awakened and the message of the gospel is clearly proclaimed, then a decisive element in that process of speaking to a congregation is missing. It becomes visible in the following listener reactions:

—He was too sure about God and the beyond for my taste.
—It's too bad she turned away from the difficult things so quickly.
—I don't really know what to do with this unquestionable faith.
—My unbelief wasn't taken into consideration.
—The solution at the end was too harmless for me.
—He didn't take seriously the resistance in me.

And positively:

—It helped me to hear that Easter is not a problem, but rather a mystery.
—[The alternative of "love" to "untarnished heroism" was important to me.]
—The image of the mountain lake did it for me.

It becomes apparent in these statements that listeners basically have something in themselves which resists understanding and accepting what is offered in the worship service, but they are hoping these difficulties will be overcome and are glad and feel spoken to if that actually happens. An alternative term ("mystery" instead of "problem," "love" instead of "perfectionism") or a clear image can overcome the resistance. If that doesn't happen, the listeners find the sermon too harmless because they don't feel taken seriously enough in their questions and resistance. That harmlessness refers now less to the fact that the preacher doesn't bring in the darker side of life, as in the dimension of deliverance, than to the fact that the preacher simply presupposes that the listeners are ready and capable of accepting the message. The people in the service want to be convinced, their opposing voices are supposed to be silenced.

A second aspect of this dimension becomes clear in the next statements:

—I couldn't find any clear thread of thought.

—I never did understand hope.
—The terms made me tired; I had difficulty following along.
—I found the images unclear.
—It confused me; I found it too complicated.
—The story seemed too calculated to me.
—Unfortunately it never really became clear to me what he wanted to
say.

The listeners are complaining here about the sermon's lack of clarity; I discussed this earlier in connection with the argument for preaching personally.
Lack of clarity has an impersonal effect, and we encounter it here in its inability
to persuade. The listeners are concerned with this: They want to be persuaded,
and the preacher's statements must thus be clear so that the listeners can see the
structure and the result. In this chapter I will speak more about the details.

It's like a game: On the one hand, the worshipers are expecting the gospel;
they know, so to speak, what is offered in the church. On the other hand, they
resist the proclamation—not to prove themselves right, but so that they are overcome in their resistance. They question everything with the intention of being
persuaded by the preacher. This game appears to me to be both very serious and
profound. It comes from the pains known only to the believer, the pains of
temptation.

A worship service, a sermon not directing itself to hearts in temptation, does
not speak to the listeners. The congregation feels itself spoken to to the extent
that it feels taken seriously in its doubts and is lifted up above them.

I am considering the event of worship service and sermon in this chapter
according to the dimension of understanding or insight. People in a worship
service want to be persuaded, they want to understand and thus gain a certain
security. It is a matter here of only one dimension, but without doing justice to
the other dimensions, without awakening trust and proclaiming the gospel's
message, the preacher will not genuinely speak to the congregation. More than
in the other dimensions where it's a matter of feeling and hearing, here in the
dimension of understanding it's a matter of comprehension and insight. On the
other hand, this dimension can be separated from the others only theoretically;
it's not identifiable, for example, as a separate section of the sermon. Just as do
the other two dimensions, it permeates the entire worship service, even though
the dimension of understanding probably becomes most clearly visible in the
sermon.

The Temptation of Faith

If we have faith, we are dealing with things unseen (Heb. 11:1). Something
existentially important to us stands there unsecured. Faith is related to our life's

foundation and connects us with primal trust, our deepest feeling; but our senses, which otherwise serve us as a dependable observer of reality, are totally excluded in our dealings with the unseen: no seeing, no direct hearing, nothing. For our experience this means a dramatic schism. Where everything—our salvation—is at stake, there is simultaneously nothing guaranteed through direct perception. Actually we don't know what we're saying when we confess Christ. This results in a tension between faith and unbelief which is, from a human perspective, hopeless. The reality of God, which we take on faith, is continually called into question by our daily experience, and faith is "completely silenced by the language spoken by facts." [1]

Believing persons can again and again doubt God himself, their last certainty; nothing prevents them from questioning God's dependability or God's active existence in general. Yet they are also never certain even about themselves as believers; they can never definitely answer the probing question of when their faith is sincere and whether it is existentially significant for them, since all faith is related to something unseen. This means it is fundamentally challenged by perception and thus experience. Immediate experience is an attack on faith, and this temptation is characteristic of Christian faith, a shadow inseparable from the light.

The believing person's experience thus stands in a perpetual tension between certainty and uncertainty. Certainty is often experienced as being complete because it's associated with the deepest feeling of trust. Uncertainty can be experienced as being equally complete as a depressed feeling of emptiness and broken illusion. The two poles of this tension are basically accessible to believers. Their memory tells them how much healing encouragement and joy can be found in faith and with God and Jesus Christ; immediate daily experience, however, its pain and absurdity, always keeps the door to uncertainty and emptiness open.

And things are even a bit more difficult. People can get caught in uncertainty—for a long time or even forever. A hardening is possible from which one never gets loose, and yet the believer can never really live in certainty either. "For we walk by faith, not by sight" (2 Cor. 5:7). Unbroken certainty has not yet come. The door to that certainty is not always open, but the door to uncertainty and doubt is always open. The highest state attainable for the believer's experience is a rhythm between certainty and uncertainty. If after an exhalation and emptying he or she can once more breathe in and be filled, then the believer has received everything possible. The God known to the church does not want to give more, and a fundamental ambivalence is left in the believer. The emptying and temptation belong to Christian faith and are the pains of that faith. That humiliation God chose for himself in Christ goes so far that God's Spirit sometimes leaves humanity, and it can then happen that people want to pray but cannot. There they suffer God, who also carries some of the responsibility for the temptation.

Whenever people hear a sermon their initial experience unconsciously moves to the side of insecurity, and they emphasize the one side of that ambivalence in which they basically stand. But now they hope the sermon will convince them anew, that they will be led away from insecurity and toward believing certainty again. They need to experience the rhythm again, especially the breathing in and being filled up and persuaded. During the hymns and prayers most worshipers turn forth the pole of trust; and strange to say, the word "God" disturbs them either not at all or much less if it comes up without further ado, whereas they are much more demanding during the sermon. Especially while listening to that sermon they unconsciously spread out all their second thoughts, doubts, questions, insecurities and disappointments in the hope that the preacher will succeed in breaking through that resistance.

The listener statements make it clear that faithful, believing people expect the preacher to fill the word "God" with something new, to be convincing in speaking of the gospel and not simply to refer to it as something self-evident. They are apparently not prepared to supply personally the persuasive force from their own experiences in life. The preacher must do that.

It looks like a mischievous game; the listners spread out all the opposing arguments in order to test the preacher. But this is no malicious game. It's the pain of temptation bringing people to listen to a sermon in this way. They want to breathe in after day-to-day life has taken their breath away, and they use a fellow Christian's gospel proclamation as an opportunity to show their wounds and lament their sufferings. They are not at all hoping to win; in fact they want nothing more than to lose, to be overcome. In principle they are cooperating with the preacher, who just needs to see how badly beaten they are in order to help them come through this great temptation with a renewed faith. In this way those worshipers struggling with some difficulty are sometimes able to take a step forward. Sermons can make a valuable contribution toward this, especially at funerals.

Temptation concerns faith as a whole, not just particular parts of it. This is not the place to go into the substance of problems of temptation, so I will simply summarize what the main points are when I reflect on temptation. It is a matter of everything comprising the relationship between persons and God, and the two focal points are precisely the Lord and we ourselves. "God," "the most heavily-laden of all human words," [2] continually needs to be made relevant for those who seek him. It won't do simply to presuppose God, something true also in earlier times, although preachers and listeners often did not notice that. Today many, but not all, listeners protest if one speaks about God as something self-evident. Not only does the word "God" designate what is most holy for some people, it has also "been worn out after centuries of negligent misuse, employed both consciously and unconsciously as a means of power, and used as a subterfuge for base interests, in a word: ravaged a thousand times over and . . .

thus rendered suspect." [3] In general this requires that the preacher not speak of God as something self-evident.

The other focal point is humanity itself. When people want to hear a sermon their deepest trust is the important thing. They need a renewal of their primal trust, and their faith is as little something self-evident as is God. It's tempted, and they want to be spoken to in that contradiction between faith and doubt, trust and uncertainty.

The preacher should not forget that many listeners are not aware of this temptation. There are certainly situations and feelings active in people of which they are not clearly aware. Temptation is a part of faith and is an active force in listeners who are not conscious of it. Listeners sense this contradictory state to a greater extent than they actually know of it.

It is this temptation which has led to the institution of the repeated proclamation and concretely to the regular Sunday worship service. The homiletical situation is one of temptation: "That situation through which the preaching church sees itself here and now challenged to proclamation," and the preacher must discover the places where a congregation is suffering under temptation. That is where the proclamation must happen with a clear reference to the questions at hand. Faith recognition must be conveyed, a new persuasion, yet the preacher can do this no more easily than in the case of security and deliverance. Nonetheless there is work for the preacher in this dimension as well.

The dimension of understanding, which deals with temptation, is not the only important one in the sermon. The homiletical situation encompasses—if I let the listener statements speak—more than only temptation. (In Ernst Lange's book I especially miss the dimension of security. His efforts are directed almost entirely to the sermon's content, and the danger of a one-sided intellectual enlightenment instead of a proclamation also encompassing experience seems to me to become unnecessarily great because of that.) I have already spoken about the other dimensions. What this present chapter discusses is a final aspect of this larger event.

Only Evidence Persuades

The listeners expect the preacher to convince them of the truth of the gospel. They have already experienced that earlier, and now they await it again. How can the preacher persuade the listeners again?

The problem is that persuasion is being required in an area of life in which logical arguments have almost no value at all. The truth sought again by the people in a worship service is not an objective one, but is rather an existential truth precipitating engagement and participation, not cool ascertainment. It's a truth giving a feeling of security. Only theoretical observation can independently differentiate the cognitive components of this truth; in the act of persuasion itself the emotional effect of the renewal of trust is inseparably connected with cognitive understanding. That process of being persuaded is thus a total experience, not just an intellectual comprehension. Experience demands more than logical arguments and explanations; it requires genuine perception. Love and trust are not awakened by assurance, but rather only by perceptible, palpable or visible warmth and sincerity. The sympathy offered becomes accessible to experience by means of sense perception, and love and trust emerge as an answer to it. That primal trust discussed in the chapter on the dimension of security does not emerge as a result of logical arguments, but as our answer to the attention given us by caring people whose skin we have felt, whose smell we have sensed, whose voice we have heard.

In a worship service this kind of persuasion is demanded precisely in the context of the unseen and unheard. An experience is being demanded in a realm where the human senses are of no use, an experience which can, however, emerge only as a reaction to sense perception. Put simply this means people want to *see* the unseen.

There is only one way the preacher can convey to the listeners this experience of being persuaded anew: by calling forth evidence. Evidence is an event; it persuades without examinable proof and effects an unshakable inner certainty. For the person who is persuaded, this evidence is valid in the manner of an axiom; it possesses the persuasive power of daylight which makes things visible and thus real for us. It normally accompanies the perceptive activity of our senses, but it can also be effective in the realm of the unseen, the only prerequisite being that the unseen becomes "seen" or evident. Only vivid, graphic language can arouse this kind of evidence, while logical argumentation reaches only our discursive thinking. Truth is grasped in small fragments, analyzed and thus cooled off, a process inadequate for the emergence of genuine experience. Graphic speech, however, touches more than the cognitive level of our understanding; it reaches the subconscious layer of inner vision where we are able to grasp truth as a totality. In this kind of evidence precisely the apparently impossible happens: the unseen becomes seen. This occurrence is always impressive and precipitates intense surprise. People are encountering their life's truth.

The specific kind of certainty conveyed by this living evidence corresponds exactly to the character of truth meant here. Rational, objective truth needs no evidence in this sense; it needs only sense perception and logical argumentation. In the worship service and sermon, however, existential truth is being sought. When it reveals itself the perceiver, the person seeing it, cannot remain cool and detached. That person is struck at the very roots, and his or her whole life is affected: feeling, thinking, inner vision and will. Evidence cannot come about without the free understanding and will of the person concerned.

At the same time, that certainty conveyed by the evidential experience is also vulnerable. That certainty can fall away at any time because the will participates in that experience, because it is not an objective occurrence which is independent of one's own will. The person involved can also think the evidential experience is *only* called forth by his or her own will and is thus only wish fulfillment or a projection.

Within that experience itself, however, no one believes one is clinging to a wishful projection. One freely gives oneself over to that evidential insight, the whole person, with will, feeling, and inner vision, and confirms that encounter with truth. Only in this total and thus vulnerable way can one grasp existential truth at all. It leads a person into its *circulum veritatis*, where wanting to be persuaded and being persuaded form an inseparable unity. This encounter with our life's truth, with God our Lord, has the characteristics of a merger. The boundaries between the participants in this encounter are no longer distinct, and for this reason such an evidential experience cannot last long. An intense encounter is so demanding and takes so much energy that it can only be a temporary occurrence.

The cognitive part of this experience encompasses an intellectual clarity or insight, though the manner of comprehension is affected by the experience itself. It is not the manner of scientific comprehension, but rather always refers to an act of encountering such as the biblical-Hebraic *jd'*. The relationships in such comprehension are clear: There is not a recognition of who one actually is, but rather of what I mean for someone else and what they mean for me. This recognition creates basically a personal association, and for this reason it must be voluntary, personally intended, personally confessed. This encounter occurring in the evidential experience of a worship service, particularly while listening to the sermon, is the clash between faith and temptation, between gospel and unbelief. The evidence of understanding is born out of this encounter, and that understanding is thus directly connected with temptation. It's the inhalation after the stresses of insecurity. If people in temptation hear only the word of deliverance, they do not yet take that deep breath because it sounds so harmless. But if the proclamation awakens an evidential insight in the middle of that temptation, there is an "aha, so that's how it is!"—a deep breath is taken, a new certainty is there. An example might make this clear:

> We then are in danger of taking the wrong path. We make the message of Easter into a *problem*. Then we no longer understand it. But the resurrection is not a problem. It's a *mystery*. Indeed, a mystery also causes us to question. But we can understand it and believe it nonetheless.

The preacher, who had just graphically verbalized the skeptical reactions to the incredible Easter message, now summarizes the temptation in the term "problem." A confrontation with the proclamation comes next in the term "mystery," and the insight into the difference between the two terms offers the element of understanding leading the listeners to the evidential experience of "aha." Their temptation is not glossed over with words such as "you just have to believe it, that's just the way it is in the Bible"; that temptation is rather taken seriously in the remark that mysteries also cause us to question. The connection between temptation and proclamation thus becomes clear, and that insight into the fact that the Easter message is a mystery is thus able to encounter the listeners in their real experience. The sermon directs itself to the unbeliever in the listener and thus does not need to presuppose faith.

This understanding is not evidential without the struggle with temptation; at most one puts up with it rather harmlessly, but it doesn't really move the heart. A preacher cannot expect to precipitate an evidential experience in the listeners simply by saying that the gospel of Easter is a mystery. The dynamics of evidence is not awakened except by the confrontation with the "problem," the encounter with temptation.

The understanding referred to in this dimension is simple but not harmless; in fact, it resides in a tension between simplicity and complexity. The resurrection is a mystery; that can be easily understood. A mystery elicits our questions and doubts. This does justice to the complexity of understanding; the miraculous element in genuine, evidential understanding is its simultaneous simplicity and complexity, and if preachers veer from this tension they will no longer do justice to these conditions of the dimension of understanding. They then either neglect the complex character of understanding, and their sermons become naïve and unrealistic so that the listeners complain that the preacher is not taking their resistance seriously, or they neglect the simplicity of evidential understanding and their preaching is too complicated. They only see the difficulties and problems, and the listeners complain now as well, because the sermons are not clear to them.

The people in a worship service want to be persuaded with evidence. Some are quickly satisfied, others more demanding, but I suspect this longing is basically an active force in all listeners at all times. Most of the listeners I questioned were relatively demanding on this point. Those not theologically or academically trained were generally satisfied with less during the inquiries concerning this. People long to be moved directly and to relinquish their resistance to a compelling power of persuasion, and they are so positively predispositioned for this surrender that they are disappointed if they do not get the opportunity to do so. In what follows I will try to show concretely how the preacher can awaken an evidential experience. But I do want to repeat one thing: All concrete methods fail to have any effect if the preacher is not personally engaged and convinced. Only those can awaken evidence who have themselves encountered truth. The content of the sentences alone will not convince the worshipers; preachers are themselves a requirement. It is not the exegetical or dogmatic correctness of their assertions, but rather their own living relationship to the mystery of faith which has that persuasive power. And—just so no one reading this book will forget—two people are necessary before the listener can be persuaded: the Lord himself—if he is not a contributing force, then nothing can help—and the listener. Preachers cannot decide whether they affirm what they encounter. These insights into the forces standing outside the preachers' control should not lead them to neglect their own work. Their task is to contribute as human beings whatever they can, and in the dimension of understanding that means—aside from the art of communication to be discussed—their own involvement. Preachers can convey that faith understanding only if the listeners can see the preachers' own joy about that understanding; only then does it pass over to the others.

In the Easter sermon cited earlier the difference between the "problem" and the "mystery" was the foundation for the persuasive insight. Many of the listeners were spoken to in an intensive way by these words, but one can easily imagine what a weak effect such words would have if the preacher were unmoved by the insight. The listener probably can tell whether the preacher is truly involved by the way he or she pronounces the word "mystery." Only if that insight is the preacher's own discovery is there hope for it to be carried on.

The Preacher as Questioning Listener

The listeners' expectations of being convinced anew by the sermon require that preachers develop a sense for their listeners' questions. While they preach *they* should be the first ones to question. The listeners must be able to find both themselves and their temptation in the preacher in order for the understanding offered by that sermon to strike home with them. The preacher's function is thus to represent the listeners.

How should preachers integrate the questions elicited by temptation into their sermons and worship services? Should they begin with questions? This is an important decision, but the listener reactions give us some help here. Beginning with the questions and problems of life seldom leads to satisfactory results. Quite a few sermons are structured according to the model of question-answer in which a human situation is depicted at the beginning, leading to a pressing question. Then an attempt is made to offer an answer to this question from the gospel. It becomes apparent that sermons structured on this model elicit the same reaction in many listeners—frustration. This is explained by the fact that the preacher usually is able to depict the first part of the sermon very impressively, but then simply fails in the second part. Human need is portrayed in gripping, often shocking images, sometimes by referring to a recent catastrophe—a train wreck or earthquake. This arouses and strengthens feelings of shock and fear in the listeners, and it naturally results in a great interest, indeed a burning curiosity to find out how the preacher will cope with these things. The question of meaning, the speechless shock in the face of blind fate—these await an answer, a solution, and an insight from a certain perspective. The preacher promises to give this by the simple act of bringing up this topic and arousing these feelings. But the second part of such sermons is almost always strikingly bland. During evaluations many listeners say they no longer even know exactly what the preacher said there. When sermons are available on tape or in writing one usually finds that the gripping clarity at the beginning is exchanged for vague allusions, catch phrases, and sometimes textbook expressions at the end. This makes the listeners feel frustrated. Wounds have been opened which are painful for all people, and several listeners say later that they were surprised the sermon was already over. They were waiting for the implicitly promised solution. Perhaps the preacher offered some solution or other in the sense of an opening into hope or a new perspective, but the listeners either hardly noticed it or did not notice it at all. No evidential insight emerged.

Young preachers are particularly prone to this kind of sermon effect. In the subsequent evaluation it often becomes clear that they are struggling with the questions themselves, but instead of struggling with them openly or choosing another topic, they simulate a solution which in reality does not exist for them or which is not yet really clear to them. They transmit their own shock and fear and yet do not lead the congregation a single step further toward an evidential understanding. Listeners who have been gripped by the portrayal of human need are depressed at the end, and others, intensely awaiting an evidential insight, are aggravated that it did not come.

I believe the reason behind listeners' frustrations after such sermons is that the question-answer model does not do justice to the structure of the gospel. It overlooks the fact that the biblical message is not an answer to human questions. The result of this is that a person who begins with questions of human self-understanding will never end up at the biblical message. Its answers are necessarily pale and bloodless because there is no path leading from human questions to the gospel.

The concern of preachers using this model is, however, certainly legitimate: to pick up the congregation in its real situation in life. The preachers have apparently seen that there are questions which the church's proclamation cannot simply ignore. They begin courageously with the difficulties of life and of understanding and hope to address people where they really are in life, not in a nice, secure faith, but in a shocked, fearful consciousness of life. But these preachers make two fundamental mistakes. In the first place, they overlook the worship service situation into which the listeners have come of their own free will. These people should not, without further ado, be identified with the questioning person unable to cope with fate. Of course, they have these questions, just as do all people, but on the other hand they *have* come to church and are willingly seeking out the Christian tradition and biblical proclamation. That belongs to their disposition as well, and preachers should not simply bracket that out at the beginning of the sermon as if they had to pull the listeners out of a corner where they can't really be found. Preachers can go ahead and *begin* with the proclamation; it is already explicitly or implicitly there in the greeting, prayer, or hymn before the sermon.

These preachers make an even larger mistake, or rather, the preliminary mistake already mentioned has even deeper roots. There are two different kinds of questions of life. There are questions growing directly out of life experience, out of the suffering and pain of existence. I call them religiously-existentially significant questions—the meaning of suffering, the suffering of mortality, the invisible quality of a good, caring guidance, the question of whether there is a God, and so on. There are also questions of temptation, but those are different questions! They also originate in the realm of immediate life experience, but they are awakened by the proclamation itself. Temptation is a part of faith; it doesn't precede faith, but accompanies it. A preacher can indeed take up these questions of temptation and in certain circumstances even answer them. But the Christian proclamation is just not suited to answering the religious-existential questions. It proclaims God's reign in Christ, and that is quite different from answering questions. If one seeks answers in spite of that, they can only be meagerly or halfway successful. And the listeners are frustrated.

Should the church's proclamation then not deal with these primal human questions at all? It should, but only indirectly, because when one begins with the proclamation one also raises questions; these are the questions of temptation. They are indeed related to more existential questions, but are different in that they stand in a direct relation to the proclamation; in fact, they are ignited by the proclamation. Whenever these questions of temptation are dealt with, the other, existential ones pale beside them. People are then less interested in seeing these questions answered because a whole new level of inquiry is opened to them through the encounter with the Lord. Those religious-existential questions are not as pressing in the encounter with Jesus Christ, first because a relationship emerges, and secondly because in this relationship the same sufferings formerly. leading to the existential questions and religious answers, are not integrated in a new way. Kornelis Heiko Miskotte impressively portrays the differences between the questions and solutions of religion and nihilism on the one hand, and of biblical faith on the other. He shows how the universally human thought schemata are broken through by the biblical proclamation: "Providence" as a pious euphemism for fate, "fear of God" as a feeling of guilt, "love" as stimulus for feeling, "one's neighbor" as just anyone, the goal of life as the blessedness in the "beyond" and so on. Biblical proclamation is always exactly the opposite.[4]

In a sermon on the question-answer model, the beginning with the preliminary question sounds as follows:

> We live in a threatened world. Something totally unexpected can happen at any moment, and it seems we are simply given over to it. This week we learned that a train derailed and more than forty people were killed. How is something like that possible? Mothers and fathers ripped away from childern, loved ones from one another. Why? That's the enormous question we face—why?

Those listening to the sermon were later either not able at all to remember the answer to that question, or they recalled it only vaguely; it came at the end of the sermon after the preacher had told the story of a man who had been sick for 38 years:

> Love has been revealed in the middle of a dark world in which many things happen which are incomprehensible. Jesus is love. That is also a task for us, so that we can see a way with and for each other.

The fears and horror aroused by the portrayal of the train wreck were by no means dispelled by the generalized, actually rather bland sentences. They simply remained, and that frustrated the listeners. They had expected to get some kind of answer to the question of "why?" The answer was that we cannot "comprehend" everything and that there is nonetheless love, but in this pallid form it's just no match for the abrupt force of the vivid portrayal of fate at the beginning of the sermon. The preacher's mistake is in programming the listeners for the treatment of a religious-existential question, and thus beginning on the wrong side of things. Strange to say, the listeners gladly fall into this trap, indicating that these religious-existential questions are easily activated in them.

But things can be different and better. What follows is a generally positively evaluated sermon which took up the pains of suffering and absurdity, but did so within the framework of temptation instead of as a theoretical problem. The text was Matthew 5:4: "Blessed are those who mourn, for they shall be comforted." The sermon began with a description of the difference between "happy" and "blessed." Blessedness was associated with hope; through God's deed in Jesus Christ persons are meant for salvation and not given over to themselves or to misfortune. This does not result in a life without suffering, but in a blessed life full of hope because of God's promise. Only then did the sermon raise the questions of temptation:

> But wait a minute! What does this "blessed" mean; what does this hope mean for an old man whose legs have to be amputated this week, or for a person who can find no peace for his yearning? Isn't it all just so much empty talk?

The questions coming from real-life experiences and precipitated now by the proclamation are presented here much more aggressively than in the more theoretical sermon. Indeed they even gain a different character, that reproachful undertone having become much more clearly noticeable. The questions developed into complaints, accusations, and impatient expressions of yearning. This is so, I think, because they now have a clear counterpart—Jesus Christ, who promises consolation. The sermon leaves these complaints and questions where they are and simply juxtaposes them to the promise:

> What he promises is renewal and consolation. Are you suffering? That hurts, more than I in the pulpit can know or understand. But it's not tragic, my friend; you are on the path of hope. Because Jesus is coming. Unbelievable, but not impossible. Look at how the dark winter has disappeared; a fresh spring awaits our astonishment. Jesus Christ is nearer and more consoling than that spring. In a hidden way he inspires those who suffer with his hope.

Theoretically even less occurs here than in the first sermon. Though no solution is offered, the listeners can still get rid of their questions and complaints much more easily because of the confrontation here. They're not fed some pale, unsatisfying theory about the incomprehensibility of God or of events in life; instead they come with their sufferings to the Lord, who gives not solutions but rather promise. From a theoretical perspective less occurs, but dynamically much more is attained.

An indirect treatment of human questions such as this is much more promising and theologically more easily understandable than the model of question-answer. Without directly dealing with these problems, Ernst Lange has also suggested this indirect method. He juxtaposes exegetical efforts and "homiletical text criticism." The preacher needs to determine what kind of resistance a given text arouses, what kind of stimulus and doubt.[5] This is probably the result of two phenomena. First, the listeners are more deeply addressed if their questions are revealed indirectly, over against a counterpart; this especially awakens aggressive feelings and brings them into a confrontation with God. A direct approach to such questions inevitably leads to a theoretical-existential treatise, and only a virtuoso preacher will succeed in then formulating the biblical message so that it does not disappear in the face of the impressively portrayed misery. Secondly, the gospel itself is already a confrontation of human questions. It's not at all necessary; indeed it's confusing and deceiving for the sermon first to raise questions to which the gospel must then give the answer.

A person conducting the worship service and doing justice to the dimension of understanding should be able to express those questions the proclamations arouse in people. Here the preacher again becomes visible as an authority, who should be able to integrate the temptations of faith into the worship service and the sermon. This authority cannot be exhausted in the traditional images of the shepherd who accepts responsibility, or of the messenger or witness. The preacher is also the questioning listener, and in a sense represents the congregation. This representation of the congregation, however, is only one aspect of the preacher's function and authority. The pastor builds authority by knowing how to portray graphically and genuinely the worshipers' questions and doubts; only then will come success in discovering and conveying evidential understanding.

The pastor needs this authority. It makes it easier for the listeners to be spoken to by the sermon if they see that the preacher, too, is acquainted with a tempted life and faith. How might preachers prepare themselves for this aspect of their authority? Getting to know temptation means simply living and experiencing the Christian faith. The ability to verbalize this correctly requires a thorough theological education, and preachers must be able to distinguish precisely between the uniqueness of the biblical message and religious or non-religious ideologies.

The aspect of authority now under discussion poses the least emotional difficulties for the preacher. Being someone who questions fits much more naturally into today's experience than does being a shepherd or witness. The adult ego, described in the previous chapter as the most promising stance for the preacher, can be most easily realized in this dimension. In fact there is something liberating and loosening about preachers who speak openly about the temptations they too feel. Today's atmosphere also lends wind to their sails, since people who openly take a position toward their own weaknesses come across with a positive, winning effect. In this way a preacher also gains respect in pastoral counseling; if the listeners see that the preacher does not just harmlessly gloss over important questions of life, they will seek out the preacher as a counselor in times of personal need. Other helping vocations lack this opportunity to introduce oneself to people before any personal relationship is established.

If *only* questions are presented, the listeners are frustrated; the following was said in a sermon:

> Many people today just don't know what to make of a bodily resurrection. I don't either.

With that the topic was finished. This kind of honesty is not able to give the listeners the feeling they are being taken seriously. They expect the preacher to have found a traversable path, otherwise he or she should not be preaching. The adult stance implies that the preacher try to fulfill the listeners' legitimate expectations, and they are expecting their temptation to be integrated into the sermon as well as overcome. A question does not necessarily have to be answered, but a path must become visible upon which one is able to live with the question.

Young preachers particularly tend to demand too much of themselves when they raise certain questions. If they are themselves unable to cope with these questions, then they open up wounds without healing them and perform a kind of half-surgery without very much promise for most listeners. One positive aspect of this is that the preacher is being modest and sincere; it still surprises people whenever preachers openly admit they don't understand everything. But this alone will not satisfy many listeners—certainly not those who already know preachers don't know everything.

The decisive question concerning this integration of temptation is always: What does the preacher do with it? It's not enough simply to mention it. I believe the most suitable solution is an evidential experience in which some insight takes one through that temptation. There are, however, situations in which no evidential understanding is possible. That can be the case at many funerals or after great catastrophes, when any effort to understand appears cheap. An adult stance is then just not suited because the suffering is too great, but preachers do have the opportunity as the listeners' representatives to activate their child egos. They can express this temptation particularly well in prayer, and many prophets and psalmists show that tempted believers cry, sigh, lament, accuse, and even scold. This also integrates that temptation. The difference between this and the stance we criticized—when in the sermon the preacher admits he "also does not understand"—is the intensity and focus on God as one's counterpart. Expressing aggressive and sad feelings in a public prayer has a liberating effect, though positive feelings also must be expressed. The recognition of God and his mysteries leads to praise, and the preacher as listener needs the child ego's spontaneity and joy in order to give expression to this praise in word and song. The groans of temptation and the rejoicing of faith thus stand very close to one another. The lament gives praise free breathing room, without strict logic.

An inner focus which balances complexity and simplicity is required of preachers as listeners. They should also give themselves over to the simplicity of evidential understanding, but can one possibly fear this simplicity? Indeed, it basically makes greater demands on us than complexity since it requires a surrender; and it requires that child in us which gives itself over with such trust that a joy which is logically incomprehensible radiates from us.

Graphic Speech

Whenever a sermon has been graphic or vivid, that is always positively noted during the evaluation. The listeners feel spoken to whenever the preacher paints a gripping scene or tells a story. Of course, it's been known for centuries that the listening congregation perks up its ears as soon as the preacher starts telling a story. This was often disparaged as sensationalism with the depressed realization that the people forgot everything in the sermon except the story. It's astonishing, however, that the educated listeners I questioned reacted precisely as did the more simple people. It is not a matter of sensationalism; what is positively coming across here is the stimulation of the imagination. In contrast to the more conceptual approach, something graphic causes the listeners themselves to become active. Concepts are finished products which the listeners simply register. They need only to think, to think abstractly. But if the preacher tells a story, the listeners themselves construct the forms of the people, the appearance of the events. Now they can experience something.

This is not just some inconsequential minor point which might have significance only for a sermon's presentation. It concerns rather the central question of the nature of the proclaimed truth. Images and stories are eminently suited to the Christian proclamation; concepts are not. This discovery led scholars to speak of a "narrative theology" in which the narrative element is not supposed to displace argumentation, but is meant rather to complement it. Narration is not only indispensable for the proclamation, but for systematic theology as well. Theology has a deeper structure which is narrative in nature. I would like to expand on this within the context of this chapter.

A preacher proclaims the Kingdom of God in this world even though it is not of this world (John 18:36). God's reign cannot be grasped, defined, or made visible. As far as our senses are concerned, it does not belong to this world; God and his kingdom are not immediately accessible. Hence temptation arises for each person who believes in this God. The proclamation, if it is persuasive, carries the listener through that temptation, and this is what happens in an evidential experience. But that evidence cannot be produced with arguments as can everything else immediately available to us; there is nothing here to prove. An evidential experience shares with proof a persuasive power, but it differs because control of the senses is impossible; in its place we find a subjective experience, an inner vision.

Graphic language about God can produce precisely what is necessary for that subjective evidential experience. It draws a picture, a picture from our own world: "Father," "friend," "one hidden." This image becomes transparent in the evidential experience. It is quite clear in its literal sense, but in the sermon it's not just this literal sense that is intended. It is transferred, in the concrete cases already seen, to God. Two quantities are thus related, for example "God" and "friend." The less familiar quantity, "God," is made clearer for us by the familiar "friend," and the clear, secular image ("friend") becomes in the process a kind of manifestation for us of an other-worldly, incomprehensible event—"God," "the Kingdom of God," "salvation." That incomprehensible event becomes accessible only in its reflection in that visible, comprehensible image. That image becomes a reflection pointing to something else, to a primal image, though the difference and distance between the two is very important. It

results in a space for free play, and this space is very well suited to the uniqueness of God's revelation in Christ. He is *in* this world and yet not *of* this world.
Such a space for free play is available much more rarely and sparsely in concepts and definitions than in visual illustrations, since graphic language is not
meant to be taken literally. It gives one's own imagination room for free play
and activates one's inner vision. The language's plasticity creates a space which
then expands for the listener beyond the limits of the image itself; the inner
vision needs this expansion if the unseen is to be seen. With one hand holding to
the familiar image, the listener ventures into the unknown. Only on this path can
a person experience existential truth; it's a seeing where nothing is there to be
seen, and there emerges a relationship with God which "doesn't exist." A person is not rationally persuaded, but rather existentially struck. Engagement is
fundamentally a narrative category.

Eberhard Jüngel describes these existential processes precipitated by metaphorical speech. The event of discovery is particularly deserving of attention in
this context. Graphic speech gives the listeners not only the results of discovering, but also the act itself, and for that reason metaphorical language is perceived as pleasant and nice.[6] The association of the two realms—of the image
and the content to which that image is referred—makes possible the dynamics of
experience. "Oh, is that the way it is!" the listener says. Jüngel attributes to
metaphors an effect which intensifies one's feeling for existence and expands
one's horizons. He discusses Friedrich Nietzsche, who made this same discovery that truth has a metaphorical structure, though for him that was negative:
Truth is nothing other than a "moving army of metaphors, metonomy, and an-
thropomorphisms." Jüngel makes it clear that one can evaluate all this positively. Truth becomes accessible to subjective experience through its metaphorical
structure since it is there that persons can encounter it.

The metaphor's persuasive power resides in the mysterious paradox that it
can be concretely presented and yet simultaneously leaves room for the unseen.
How does this look concretely? Until now I have only discussed basics; but how
does all this appear in broad daylight? There are two main forms of graphic
language: narrative and image. I will now give some attention to each of these
concrete forms.

1. Narrative

Whoever has told stories to groups of children knows the phenomenon well:
They listen with wide eyes—thoroughly engaged—all the way to the end of the
story. If the narrator then wants to add something, a summary, a teaching or an
admonition, they suddenly get restless. Chairs are shuffled, heads turned
around; there's no more interest in what is most important. Children are far and
away the best teachers of rhetoric because they are still capable of immediate

bodily response. As soon as a speech bores them, that spell of engagement crumbles notoriously. Adults react differently only on the surface; they apparently keep on listening, but inwardly they are no longer engaged. Children make it representatively clear for us that narration precipitates tension and engagement, and that afterwards people generally are not interested any more in something extra.

What happens in listeners while listening to a narrative? In the first place their imaginations are activated, and their reactions attribute to the preacher what the listeners actually have done for themselves:

—I thought the plasticity was good; I saw it all right before my eyes.

—The hackneyed topic in his first sentence aggravated me (''what is faith?''), but the fear went away immediately because of the exciting story about the school class.

—The portrayal really gripped me. The sons (in the story) became living people for me.

The preacher's allusions were apparently enough to set these listeners' fantasies into motion. The fact that this is what happened is no doubt to be credited to the preacher, and the listeners are glad they themselves have been activated. They sense their own participation and the fact that they are being directly addressed.

But there is also a danger here. If the preachers do everything themselves, they are not really communicating. The listeners must have the freedom and opportunity to be formatively creative in all this; otherwise they feel as if they are in a theater, where comparatively more is portrayed than in a sermon. Reactions are then negative, or else positive but suspicious:

—I thought the preacher really got involved in the story; it was impressive.

—He was entertaining; I didn't get bored.

—Good entertainment, but after a while I was getting bored.

—I thought the portrayal of the prophets was exaggerated; it put me off.

The sermons referred to here were too extensively worked out, and the listeners were only able to register what was said; this cripples instead of activates the imagination.

A good narrative awakens even more than one's power of imagination. The listeners recognize their own lives in the story, their own joy, pain, disappointment and hope, and without being clearly aware of it they think and feel their way into the story's situation and characters. A kind of identification occurs between the listeners and the person or situation portrayed in the story, and that is actually the narrative's source of power. Without directly speaking about the listeners, the sermon nonetheless comes across to them as if meant for each of them personally. Every preacher has experienced people coming up after the worship service and asking whether the sermon was intentionally directed to them. This clear identification has embarrassed unsuspecting preachers.

The listener's criterion for a good sermon is not (as many theologians mistakenly believe) whether I, the listener, am able to believe or accept the sermon, but rather whether it goes beyond me, whether I recognize and experience what is narrated. Lorenz Wachinger writes that a dogma or commandment soon leads the listeners to rebel, while a story encourages them to examine their experiences and have new ones. Ernst Lerle has described in detail what happens in the listeners when they recognize their own experiences in the sermon narrative.[7] He calls it projective identification. He's cautious about taking the concepts "identification" and "projection" over from depth psychology because they are normally used to refer to pathological processes. Persons who identify no longer see themselves, but see rather only the other person in themselves. Persons who project no longer see the other person, but see rather only themselves in that other. Both are unrealistic and are a disintegration of the ego. But what happens during the hearing of a story cannot be described as pathological. Neither is there any identification or projection in the strict sense, since the listeners always know they are not Abraham or Zacchaeus; they are aware of the "as if" reality as such. The cognitive distance from the story remains, but the emotional boundary is broken down, and the listeners project their own experiences into the narrative. This occurs when, for example, they recognize themselves in Abraham.

> Abraham goes. With trust, clearly, otherwise he wouldn't go. But that's only one side of it! Who wouldn't like to know what is coming and what the future holds? "Maybe what I sometimes fear won't happen! Or will it suddenly one day, on the contrary, really happen to me?" Abraham goes. With apprehension and trust.

This sermon only alludes to what Abraham "sometimes fears," and thus gives the listeners an opportunity to integrate their own fears into the process of listening, so that they no longer only see Abraham. They project themselves into him. An identification can also take place:

> These words give him courage. The apprehension returns, the worries and fears, but this Lord who speaks awakens him and rouses him again and again to trust, and to continue on.

The listeners have the opportunity to relate this event awakening trust in Abraham's life to themselves. They no longer only see themselves and their own fears, they also experience something of Abraham, who let himself be encouraged. That is an identification. They can re-experience the events portrayed by empathizing with them.

By means of this particular identification the listeners infuse the sermon with "personal content," and they personally experience the narrated events. That is active listening, and in this way the service and particularly the sermon becomes an experience. Although people also experience the proclaimed gospel in their daily lives, outside of the worship service, the initial experience is that of the gospel itself, that deep experience of being spoken to. This happens most directly while listening to a story. "The narration is itself an event; it is consecrated like a holy ritual." [8] It becomes clear here that the criticism is psychologically untenable that in the traditional worship service and particularly during the monologue sermon listeners are nothing more than consumers. When Martin Kriener says that the person in the worship service is as a "mere listener" very close to being a consumer,[9] he overlooks the active process of genuine listening. A great deal of activity takes place whenever listeners recognize themselves in the sermon in the sense of an identification. They become bored only when they can no longer identify, and that has very little to do with the clock.

Listener statements point out various laws which will not go unpunished if transgressed during the sermon narrative. Narration is not just the simple reproduction of the content of a text. I will now present two listener reactions made after a narrative sermon:

—Its nearness to life really spoke to me.
—I didn't really know what the story had to do with me.

It's clear the listeners recognized themselves in the first story, but not—or not enough—in the second. Preachers can count on having a good effect only when they tell the story so that the listeners' experience can be integrated into it. They must touch that level of existential feelings, of expectation, disappointment, yearning, joy, sadness, and desire; only then do the people in the service hear their own story. This touching of existential feelings is more important than a similarity of situations; fathers and mothers without children can also participate in the experience of motherly fear and relief. There are always listeners who say during the inquiries that, indeed, they felt spoken to, but they fear others were excluded because the preacher depicted a situation unknown to them; very seldom do any listeners complain that they were unable to feel their way into the narrated situation because they had not yet experienced it personally. Those fundamental feelings and existential situations making the story significant are universally human. Everyone knows what the yearning for freedom is, so a story about imprisonment can also speak to people who have never been imprisoned. The experiential situation, not the external situation, is decisive for the listeners' participation. In fact, external similarity often has a negative effect; premature identifications arise if the listeners sense a direct allusion to a particular person. It's not good when the listeners are asking themselves who is probably meant in the allusion. They then become spectators, and their own inner participation is excluded. In fact, externally there should reign a certain unreality, since only then can the listeners leave behind the role of spectator and recognize themselves in the story. Gert Otto argues for a poetic speaking style over against the tacky factual one. The latter is only seemingly realistic. Reality in multiplicity can only be communicated poetically, that is, in a seemingly unrealistic way. Only the category of unreality gives the listeners' identification a chance.[10] Thus the preacher should be careful with geographical and personal information. The phrases "someone in our congregation" and "I know someone" sooner arouse curiosity than identification. The sincere openness in these examples is meaningless for the listeners at this particular moment, and the same thing applies when the preacher talks about himself or his family. Naturally a historicizing narrative also makes the listeners into spectators. The preacher should tell how things "were" in a way that enables the listener to understand how it is now, how things stand between God and humanity.

People listening to a sermon do not just expect the sermon to be life-like and to be able to identify with it themselves; they also expect the miracle, the proclamation. I discussed this at the beginning of the chapter about the dimension of deliverance. A narrative sermon which is only life-like is not enough. After such a sermon the listeners complain they did not quite understand what the story had to do with faith. And they are not just expecting to hear words such as "faith," "God," or "Jesus"; the dimension alluded to in these words, however, is so important to them that they won't stand for it if it does become clearly visible. In this instance the listeners I questioned were relatively tolerant. Most listeners are not that subtle in their understanding of stories. It must become quite clear to them what the point is; sophisticated subtleties are for sophisticated ears. The danger of the narrative sermon is precisely that too much of what is essential may go unspoken. The problem in such illustration is the loss of theological reference. Here we see the limits of the narrative: it hardly works or does not work at all without conceptuality. What is experienced in the story must be summarized or at least alluded to in clear words or concepts; otherwise people will feel confused. I will come back to the possibilities of conceptual speech in the next section.

The narrative sermon also requires a personal framework. With a listener group, which later gave an evaluation, I once heard a sermon in which the preacher only told a story. One never heard directly what he himself had to say; everything was packed into the narrative, and the people portrayed in it were speaking to the congregation. People will not accept this kind of theater-playing, at least not in the traditional worship service. They want direct contact with the preacher, as I discussed in the chapter about the dimension of security. Someone hiding behind a story will not reach the people in the worship service, and here the sermon's prerequisites differ from those of a lecture or theater performance.

When a preacher wants to tell a story, it's obvious he or she will choose a biblical story. The Bible is an inexhaustible source for the narrating preacher. However, what I have already written about narration in general also holds true for non-biblical stories. Anyone choosing a generally *well-known* story must take some things into consideration. Listeners are normally willing to hear an old story again; after all, it's not a matter of content, but of a re-experience, something a person can do again and again. One always gladly hears a beautiful symphony again because experience can be repeated and is always new. Information, on the other hand, has only a one-time effect as far as participation is concerned. When a well-known story is announced, the listeners often worry whether the preacher will be able to tell it in a surprising new way. They expect nothing new in the content; it's rather the new experience that determines the success. There is also the problem that the listeners already have a certain view of the story, and the preacher should go ahead and call this view into question. But it should not be overlooked. "Is Martha that dumb?" is the criticism some listeners have after a sermon in which Mary is only praised and Martha only criticized (Luke 10:38-42). The classic interpretation also attributes understanding to Martha, but the preacher had overlooked this. If such interpretative variations are not explained they will disturb the listeners, and similarly if too little of a well-known story is used it has a negative effect. The listeners are then expecting more than is offered to them, and at the end they are disappointed. "I expected something more, and then it was already over."

A narrative not seen, but rather constructed, has a much weaker and often even a negative effect. By this I mean exemplary stories designed to illustrate certain thoughts and topics. The listeners sense that they are not able to identify freely, but are rather supposed to pay attention to a particular idea; the narrative then does not have an effect inviting participation. Basically, the exemplary story belongs to conceptual speech; the preacher wants to explain something, not arouse someone to an experience.

A general listener reaction often heard is that one's interest dissipated quickly as soon as the story was over. The scope of the material from which I am drawing is not broad enough to allow clear conclusions, but I will relate some of my conjectures:

Because of the strong listener participation during a narrative it's not a good idea to say a lot after the narrative is over. It's better to introduce whatever falls outside that progressing narrative before the narrative itself is finished. The story's tension has then not yet dissipated. The most promising way of all seems to me to be to remain in the story from beginning to end and to integrate the treatment of the listeners' existential feelings completely into the narrative portrayal.

In this business of narrating the preacher is, by the way, on proven and even holy ground. Within the Old Testament we see how new generations have retold the old tradition with significant variations, new accents, and with insertions. Gerhard von Rad thus considers it legitimate to tell the story of Jesus in an identification with that old transmitted tradition.[11] Many exegetes are put off by the way the New Testament claims the old tradition for itself with the scheme of promise and fulfillment and with the innumerable citations from the Old Testament. But precisely this adaptation—impermissible from the historical-critical perspective—keeps the transmitted tradition alive. The spur-of-the-moment element in these adaptations, that element given by the particular moment, and the *ad hoc* associations make every observer demanding preciseness nervous or unaccepting. "The whole way by which old traditions are actualized," already in the Old Testament itself and then also in the New, "can only be understood as fundamentally charismatic procedure, or, to put it more exactly, as a eclective process based on charisma." [12] The connection with the Scripture, with the text, is not entirely comprehensible. It's a limitation in freedom, something which does not necessarily have to mean arbitrariness. Only for a forced understanding is limitation in freedom equated with arbitrariness. "Wherever the Spirit of the Lord is, there is freedom," and this freedom is something different than arbitrariness or perfectionism. For narrating preachers this means they are free to tell the text's story just as it is given to them in their own *ad hoc* associations and inspiration. Their self-examination protects them from error, but not from spontaneity and risks; there is no sure system of control.

2. Images

There are various speech structures rich in imagery. We find preachers with a generally graphic language; images are used in almost every sentence, very brief, very colorful. Then there is the method which from time to time selects an image and dwells on it a while before the stream flows on. There are also sermons carried by a single image recurring again and again. The different methods, I suspect, reflect different personalities, and I have not gotten the impression from sermon analyses that one way is any better than the others. The listener reactions which refer to a sermon's images show basically three tendencies. Just as in narration, interest is almost always aroused by imagery. That graphic element brings the listeners in, who then activate their own powers, especially that of imagination. But then something different happens during the concentration on that image than what happens during a narrative. Individual characteristics are not grasped one after the other, but rather as a whole, all at one time. The activity of projection and identification can take place much more freely than while listening to a story. The listeners are able to recognize much of their own experience in that image, and they are also able to refer the image's characteristics to themselves.

—The mountain lake has dangerous, deep places, but it is supported by
strong rocks.

The listeners can project their own riddles and burdens into the "dangerous,
deep places," and can also refer that "being supported" to themselves. They
can find themselves in the security alluded to in the image.

Negative listener statements refer on the one hand to the digressions to
which an image can seduce one, on the other hand to the confusion and fatigue generated by too much imagery. Digression in itself must not always be
evaluated negatively; in fact, a gripping image can cause listeners to order, re-
orient and thus cleanse their own experience. But this requires two things not
normally offered by the traditional worship service sermon: freedom and time.
When an image really strikes the listeners, they employ both of these, let their
own associations flow, and tarry with their own ideas about that image. The
only disturbing factor is that in the meantime the sermon goes on, and the
listeners engaged in this way no longer have the energy or interest in it. So
preachers must be clear about what they intend to accomplish with powerful
images; either they accept that several listeners will leave them and follow
their own associations, or they should leave a space for those free associations. There is good resonance concerning image meditations, but that takes
us outside the framework of the traditional worship service. The integration of
an image meditation into a monologue appears to be extremely difficult if not
impossible.

The second negative reaction concerns the *multiplicity* of images often dominating a sermon. Listeners gladly come up with the energy needed to get themselves into an image, but it's such a tremendous amount that the preacher cannot
begin with something new a second, third, and certainly not a fourth time. The
worshipers then merely listen without being inwardly engaged. It's like a love
game—that can't endure too many new beginnings either. The result is that
people become frustrated and give up. Otto Haendler writes: "Anyone piling up
images should suspect himself of working with an imagery that's not genuine. A
genuine image coaxes one to use it sparingly but effectively." [13]

Just as a narrative, an image works only if the preacher has actually seen it.
One cannot make an image; one must discover it. That is, by the way, not
difficult. There is a layer between our conscious and unconscious realm in
which inner vision takes place, in which there are only images. The preacher
must simply get access to this level. Anyone wanting to construct an image
intellectually will certainly come up with something. But this image has no effect because it's construed, and is dominated by intellectual intention. It cannot
live freely; as a matter of fact it sooner confines the listener than offers the
freedom for inner participation.

Great possibilities for the monologue sermon can be found in imagery and narrative. In spite of the critical statements just mentioned, the listener reactions are almost always positive, and I consider this a welcome encouragement for those who must preach. Clear paths are shown here along which listeners will gladly follow the preacher.

Graphic speech, particularly in reference to biblical images and stories, requires of the preacher two inner attitudes which—more even than technical know-how—decide whether he or she will really preach graphically.

In the social realm, the preacher is required to remain aware of speaking in a certain community, namely, within the church. The stories and images have been transmitted in it and enjoy a certain esteem in it, and whoever picks them up and relates them can count on the believers' participation. Those listeners are hoping that the time-proven tradition will convince them anew, but those not really participating, those at a distance, the outsiders, will not be persuaded by this graphic language. "The stories are not supposed to convert unbelievers, they are not a means of proof; they are the game of the initiated, a gift and offering for those listening, poetry which wants to be taken according to its own laws; they contain their own truth and seriousness—except whoever demands too much from them, whoever unburdens himself at their cost, ruins them and exposes them to mockery." [14] One speaks of God and his salvation differently inside than outside that community; I do not need to answer here and now the question concerning how one is then to speak outside the Christian community, since we are here concerned with the traditional worship service. This traditional gathering loses its dignity and with it its credibility for outsiders if the playing rules are changed for their sake. Neither does one change the rules in a football game if there are uninformed spectators; indeed precisely these spectators want to get to know this as yet unknown quantity. Things mean more to spectators if one does not expressly take them into special consideration.

Many sermons suffer from the preacher's trying to speak to the reason of the world, seeking persuasive proofs or only taking up aspects of the gospel which can be broadly recommended. Such a preacher will hardly dare to tell a biblical story in an unaffected manner. Graphic speech has an axiomatic power and is neither able nor needs to offer proof. But it does presuppose a community upon which this axiomatic power depends. For the worship service this means that only those people will be persuaded who already have been. They would like to find again what was already of value to them. Evidence only carries one through temptation, not through apathy.

In the personal realm, a preacher who speaks graphically is required to be naïve in a positive sense; graphic language presupposes graphic vision; otherwise, it's artificial and the listeners will notice that. Actually seeing graphically is more an experience than an activity; a person must be overcome by it, and this requires surrender and willingness to let oneself be driven—no small task for someone who became a pastor precisely in order to "do" a great deal. But graphic speech presupposes not activity, but rather something a person can only "let happen"; only then do images and stories with life emerge. Listen to the way simple people portray their experiences. They not only tell the main line; they also portray the cheerful curls in the hair of the people they like, and the stumbling step or big nose of the people they find unsympathetic. Primitive, but graphic. Intellectuals have to a large extent lost this gift, probably through excessive demands on their energy for rational activity. Inner vision diminishes in that process. Perhaps spontaneous story-telling is also a threat to intellectuals; this would be expected, since a person who really tells a story cannot always keep everything under control. The autonomy of that graphic element limits the speaker's power, and in that sense one can say that graphic speech diminishes the speaker's authority.

Narration leads to other phenomena which intellectuals find suspect. Many times repetition is highly effective, either in synonyms or in exactly the same words. Again, pay attention to the way uneducated people repeat a story's magic point four or five times and how the listeners take part in it again and again with increasing pleasure or even horror. People can't digest great or decisive events all at once; they must be told several times. This is a well-known phenomenon in the grief process. The grieving person can at first not believe the beloved is no longer there; the person really believes it only after relating the details of the last encounter and of death several times. This is also the case with graphic language; anyone forgetting that it's a matter of experience and not of comprehension of some content will tend to leave behind the story's salient points much too quickly.

However, an intellectual examination of a particular image is also necessary; it is, after all, a matter of some content or other in the final analysis, and not of mere words. For that reason the graphic words must be disciplined, though the control of understanding must remain true to the structure of graphic language and aid it towards the required clarity and sober self-limitation.

Conceptual Speech

It would be an oversimplification to remain only with graphic speech. The promises which are obvious for narrative and graphic sermons are fulfilled, strange to say, only when a certain counterpart of conceptual speech is offered. This is not the case with all graphic speech, but I am concerned here with such speech in a worship service. Vividness may be enough in a theater situation, but it's not enough in a church. People in a worship service are not coming in order to hear a story; in and with that narrative they are hoping to hear a clear message concerning their own lives. Precisely this reference to their lives must become clear—the listeners want to pack that vivid illustration up and take it with them; they would like to have a certain access to it.

Graphic speech alone cannot meet this demand. Listeners complain that "the image just remained an image" or that they don't really know what to "do" with the story if that imagery is not clearly profiled and identified. Perhaps there are exceptions; sometimes the reference to life is so clear that the listener easily knows what to "do" with the sermon.

The right concepts are able to summarize the relevance of an image or an experienced narrative and to give a name to the whole; that gives the listeners access to their experiences. During the narrative the conceptual language is already creating a link with the listeners' experience, and at the same time the listeners are filling the narrative with their own experiences. This makes the narrative transparent for them. Concepts then give this entire process a name and emphasize precisely what in that narrative or image agrees with the listeners' experiences. They thus point out where the listener can personally become part of the narrative. After an introduction to the sad life of King Saul, Hannelore Frank says the following in a sermon:

> As always in such cases, people asked about reasons and motives, sought them and believed to have found them in the time-tested scheme: Punishment follows guilt.[15]

Conceptual speech interrupts the narrative here and shows where the listener might find the story's relevance: the universal problem of failure. "As always in such cases" suspends the concrete element for a moment, offers a generalization in its place so that each person can project his or her own life situation—which has not been explicitly portrayed—into the story of Saul. "Punishment and guilt"—that is the story's point. These concepts profile the universally human element in the concrete story.

Concepts help orient the listener. Vivid, graphic speech portrays life, but not all of life at one time. Concepts show the place in life where the story takes place; today we are not speaking about love, boredom, yearning or freedom; today we are talking about "punishment and guilt."

The preacher can expect the optimum effect only when there is a balance between graphic and conceptual speech. The vivid, graphic element makes it possible to carry through the experience; the conceptual element makes it possible to get into that experience. Pregnant formulations and unusual expressions have a strong effect. Sometimes the listeners discover the relevance of the proclamation in such a conceptual sentence as this and are able to keep it for themselves, thus maintaining access to what they experienced while listening. Whenever there is a main point, a salient point in the proclamation, a certain amount of conceptuality is needed precisely there so that the listener can grasp this important element in a summarizing concept. Here is another sermon by Hannelore Frank; the ending goes as follows:

> We are tempted like Gideon to ask for proof. And just as he was, we also are thrown back on ourselves, on our own faith and our own decision—for God or against Him, for changing the world (in God's name) or for bearing what he has laid upon us. Nobody relieves us of this decision. And that's the way it should be.[16]

The whole result of the sermon is summarized conceptually in a few words. Offering only these words would be weak and ineffective, but as a small unit following a vividly narrated story they summarize clearly what has been "seen." The concepts are meaningful precisely as this kind of profile.

It ought to be clear that conceptual speech is more effective the less graphic it is. Precisely that non-graphic, abstract element makes its universal application possible.

I do not intend to say anything more about the importance of conceptual speech. One shouldn't take water to the ocean, and the oft-heard complaint of worshipers about the excessively conceptual nature of sermons shows that preachers need something other than encouragement to be conceptual. Here the problems are exactly reversed compared to graphic speech in which one can for now encourage preachers almost limitlessly; as regards conceptual speech, one must try rather broadly to put the brakes on them. The previous paragraphs show, I believe, that I would like to do this not quite so broadly, but rather with some attention to specifics.

One form into which conceptual speech can degenerate is alluded to by the following listener statements:

> —I've already heard that so often.
> —A nice saying to hang on the wall.
> —I agree entirely; but it didn't really engage me.

These statements refer to conceptually clearly worked-out sermons; what was offered in those concepts was so flat and well-known that it elicited in the listeners reactions similar to those one has toward quaint sayings and platitudes. They were spoken exclusively by the "parent ego" with its traditional value system, without any freshness or element of surprise. "God accepts us" was emphasized again and again in one of these sermons, yet the paleness of this all-too-familiar gospel summarization just didn't touch anyone's heart; the listeners all agreed, but they were not moved.

The form of conceptual speech most often evaluated negatively is the intellectualistic; listeners say:

> —It was too complicated for me.
> —I didn't think it was clear.

One may recall here the complaints already heard about the impersonal character of the worship service. Remarks such as "empty phrases," "pale," and "too general" almost always refer to both aspects: the lack of both personal and graphic elements. A preacher can hide behind concepts much more easily than behind vividness. Intellectualistic speech thus causes damage in two dimensions: worshipers are not able to experience feelings of security because intellectualism is not personal enough, and there is no understanding because it is too complicated and too one-sidedly speaks to the rational faculty. That one-sided orientation toward the rational side of understanding is experienced so intensely negatively that the adjective "intellectual" in listeners' reactions to sermons invariably is used as an equivalent for "incomprehensible," "abstruse," and "meaningless." The analyses confirm this observation. The congregation obviously expects a sermon to address spiritual areas other than merely the intellect. The characterization "intellectual" is for this reason a negative qualification; the listeners have not felt spoken to in their entirety and are disappointed about it.

The relationship between intellectualism and abstractness is obvious. Concepts aim at a rational comprehension, and I have shown that they are necessary if the listener is to be able to enter into the graphic language. That language becomes intellectualistic when the concepts no longer have a clear connection with the graphic, vivid element. Only that vividness makes an experience possible, and it must continually encompass or cover those concepts, otherwise they become intellectualistic. Then only the rational level, no longer the visual one, is addressed, and this quickly fatigues the listener. Robert Leuenberger remarks in this context that intellectualistic words and ideas betray a relationship to reality which is not genuine because it's not commensurate with any experiential reality.[17] Even the "most witty application of theological abstractions does not protect the congregation against boredom." [18]

Identifying the torture of intellectualism is one thing; getting rid of it quite another. There is resistance. University education is strongly oriented toward the cognitive realm. "The structure of the entire university rests on an anthropology which considers the cognitive realm to be the essentially human element in persons and which is directed towards eliminating or overcoming all subjective and affective elements with its ideal of science." [19] Preachers are above all taught to prepare their sermons with books. Their commissioning to a church office is attained primarily by means of intellectual ability, and changing this system is no simple matter. That questionable intellectualism protects theological education from other problems. The main question would be how the church could otherwise test its office-holders' competency.

At the same time the listeners' sufferings are growing more and more because the inclination of the day shows us that people strongly prefer experience over information. Television in particular makes possible an interest in public personalities which is permeated with experiential elements; on television they are not cool, intellectual, well prepared and precise, but rather strongly influenced by immediate emotions, loose, spontaneous, and improvising. That informal improvisation comes across personally and makes a certain intimacy possible, since it's not logical ideas which determine the effect, but rather a total co-experience with living people. This kind of communication is offered publicly today much more than in previous decades, and intellectual speech has a difficult time asserting itself against this competition. People want to experience something in a worship service, not hear a lecture. One-sided emphasis on rational understanding arouses basic resistance today more than ever.

In this context it's instructive to see how several psalms place the call to God into a concrete story. That *Sitz im Leben* is graphically portrayed in the superscription, "A Psalm of David, when he fled from Absalom his son" (Ps. 3:1) though the psalm's formulation is simultaneously general enough to permit each person to enter into the situation.

The often heard accusation toward the church, that it uses incomprehensible words which it should finally modernize, appears to me unjustified in this form. The proclamation will very likely not be able to do without certain concepts such as "grace" and "mercy," "Lord," "Father," "faith," and "peace." Every realm of life has its own peculiar set of terms. Is it not that the accusation really wants to say the preachers do not use these concepts often enough in connection with experience? No listener will complain about concepts if the related experiences are also vividly portrayed in the sermon.

Analyses of worship services and sermons have shown me that those in a worship service are quite willing to acquire knowledge and understanding, but their condition is that it not be a rational understanding, but rather an understanding or recognition touching on the existential realm. This kind of understanding is possible only in the interplay between graphic and conceptual speech. If they are really engaged, listeners become quite open to concepts; indeed, they need them and are glad to be instructed in this way.

CHAPTER 5

The Personality of the Preacher

The Basic Posture of the Preacher

In the previous chapters I have followed the listener reactions to worship services and sermons. Three dimensions of experience in that worship service became visible, as well as continually new aspects of the reactions to what was offered in worship services. My impression is that this procedure has not left very much of fundamental homiletics untouched.

An unambiguous discovery in each analysis of worship service and sermon concerns the close relationship between the preacher's concrete modes of behaviour and his or her personality. It is no accident when a preacher says "I" often, too often, or seldom, or if a preacher speaks extemporaneously, preaches legalistically or speaks graphically. These visible and audible elements are all deeply rooted in the personality. Anyone wishing to change them must not only change the externally perceivable facts, but must also take into consideration the invisible roots.

An adequate fundamental posture for the preacher has emerged in fairly clear outline from the presentation of listener reactions and my accompanying reflections. I wish to summarize this now, although it may seem presumptuous to attempt a definition of the "correct" preacher. It could imply that one expects the miracle of the worship service from the preacher and not from God, but I don't think this kind of distortion is a temptation for me. Those suspecting presumptuousness here have probably brought it themselves. The "correct" preacher is a standard for measurement which does not actually exist, and I personally do not claim to do justice to this image myself at all times and in all aspects. One needs a great deal of humor, a bit of the ability to laugh at oneself, and a great deal of trust in God's far-reaching activity in order to write and read about the ideal of the correct preacher. Otherwise it will just be discouraging. So the image is meant as a point of orientation and as an aid. It helps those who believe one's entire vocational life is also a kind of atonement, and it may frighten off those who indeed are conducting worship services and preaching, but who should not be. Being a preacher is not for everyone.

I will list the aspects in which that basic posture of the preacher has emerged from the dimensions already discussed. (I will draw some parallels to Fritz Riemann, *Der Prediger aus tiefenpsychologischer Sicht.* Riemann describes four main types of preachers with their respective good and bad character traits, but that's too systematized and construed for my way of thinking. In reality the personalities of preachers cannot be divided into these main types, since most people exhibit strong characteristics from various types. Nonetheless I find it good that Riemann has directed attention to the preacher's personality.)

1. A Sense of Calling

When God wishes his word to be proclaimed, this does not exclude the possibility that the person doing the proclaiming genuinely wants to do it. Considered theologically, this calling is the connection between the two. For the preacher's experience this means he or she feels personally spoken to and engaged by the gospel and called to proclaim it to others. A preacher would be crippled without a consciousness of being called. The feeling of being touched inwardly by the gospel, and the conviction that others should also experience that in their own ways, give the inner motivation to fulfill various preconditions necessary for conducting a worship service properly. The preacher will speak clearly to the congregation and thus come across personally, something indispensable for awakening trust in the listeners. This attitude will show that being spoken to cannot come just from the preacher, but in a decisive way from God; this expectation will become clear in prayers and in other ways. If the preacher personally feels spoken to and engaged, he or she will be able to convey the astonishment resulting from that and will awaken among the listeners a similar astonishment in the face of the gospel. Being engaged will produce the courage to proclaim that gospel, to say things that cannot be rationally supported.

The fact that the preacher feels addressed by God will also have consequences for the content. Fate will not be granted too much respect, but neither will the claim be made that the church proclamation has the answers to the world's riddles. That personal feeling of being spoken to gives access to the substance of sermon and prayer, and leads to that total seriousness with which the preacher's work is performed. The worshipers will be captivated by that seriousness.

In this feeling of being spoken to and of being called, the preacher is not basically different from any other Christian. The calling pertains to the *imitatio Christi,* not necessarily to the office of the pastor. Personal, social and other factors give this calling a form which for some people means choosing the vocation of the pastor, though the same calling is realized by others in other forms. In a broad sense it can be said that every Christian is called to proclaim; this common task becomes most clearly visible in the preacher.

One of the most terrible agonies a preacher can experience is becoming inwardly unsure about whether to preach or not. The spiritual energy for this task is given by a feeling—perhaps even deeply hidden or unconscious—of being called inwardly to the work of preaching. If this feeling is missing, the sensitive preacher has a sense of being placed in an impossible situation. Externally this may show up perhaps as a missing address of God or in lifeless prayers.

As far as I can see there are basically two spiritual situations in which this agony arises. First, there are men and women who too rashly choose a vocation requiring them to preach. This is an especially sad situation for pastors, since the foundation of their entire vocational existence is missing if they are not personally engaged. Their training offers them almost no alternative work possibilities, and who wants or can start all over again if one already has a family and an established lifestyle? The solution of preaching in spite of the uncertainty is more than questionable. Church authorities have no real way of finding out whether young theologians are personally spoken to and engaged by the gospel. This would require a more intensive acquaintance with the students instead of an examining commission. As long as that remains an unrealistic wish, the agony will come up again and again: preachers without inner motivation.

The second situation, one that occurs much more frequently, is that of an alienation from oneself. The bad part of it is that it's too much trouble for many people to talk with young theologians about being engaged by God. In formal training the word "objective" is quickly equated with "avoidance of existential areas." Faith can quickly be reduced to theology, and thus life to a theory, and for young theologians this often means they lose contact with the roots of their vocational choice. They would be ashamed to refer to inner processes not discussed in learned texts. However, in pastoral training situations with students and young pastors it has become clear to me that beneath that normal skepticism concerning one's calling there is often a discarded consciousness of a very great inner involvement, a *vocatio interna*. This consciousness only dares come forth a bit in a personal atmosphere of acceptance and understanding.

Only very rarely, I believe, can one find absolute certainty concerning the calling to the pastorate. Indeed, it would even be a very questionable certainty. The heritage of pietism, with its overemphasis of a calling as only an inner and thus irrational experience, still affects theologians in that they have a bad conscience if they have not had this experience. However, the question is legitimate whether a preacher is personally engaged by the gospel. This engagement is fundamentally synonymous with the *vocatio interna*. The path to the pastorate is for many preachers simply the social framework of their faith, and as soon as they find this access to their faith again the former joy in their vocation awakens again. Preachers must be able to speak about this deepest root of their pastoral existence. It is a matter of their relationship to the Lord they are to proclaim, and they are crippled before they begin if there is no clarity about this.

2. A Feeling of Responsibility

In a harmonious growth process people not only learn how to become independent themselves, but also how to accept responsibility for others. Accepting responsibility involves more and is more difficult than being independent, just as being a father or mother is more than just being an adult. Only a person willing and able to support others will be able to take on an authoritative function. A supporting, caring attitude is indispensable for awakening trust, though today this is not one of the most popular roles. To the extent that a preacher has schizoid tendencies, he or she will have difficulty at precisely this point. A merciless manner will sooner shock than awaken trust.[1] Hysterical characteristics also make it difficult to be involved and carry responsibility. In the chapters on security and deliverance I have tried to show how difficult it is for young preachers as soon as they discover they are an authority figure in the traditional worship service. The external structure of the worship service requires a preacher able to find the proper stance as an authority.

The content structure of the proclamation also demands this feeling of responsibility; otherwise, the realm of humility and obedience, of law and of involvement in faith disappears from view with the consequences described in the third chapter. That feeling of responsibility guards against a naïve, unrealistic avoidance of problems and opens one's eyes to the complexity of life. The responsible preacher will try to discover clearly the structure of the biblical message and not just be given over uncritically to flights of fancy. He or she seeks words which will show people clearly where the proclamation wants to speak to them. Neither does the preacher make things too easy for the listeners, but rather shows them the realistic ways to go, even if there is accompanying pain. In this way the preacher is dependable and can awaken feelings of security.

3. Seeking Contact with Oneself

Human life offers the somewhat unnerving possibility of taking over the values of others and thus losing contact with oneself. Those whose values and traditions I take over are then so important to me that I basically forget myself. I am only a mouthpiece, and no longer a person, and I love myself only to the extent that I correspond to those ideal standards; I don't love myself for what I essentially am. In such a situation, however, I cannot really feel love for others; there is no longer an "I" capable of love, but only a mouthpiece, a copy. I am able to preach personally if I accept myself; only then will I dare show myself and be open.

I will awaken deep experiences in others to the extent that I am able to reach myself. If I overplay feelings of revenge because they are indeed terrifying, or if

I rationalize a pious faith in order to agree with a theological theory, then I am closing myself off, and in the worship service I am drawing from a well which is going dry. That level of yearning and security is reached only by preachers who also seek access to their own interior, an interior which at first glance normally appears comical, childish, and not really ready to be shown in public. Preachers with compulsive tendencies become so afraid that it's painful for them to find that path to themselves.

Contact with oneself is of decisive importance while preparing a sermon. The idea for the sermon emerges only in a creative restlessness, when the preacher dares ignore those constricting thoughts acquired elsewhere, thoughts that will be needed again only when it is time to examine the ideas.

I have shown how poorly preachers come across when they overplay themselves. Precisely the thing they are suppressing inside ends up having an effect on the listeners, and that is what is tragic about suppression. It has an effect on others without our wanting it to, and does so much more strongly that we think is possible. That suppressed element becomes autonomous, slips from our control and takes on a demonic power. Everyone has problems and confusing forces inside; that's not so bad, it's a part of life. Disturbances in communication don't begin in life's problems, on the contrary, difficulties can bring people closer together. Disturbances arise where we don't admit to them. Preachers not willing to admit their insecurity will preach so securely that the listeners will in the first place not be able to identify with them, and will in the second place be aggravated with their style. Their insecurity, on the other hand, would create a link wherever they brought it in. Instead of preaching human security, they would preach God's promise, which comes to the aid of those of us who are insecure. Persons finding no contact with themselves will offer something foreign which may be right, but also boring.

The question of to what extent preachers should reveal themselves cannot be answered with simple rules. Not all openness is useful, but a facade certainly does very little for communication. Emotional openness invites participation, and extemporaneous speech is generally a decisive step towards such openness.

Preachers must also find access to themselves as an aid to vividness, an element decisively important in the dimension of understanding. Real vividness emerges in communication only if the preachers see inwardly; those not seeking access to themselves will hide behind the images of others or behind abstractions.

Preachers sometimes invent an audience which actually is not even present. This, too, is a direct result of not being in contact with oneself. If I don't recognize the strife inside myself, I will preach against strife and thus only be addressing myself instead of the actual participants in the worship service. The preacher's suppression then shows itself as legalistic demands which are mercilessly laid on the congregation. This legalism quite possibly betrays an unresolved problem within the preacher, who may simply be unconsciously dealing with that problem.

Persons in contact with themselves and liking themselves will have no trouble recognizing the emotional realm of the worship service and then speaking to the worshipers in this realm.

4. Giving of Oneself

Anyone seeking community with others is self-giving toward these people, and this is also true for a preacher conducting a worship service. Some people have a great deal of trouble with this act of giving of oneself. It's probably most difficult for people with a compulsive or schizoid attitude toward life.[2] The danger is then too much reserve, and the preacher will not be fulfilling all the conditions necessary for a worship service. Intellectualism is a notorious form of reserve. One speaks to others only rationally; there is little risk because the trained pastor is intellectually fairly superior. In this way few mistakes are possible, since the pastor puts a stop to any self-giving. The people in the worship service, however, are disappointed because they are not fully spoken to or addressed.

Only very few preachers give much thought to the relationship between theology and faith. Far too many consider them to be the same thing, something I find scandalous. Theology is a rational undertaking; its justification, power, and limits all reside in the intellectual realm. Faith is an existential act encompassing the entire person. Theology belongs in the sermon preparation and examination of ideas, but has no business whatever in the pulpit. "Only a person who has already dealt with theology and become a total person again with theology's rich yield is able to come up with a sermon structure capable of speaking directly to people."[3] Cooking pots don't belong on the festively decorated table. In the pulpit a believing—and again and again unbelieving—Christian proclaims Christ the Lord, from whom a miracle is expected. That is not a theological undertaking, but rather an existential communicative act. It is the parallel to the appearance of Jesus, who did not teach as the scribes, but as one who had authority (Mark. 1:22). Proclamation often leads to one-sidedness and exaggerations not allowed in theology. Theology lacks the concrete reference to time and place, and should thus be more balanced and generalized than the individual sermon. Proclamation requires of the preacher not thinking, but first of all self-giving, which includes speaking extemporaneously. Without this kind of involvement there will be none of that feeling of consecration and intimacy so essential for a worship service characterized by encounter. Of course, the Lord himself can make up for the preacher's inadequacy, but it's unreasonable to expect too much, even from God.

Intense involvement is a part of faith. God's promise requires surrender and a trust in his capacity to make things right. Rigidness and legalism arise if there is no carefree joy. Richard Riess maintains that a legalistic sermon always points to a compulsive personality.[4] That is not confirmed by the analyses presented in this book. One finds legalism in other personality types as well. The preacher who gives of self will be able to come across vividly and narrate well because he or she is not held back by the fear of being misunderstood. The joy found in surrender will eliminate precisely that pressure sometimes caused by the feeling of responsibility.

5. Standing in Belief and Unbelief

It will be hard to decide which is more difficult to cope with—belief or unbelief. The step into faith in Christ means an existential surrender and is paid for with the loss of many old and secure habits. Consciously admitting unbelief—something which for better or worse is invariably recurring in every person—means becoming insecure as regards that ultimate trust. Neither is very easy, but both are necessary for preachers. With no relationship to their own unbelief they do not take seriously the resistance of others to God's commandments and promises, the result being a harmless proclamation. Preachers with what Fritz Riemann calls hysterical tendencies[5] are most likely to make this mistake. Riemann also mentions depressive characteristics which lead to this kind of harmless proclamation.[6] The listeners are not able to integrate the temptation they experience into the worship service, and those for whom this is important are not spoken to. Preachers holding their ground in that tension between belief and unbelief will speak to the listeners' aggravation with God, their complaints and accusations and their apathy because the preachers are able to see those things in themselves as well. They do not identify with the biblical text; rather, they examine the reality of experience to see just what reactions God's word elicits in people. Only then can temptation be overcome. The preacher then represents the congregation as a questioning listener and is its credible counterpart when he or she finds peace in the midst of that questioning.

6. Both Leading and Letting Alone

Concerning good contact, it's of decisive importance for anyone in a leadership position to find the proper rhythm between leading and letting alone. Someone who only leads will become a despot. Someone who only lets alone will become uninvolved. Leadership is promising only in a balanced relationship between these two contrasting positions. It's probably not easy for anyone to find this balanced relationship. Compulsive preachers are inclined to lead too strongly.[7] This is already of significance in the question of being genuine. A person who is *only* genuine quickly becomes an exhibitionist. Distance and respect for one's counterpart are both also a part of proper sincerity. A preacher

150

PRESENCE IN THE PULPIT

who is too personal does not leave the listeners enough free space, but if there is not *enough* leadership, then the listener feels neither taken seriously nor spoken to.

The art of narration presupposes that the preacher not only presents, but also leaves some things open to conjecture. The preacher should portray accurately enough to be vivid, and vaguely enough for the listener to become activated inwardly. A person who leads too gladly will tend to narrate too thoroughly and become theatrical. A person who does not gladly lead will tend to narrate unclearly.

7. Performing the Task Decisively and Without Presumption

In a worship service we are dealing with existential matters in which there is no hierarchy among people. Over against God they are all equally small. Nonetheless, the preacher conducts the worship service and the listeners are led. This means the preacher will come into a tension in which all stand *primi inter pares:* the polarity between the normal worshiper and the official.

Today a balanced relationship between these two roles leads to an execution of authority from the perspective of the adult ego, not of the parent ego. A lack of involvement threatens whenever a preacher does not want to be that *primus,* and presumptuousness threatens whenever one no longer experiences oneself as being among *pares.* Even more so than for listeners, it's important for the preacher's feeling of identity to find the proper balance here. Depressive tendencies sometimes hold back the proper decisiveness, hysterical ones the proper modesty.

The danger of presumptuousness arises when preachers identify too strongly with the biblical text, as if the gospel is no longer scandalous for them. An abuse of the pulpit also threatens wherever they overestimate their own function. Political sermons are especially vulnerable to this temptation. Finally, we need to mention hidden attacks on certain groups or persons sometimes found in sermons. They don't seem structured in an authoritarian way, but an aggressive undertone betrays the preacher's desire to push a personal opinion through from the pulpit. One might even maintain that hostility and aggression are the most obvious characteristics of pastoral emotion.

In these seven dispositions I have now summarized the basic posture a preacher must strive for in order to give the listeners in a traditional worship service what they expect. This summary is a model which is unlikely ever to be fully realized in a single individual, but the capacity to be totally realized is no prerequisite for a valid model. It serves as a point of orientation, and a preacher should know at which points of the model to exercise caution. It's likely that some kind of effort is required at one point or another just to stay in motion, which means that it would not really be favorable if the preacher were indeed able to realize the optimum posture.

If a preacher is able to make the worship service participants feel truly spoken to and engaged, it's a basic posture rendering that possible, not the technique used and not the content of the words spoken. The relationship between preacher and listener is the place where the decisive element in the worship service takes place. To be sure, factors other than merely the preacher do play a role, but the personality of this man or this woman is so determinative that if it comes across negatively, there is almost no hope that the listener will feel spoken to. A preacher's positive self-presentation enables that homiletical technique and the meaning of the spoken words to have a promising effect. "Morality loses its legalistic element and becomes an ordering factor. The teaching loses its rigidity and becomes proclamation. The beyond loses its alienating characteristics and becomes the present world of God." [8]

The Competency of the Preacher

In the ideal preacher one can find a unity between personal self-presentation and liturgical and homiletical technique. Whenever this preacher says "I," it's not because of trying to fulfill the most current homiletical rules, but because it comes out spontaneously. By speaking vividly, this preacher is telling what has been seen with the inner eye and not just what has been read in a book. An agreement reigns between visible and audible behavior and inner attitude. The ability to conduct a worship service has a two-fold structure. First, the preacher has a facility with language, with the liturgical progression, and with spatial relationships. On the other hand, he or she stands behind what is said and does so with the whole person, with enthusiasm, and with seriousness. The preacher's work is a simultaneous occurrence of physically perceivable forms of expressions and intuitively noticeable inner participation.

What I am calling the two-fold structure is in reality a unity, though a separation is necessary for theory and reflection. Our culture lacks a system of thought which does justice to the human being's psychosomatic unity, which is not particularly tragic as long as we do not forget that the separation is actually unrealistic.

That two-fold structure of competence requires that the preacher's training run along two tracks, encompassing technical and methodical aspects—more general factors—as well as the personal or individual element. Each preacher's training should be tailor-made because each is unique and because this uniqueness is essential for the sermon. As soon as the training becomes one-tracked, things don't look as promising. Homiletical books, including this one, don't really contribute to the actual structuring of worship services and sermons; at best they may make extremely small contributions. They serve rather the scholarly discussion *concerning* the sermon and are accordingly read by the more learned among the preachers. But one cannot necessarily say that these more learned pastors engage their congrations better or speak to them more fully. All the objective, universal aids concerning what one should say in the sermon do not help the preacher enough because his or her own uniqueness is not taken into consideration. Although I generally value very highly the work of Manfred Josuttis, it's for this reason that I think he underestimates the difficulties when he expects better sermons if preachers will just prepare themselves better on a critical and exegetical level and take reformation theology more seriously.[9] The same applies to Gert Otto, who looks for the cause of ineffective sermons not in poor theology, but in the "linguistic disinterestedness and incapacity of many preachers." [10]

This does not mean to say the homiletical essays and publications are meaningless. In the first place the theoretical discussion is not superfluous, and in the second the technical, i.e., exegetical, systematic, and rhetorical suggestions are meaningful in and for themselves. It's just that they must be complemented by something tuned in to the personality of the preacher.

The other aspect, if isolated, is just as unpromising. One can work with the personality within a good group therapy or in individual discussion with competent psychiatrists, or one can do it in the circle of one's own friends, relatives, and colleagues. Who would dare doubt the value of this work in and for itself? It's just that it does not aid the training of a preacher, or at most only makes a very small contribution.

All this training is effective only when the two work structures encounter one another; homiletical and liturgical training emerges within that tension between theological and rhetorical guides on the one hand, and the concern for the personality on the other. Only the vocational problems touch the preacher's personality at a place where this work with that personality becomes fruitful for the sermon. It's like building a tunnel—one must dig and put up supports at the same time. First dig a bit, then erect some more supports; one activity without the other would be meaningless. The same is the case in a preacher's training. As soon as someone conducts a worship service and thus realizes all the theological and rhetorical suggestions and advice, one also shows one's personality. The listener reactions do not only show clearly which theological and rhetorical rules have or have not been kept; they also show which basic stance or posture of personality is coming across. There is then work to be done on two fronts.

For homiletical and liturgical training this means one must pay much closer attention to the preachers and theology students personally, since there is certainly no dearth of technical, theological, and rhetorical advice and the production of further editions will no doubt go on. But the personal interest in the men and women preparing for conducting worship services must be expanded with continual reference to the problems of content of exegetical and systematic theology. The analyses of worship services and sermons show how

much influence the preacher's entire person has, and even someone who re-
grets that should for the sake of reality recognize that this person deserves
attention.

In the experience of most pastors it becomes clear how strongly their worship services, and particularly their sermons, as far as their own feelings are
concerned, are tied in with their own personality. Almost all preachers are
basically very sensitive to criticism and—even more significant—embarrassed
and defensive when listeners enthusiastically thank them for what the preacher
has given to the listener through the sermon. In the last century Christian
Palmer said, "the sermon is the full manifestation of the personality." [11]
Even people who theoretically argue against this or deny it also perceive this
to be true. Many pastors gain their identity precisely as preachers. On the
average, pastors spend more than thirteen hours a week in preparation for
sermon and official duties. This expenditure of time also makes it clear why
preaching is experienced as an expression of personality. It is only traditional
homiletical theory, not the congregation or the preacher's own perception,
which overlooks the enormous significance of the preacher's personality.

Two fundamental questions arise as soon as the training of preachers becomes serious about the personality. First: Who is to conduct this training?
Second: Do all preachers want to have personality taken into consideration
during training?

The development of personalities should never be put into the hands of
only one person, because every person has blind spots, weaknesses, and
prejudices. That is not so bad in and for itself, but it is reason enough to
delegate such development to several people. Within the framework of
clinical pastoral education, which is able to make a small contribution to homiletical and liturgical training, this problem is solved by having the preacher's
accompaniment be a circle of colleagues under the supervision of a leader.
The colleagues become each other's trainers, but always together, and the
leader is not the only authority. This clinical pastoral education is, however,
basically intended for pastors who have already worked independently for a
few years. In addition, pastoral relationships are of more primary importance
there. The import of worship services demands an essentially broader treatment and expansion.

In such courses the connection between technique and personality is se-
cured by the nature of the work and supervision. In this way this training does
justice to the two-fold structure of the competency necessary for worship services and sermons, though it might also be feasible in another framework.
The supervisor, as the leader who is trained and sensitive to technical competency as well as to personal growth, seems to me to be indispensable. From
this person one also gets that combination of technical and personal remarks
not always available in a circle of colleagues without a leader.

The Elimination of Wrong Behavior

The analyses of worship services and sermons presented in this book set a process into motion in the preacher concerned which led to a change in behavior. Sermons did not always improve. (One preacher was told he seemed rather impersonal. The symptom was that he only used the personal pronoun "we." Two years later he gave another sermon heard by the colleagues; he said "I" so many times that everyone complained about it during the evaluation.) Anyone healing symptoms must use medicine which often has bad side effects, and in that case one would have done better to change nothing. It is encouraging, however, that in many cases the analyses led to developments in the preacher which slowly but surely had a positive effect. The analysis is the initial step, indeed for many pastors the willingness to have their worship service or sermon analyzed is already an initial step costing a great deal of effort. However, the job is not finished with the analysis. In many cases one or several individual discussions follow between preacher and analysis leader. The preacher often feels the need to discuss things further on a more personal level, particularly if the problems becoming visible through the analysis have deep roots. Counseling then begins with the character of vocational accompaniment, though most preachers do not need that. They consciously internalize the analysis results and then wait to see what happens. After an extended period of time it's their turn again, and the second analysis then becomes an extremely interesting affair.

I will describe two such processes elicited in preachers by such analyses. The first deals with a young pastor with relatively few vocational problems. The second pastor has more difficulty in his work and is asking himself whether he will be able to continue in it if something is not fundamentally changed. (The persons concerned have become unrecognizable because of a change in names and a few details.)

1. Erich was 36 years old when he experienced a discussion of one of his worship services within a group of close colleagues. He had been a pastor for eight years, and he loved his work as well as theological reflection. In the colleague group he came across as a person who takes the initiative. He was married and the father of two children.

Every one of the colleagues said that the worship service had truly spoken to them, and they had listened to the sermon with great interest. To be sure, some thought the sermon and prayers had lasted rather long, and though no one had become bored, a growing feeling of excessive demands had come upon some of them.

Two things had a clearly negative effect. One was a section of the sermon about the sentence "born of the virgin Mary," in which Erich had refuted—in a fanatic tone of voice—a recently published liberal interpretation. Even the colleagues who agreed with his arguments on an objective level had been surprised at his sharpness and sarcastic word choice. Most of the listeners had found Erich to be rather unsympathetic in this section.

The second aspect seemed even more important. Although Erich sometimes used dramatic words, the listeners found he lived in a rather sound, carefree world, and they did not really feel taken seriously on the dark side of their lives. A strong optimism had come across to them.

Erich was particularly surprised at that second point. The first had seemed immediately clear to him, and he admitted that he had difficulty coping with criticism of old and proven church dogmas. He understood this criticism was less important to the other listeners than to himself, and saw that he conjured up the image of an executioner with his intensity. But optimistic? They say he is optimistic? That was not at all his intention, and he knew full well Christian hope was something different from optimism. He had to ask what specifically had sounded optimistic, and the colleague group was able to name two things. In the sermon he had spoken only weakly and obliquely about suffering and misery, or even briefly, and then it was all done away with very quickly. Erich had very strongly emphasized Jesus' suffering, but had only paid cursory, superficial attention to the pain accompanying the sufferings of contemporary people. That had come across as being optimistic. All the weighty aspects of life then didn't seem so bad. A second element was the intercessory prayer. Erich had indeed named concrete suffering, but it all sounded so forced, "the sick, the lonely, the dying." That personal tone which had so spoken to them in the prayer preceding the sermon was missing in the intercessions.

What was it that drove this preacher into an optimistic glossing over of the gospel and into fanaticism for the confession? Was it unconscious fears he was trying to ward off in that way? Erich said that he had had a relatively problem-free life until then and had only rarely had difficult experiences. Was it a lack of practical experience? In the conversation, someone mentioned that fanatics and optimists have a common fear: the fear of being made insecure. Erich was grateful for the analysis and said he would take the words "being made insecure" home with him. That had really hit home with him, and he sensed he had problems in this area which perhaps needed to be dealt with.

In a conversation with the analysis leader some months after the discussion, he told how things had gone for him since then. He had noticed how he honestly did react peculiarly whenever he was made to feel insecure. He noticed now while driving how he became unjustifiably angry with people, mostly only to himself, even though he actually knew they were not really to blame. And in his family life he discovered how uncontrolled he behaved whenever his children did or wanted to do things he considered dangerous. He just did not cope well with precarious situations, and he usually reacted aggressively, either with silent accusations or strong measures.

In this conversation it became clear why he had trouble coping with criticism of the church's confession. Erich had discovered the church while in puberty, and it had become a support for him during that time of easing away from his parents. Any threat of the *mater ecclesia* elicited irrational reactions from him, and he became aware of a strong need for security at this point. That need is in itself not abnormal, but it becomes cramped if one tries to satisfy it through church institutions. He noticed that not only the gospel's truth was important to him, but also the literal security of the old and traditional values he had gotten to know in his youth. This need for security made him closed-minded here and there to anything unknown, and rather than soberly examining what was new, he would cling unyieldingly to the old as if salvation were bound to old formulations. Fruitful, creative insecurity was inaccessible to him to the extent that he had bought into a false security. And that false security was only an appearance; otherwise he would not have felt threatened by new challenges and the fanatic reaction would have been superfluous.

The unconscious optimism was rooted in precisely the same defense against insecurity. As soon as all-too-painful suffering became visible to him he closed his eyes. These insights at least partially collapsed a certain view of life for Erich. He had to rediscover what God's guidance and reign meant. The changes which took place in his life were externally not particularly exciting, but were relatively important enough. Developments in his marriage indicated difficulty there as well which had been overlooked; in any case he now felt warned.

A sermon evaluation more than three years later also showed that some listeners still thought he spoke rather long, and again not in a boring, but rather an excessively demanding sense. Erich's sermons, however, no longer came across too optimistically. One sensed in the sermon a great empathy with life's sufferings, and it became clear that Erich had made progress in the four intervening years. He now risked letting insecurity and suffering get close to him, and this resulted in a deepening of his proclamation. Liberation in Christ no longer suggested the characteristics of being glossed over in his sermon, but rather stood there surrounded by humanity's unanswered questions and suffering. He had thus come closer to the gospel and to people.

However, Erich still had homework to do. He was aggravated that there were always listeners who felt overextended by his sermons. A more precise analysis revealed that he spoke too graphically; he came across with so much vividness that many listeners could no longer handle it and simply tuned out from sheer fatigue. Here, too, a certain strictness could be seen in Erich's manner. A strong will had tried to drown out the insecurity, and that had led to confessional enthusiasm and optimism. Now, however, that was no longer in order, but that strong will still asserted itself in the excessively graphic speech. Too little free room was left for the listeners. Erich continued to work on this.

This report reveals the following:

—A preacher's effect is not always predictable from his or her own perspective. Erich did not want to make propaganda for optimism, but he did it without knowing it. He needed his colleagues to help him discover this.

—The results of the sermon analysis set an inner process into motion in the preacher. In various aspects of his behavior he began to discover for himself what his colleagues had told him.

—That positive change in preaching style was not accomplished by direct adjustments, but rather internally. The change in style was the result of personal development.

—That entire process necessary to remove the sermon's negative effects and make possible a deepening effect was so thorough that it could not take place in a single worship service evaluation. A helping conversation and particularly a great deal of personal, conscious practical experience was necessary in order to overcome the excessive optimism.

—That disturbing element did not disappear entirely. The excessively demanding style of speaking was still brought to his attention by some listeners. In some way we are always struggling with the same mistake.

Martin had been a pastor for four years. Now he was 32 years old, and had a wife and three boys. He participated in a pastoral group which met for one day every two months in order to talk about vocational problems. He wanted to present a sermon because sermon preparation always cost him a great deal of effort. The whole business of having to preach each week was a source of perpetual torment for him.

The colleagues were decimated after the sermon. There was hardly any reference to a biblical text, though in itself that would not really have disturbed them. The sermon was based on an excursion the pastor's children had made with their grandparents. The topic was "being spontaneous," and spontaneity was portrayed in numerous examples from the excursion experiences. "What's the purpose of all this?" was the astonished question of almost all the listeners. They said they became increasingly aggravated at these private stories. For two or three minutes it had been funny, but then it became embarrassing and uncomfortable. They just didn't know what they were supposed to do with all this related information. As regards content, it was just too harmless.

The preacher's initial reaction was that he wanted to preach personally and say only what he could stand behind. To his astonishment, his colleagues told him they did not at all feel personally addressed by his sermon, but rather uncomfortable and embarrassed. It became clear that the preacher had mistaken exhibitionism for personal style. He had wanted to preach about spontaneity, but no one had noticed the slightest trace of spontaneity in him, but rather only a condescending tone reminiscent of fairy tale narration. In addition, the fact that he had read set liturgical formulations aloud as prayers also did not come across particularly personally.

The group then tried to pin down the difference between "personal" and "private," between "relevant" and "indiscreet." Something too personal will only appear personal, but will not really deliver the personal message.

The framework and time for a longer conversation with colleagues was not available in this group, though the preacher concerned wanted to speak further with the group leader. A number of counseling discussions followed, of which I will relate the first.

In this conversation Martin mentioned again that he found preaching very difficult. In moving words he described the painful process of his normal sermon preparation, into the wee hours of Saturday night and Sunday morning, and his general uneasiness in the work. In his teaching he also had only marginal success, though his pastoral counseling went fairly well. But preaching was the most terrible thing in the world for him, and at any rate the whole institution, he said, was outmoded. When asked what God meant to him, and what a liberation gospel meant, he became quite still. He became aware that for a long time now he himself had no longer had access to the gospel, and his vague statements about spontaneity in his sermon paralleled his vague, pale gospel. When asked why he had chosen the pastoral vocation, he said that as a 19-year-old student he had no realistic understanding of the vocation. He spoke about his parents, and the fact that his father was not quite in agreement with his study of theology. At that time, Martin said, everything was still rather romantic. I asked him what he meant by "romantic." He didn't give a clear answer, but rather looked at me with a kind of forced embarrassment, as if adults surely knew what happens during one's liberal, even radical youth. He alluded to something like "fanatical ideas."

I, however, tried to keep my distance because I had the feeling I was being made into an accomplice. I told him I had no idea what his words meant. Martin became increasingly restless, and tried to enlighten me with the cynically spoken words: "our *dear* saviour," with the emphasis on "dear." He looked at me as if I ought to say: "Ah, of course, this fairy tale from kindergarten!" But I didn't want to play along. I only repeated the words "our dear saviour," but without the sarcastic emphasis. Martin became very quiet then and just stared silently ahead for a long time. He said that memories of his youth and his image of God and particularly of Jesus evoked strong emotions in him. His "theology," he said, was now more atheistic, "God is dead," secular, totally in contrast to what had been holy for him, especially in a former youth group. We tried to understand what had taken place in him, and it became clear that his theological education had basically demanded too much of him. He had, however, been able to adapt, had sought a place for himself in the middle of all the theories alienating him, and had finally found one in a kind of theology which did not demand a clear proclamation. He had totally left behind his former, youthful enthusiasm for "our dear savior." The immature but existentially active images from his puberty had not matured, but had rather been covered over by concepts alien to him, and he had been despising his old faith instead of developing it. A part of his most personal experience had thus been cut off and denied. In the conversation, however, we came across this discarded portion, and it lay there exactly as it did 15 years ago: "Our dear saviour." The sarcastic emphasis was a disguise for strong emotions.

The catastrophic part of this defective development was that Martin had been alienated from his motivation for the pastorate by the denial of those experiences he once considered encounters with God. He could no longer be personal in his vocation because he would not accept its personal roots, and in that context it is no accident that he accepted a theology not requiring him to proclaim the gospel.

Martin now understood why sermon preparation was so torturous for him. Any self-contact was blocked by that denial of his deepest feelings and experience. This was also the reason he tended to give his sermons an allegedly "personal" facade.

The open question was whether his "dear saviour" was still capable of life after years of incarceration. Can Martin succeed in making the connection again to an experience within himself which has been dormant for so long? The analysis of his worship service had made it clear to him that he now lacked the prerequisites for the pastorate, and the individual conversation revealed what precisely was missing: access to his own experience of God. Only if he is able to gain access to this experience again will he have that authenticity necessary to conduct a worship service credibly.

I will not tell more of this story. What is important for this book has been given. Analyses and vocational-personal conversations can rarely solve personal problems, though they can show preachers with relative clarity just where they are unconsciously suffering and making mistakes. That sometimes points out the direction where a solution might be found. An eventual happy ending depends on more factors than merely the good will of a group of colleagues and the empathy and support of a supervisor.

General Conclusions for Education

After so much hindsight, I wish now to look forward in this final section of the book. I will try to answer the question concerning which conclusions may be drawn from the worship service analyses for the education and training of preachers. I will forego trying to outline any thoroughgoing education model, because for me that would be presumptuous. The analyses, however, enable me to come up with several fundamental theses which can be realized in many different forms.

1. The Clarification of Motivation

Conducting a worship service requires an existential involvement on the part of the preacher, and without it he or she cannot offer the congregation what it rightfully expects. Personal authenticity is particularly necessary for awakening trust in the listeners, since very few vocations require this personal identification with the element represented in the vocation the way the preacher's does. Preachers should know this; it should be said to them before they even begin their education. Precisely something as self-evident as this should be made clear.

The realization of this motivational clarification can take a legalistic, clerical form as a signature on a confessional statement, but it can also take place in a pastoral counseling situation. In the first case one will likely bring a great many Pharisees into the pastorate; in the second the church or university must choose people who are themselves capable of undergoing this kind of counseling and who know from practical experience what the pastorate requires.

2. Learning Through Doing

The preacher can only learn how to conduct a worship service and give a sermon by practice, not by thinking and study, since both encompass the entire person and are thus individually determined. Theoretical reflection is always necessary afterwards in order to examine and evaluate the practice, and for this the preacher needs listeners capable of telling what effect the worship service had on them. In the beginning preachers will need advice from experienced preachers; later, they will probably only be able to find answers themselves. But they will always need others to show them where they come across negatively.

Any preacher can take on the role of the listener again at any time, and this book has clearly shown how different the worship service looks from this perspective. In this role the preacher finds the listeners' needs which must be addressed as soon as he or she is the preacher again. Ernst Lerle points to this personal participation in the worship service as the decisive factor in one's preparation for the pastorate. "Whoever has not learned to hear the preaching of God's word . . . does not have the preparation for the theory of the sermon." [8]

3. Integration of Theological Study and Practice

The widespread separation of theoretical and practical education of pastors does not do justice to the demands of the worship service. There is much too little time for reflection on that practice if yet another year of practice is squeezed in between the university and independent pastorate. The preacher's education needs some time in which to weave together the theoretical knowledge with personal and vocational growth. For most pastors this now takes place only in the initial years of vocational work, and then without supervision.

The entire theological education could gain in intensity and significance if the students were immediately placed into practical situations, and this cannot be limited only to worship services. Pastoral counseling and teaching require in this respect the same educational possibilities as the worship service and sermon. They could probably often be combined, and indeed nursing homes— pastorally so often neglected—certainly offer possibilities in this respect. Sunday school is already a proven training ground for future preachers; the children are direct and precise with their responses.

Helmut Thielicke suggests the practical employment of theology students in various kinds of proclamation.[9] But this needs some amplification. During their training, preachers not only need the opportunity for practical experience; this work must also be reflected upon. There lies the connection between theology and practice. For example, students can suddenly become interested in the doctrine of justification if they must be told they are preaching legalistically. The relevance of the central topics of theology becomes visible in the worship service and sermon. Here lies an important stimulus for theological reflection in general, but only if thorough evaluations of practical work take place; otherwise one will not discover that relevance.

4. Regular Evaluation of One's Work

Because the leading of a worship service is rooted deep in the personality, there are only very few elements of a preacher's work which can be learned once and for all. Each personality has its own history, and thus each preacher's own way of conducting a worship service also has a history. Response from other worship service participants is continually necessary in order to protect the preacher from fateful developments, so the responsibility for the worship service and sermon resides in the congregation as a whole. This means the listeners should not only help the preacher with their loyalty and prayers, but also with their responses.

In the first chapter I described the difficulties involved in collecting such responses. A correctly led circle of open and participating people is indispensable in the search for a dependable overall picture of listener reactions. In the courses for clinical pastoral education, preachers have the opportunity to examine the effect of their sermons through the help of colleagues. However, other possibilities can be found as well. A cooperative team within a church congregation, church counseling, a pastoral retreat, and homiletical work groups already offer externally the opportunity for such discussions. The prerequisites are an atmosphere of participation and openness and a properly supervised group. Otherwise either there is nothing said of any importance, or the discussion degenerates into a theoretical discussion. Reuel L. Howe, with an eye on American church communities, says the preacher should formally activate the congregation for cooperation and response concerning the sermon,[10] and he mentions two forms which have already proven successful in several congregations. First are discussion circles which regularly deal with topics important to the congregation. In this way the sermon is not the only place where the problems of life and faith are brought to consciousness, and the preacher then has a significant source of sermon material. Such groups can even collectively help the preacher prepare a sermon. Second, Howe suggests that the preacher invite a few congregation members to a post-sermon discussion from time to time, a discussion in which the preacher, however, does not participate. A tape recorder is used to record the listeners' discussion about the worship service, and the preacher later listens to this recording. Such a discussion does not require a supervisor.

In these suggestions one notices the great trust placed in the competence of the congregation members. Howe naturally does not mean that the listeners are always right in their reactions, but he does apparently trust them a great deal. The suggestions made by the European Richard Riess as aids to the preacher limit the competence—in contrast to Howe—almost exclusively to experts in the field. Riess mentions accompanying counseling, lineal investigations, an intensive practicum with individual therapeutic treatment, psychoanalytical therapy, group dynamic training and seminars, and finally dialogue sermon work in the form of pre- and post-discussions.[11] In none or few of these models is there room for listener reactions. Only a great deal of experience will show in which way the congregation and preacher can best profit. The more important question is whether the preacher is willing in the first place to submit to the listeners' responses. At any rate, preachers really wanting an echo to their work have access to several feasible models.

Everything preachers can learn from listeners, colleagues, and books would be useless if they were to forget that in spite of all their ability they basically remain "unworthy servants" (Luke 17:10). Only this faith can ease the effort and put it in the right perspective. Only the Lord himself can bring about that miracle the worshipers hope to find in church. It is not part of the task of the preacher or of homiletics. Thus a carefree relaxation stands both at the beginning and at the end of all homiletical considerations; preachers are in the final analysis not responsible. "Doesn't that make people thoughtless and wicked? No, because it's impossible for those given to Christ in true faith not to bring forth fruit and thankfulness." [16] The effect a preacher has is a very important factor in the worship service. God does not exclude it, but sometimes he outdoes it.

"You have spoken to me." Who is meant with "you"? Is it God? Is it the preacher? Both of them? Let us not put asunder what God has joined.

Notes

Chapter One

1. The limitation many sermon analyses assume by dealing only with the intellectual content of the sermon does not, by the way, necessarily mean they are without value. The analyses of Manfred Josuttis especially yield important results; it's just that the *effect* of the sermon on the listeners does not come into view in this manner. We hear only the author's subjective evaluation of printed sermons; the author cannot claim universal validity for this evaluation. Rudolf Bohren, for example, does this in *Predigtlehre* (p. 418) when he encounters expressions which he considers "emphatic." From this "emphasis" he then concludes that the preacher expresses "nothing but hopelessness." This is an impermissible universalizing of his private evaluation. It is certainly conceivable that the listeners at that time did not at all find the sermon emphatic, and that they indeed were made hopeful by it. Joachim Konrad is more cautious and himself points out that serious limitations apply to the analysis and criticism of only printed sermon texts *(Die evangelische Predigt)*.
2. Otto Haendler, *Die Predigt*. Tiefenpsychologische Grundlagen und Grundfragen. Berlin, 1960, p. 145.
3. Christian Moeller, *Von der Predigt zum Text* (Studien zur Praktischen Theologie 7), Munich, 1970, pp. 112 ff.
4. Ernst Lerle, *Homiletische Forschung zwischen Hermeneutik und Psychologie,* KuD, 12. Jg., 1966, p. 79.
5. Ernst Lerle, *Grundriss der empirischen Homiletik,* Berlin, 1975, p. 62.

Chapter Two

1. Ronald D. Laing, *The Divided Self,* New York, 1969.
2. Erik H. Erikson, *Identity, Youth, and Crisis,* New York, 1968.
3. Walter Neidhart, *Psychologische Überlegungen zur Gestaltung von Gottesdiensten für die Gegenwart,* Thpr. 5. Jg., 1970, p. 234.
4. Manfred Josuttis, *Praxis des Evangeliums zwischen Politik und Religion.* Grundprobleme der Praktischen Theologie. Munich, 1974, pp. 184 ff.
5. Karl Barth, *Homiletik.* Wesen und Vorbereitung der Predigt (ed. G. Seyfferth). Zurich, 1966 (1932/3), p. 50.

6. Karl Barth, *Church Dogmatics* II, 1, p. 507.
7. Manfred Josuttis, *Praxis des Evangeliums zwischen Politik und Religion,* pp. 91 ff.
8. Rudolf Bohren, *Predigtlehre.* Munich, 1974, p. 409.
9. Paul Watzlawick, et al, *Pragmatics of Human Communication.* New York, 1967.
10. Otto Haendler, *Die Predigt,* p. 144.
11. Manfred Mezger, *Verkündigung heute.* Elf Versuche in verständlicher Theologie (Stundenbucher 65). Hamburg, 1966, p. 49.
12. Wolfgang Hammer, *Die Sprache der Verkündigung im Prisma moderner Literatur.* In: J. Roloff (ed.), Die Predigt als Kommunikation, 11-27, Stuttgart, 1972, p. 12.
13. Gerhard Krause, *Anredeformen der christlichen Predigt.* Thpr, 2. Jg., 1967, p. 132.
14. Quoted in Albert Schadelin, *Die rechte Predigt.* Grundriss der Homiletik, Zurich, 1953, p. 66.
15. Otto Haendler, *Die Predigt,* p. 303.
16. Ernst Lerle, *Grundriss der empirischen Homiletik,* p. 65. Concerning the neccessity of extemporaneous speech see also Reuel L. Howe, *Partners in Preaching.* Clergy and Laity in Dialogue. (New York, 1967), p. 88.
17. Richard Kliem, *Die katholische Predigt.* Texte und Analysen (Sammlung Dieterich 313), Bremen, 1967, pp. 387 ff. He gives simple guides for practicing this speech-thinking, combining practical applicability with intellectual justification.
18. Marshall McLuhan, *Understanding Media: The Extensions of Man.* New York, 1964.
19. Karl Barth, *Church Dogmatics,* I, 1, p. 65.
20. Heije Faber, *Profil eines Bettlers?* Der Pfarrer im Wandel der modernen Gesellschaft. Göttingen 1976 (Meppel 1975), pp. 63 ff.
21. Yorick Spiegel, *Erinnern Wiederholen, Durcharbeiten.* Die Sozialpsychologie des Gottesdienstes, Stuttgart, 1972, p. 20.
22. Elmar Maria Lorey, *Mechanismen religiöser Information.* Kirche im Prozess der Massenkommunikation (Gesellschaft und Theologie. Abt. Praxis der Kirche 2). Munich/Mainz, 1970, p. 127.
23. Wolfgang Steck, *Die Angst vor dem Text.* Skizze einer homiletischen Erfahrung. WiuPr, 65. Jg., 1976, p. 512.
24. David Riesman, Reuel Denney, Nathan Glazer, *The Lonely Crowd.* A Study of the Changing American Character. New Haven, 1950.
25. Die Predigt, p. 236.
26. *Het verschijnsel preek.* In: Praktische Theologie, nederlands tijdschrift voor pastorale wetenschappen, 3. Jg., 1976, p. 263.

27. Martin Kriener, *Aporien der politischen Predigt*. ThEx 180, Munich, 1974, pp. 7 ff.
28. *Der Theologe zwischen Text und Predigt*, EvTh, 18. Jg., 1958, p. 296.
29. *Het verschijnsel preek*, p. 262.
30. Kornelis Heiko Miskotte, *Om het levende Woord*. Opstellen over de praktijk der exegese. Den Haag, 1948, p. 238.
31. Leonhard Fendt, *Homiletik*. 2nd ed. newly revised by Bernhard Klaus. Berlin, 1970, p. 19.
32. Karl Barth, Homiletik, p. 112.
33. Die Predigt, p. 285.
34. In Helmut Thielicke, *Vom geistlichen Reden*. Begegnung mit Spurgeon. Stuttgart, 1961, p. 278.
35. Münster, 1975, p. 133.
36. Gerhard von Rad, *Old Testament Theology*. New York, 1965, pp. 80 ff.
37. Karl Barth, *Homiletik*, pp. 99 ff.
38. Friedrich Schleiermacher, *The Christian Faith*. Edinburgh, 1928, p. 76.
39. Emil Brunner, *Das Mystik und das Wort*. Der Gegensatz zwischen moderner Religionsauffassung und christlichem Glauben dargestellt an der Theologie Schleiermachers. Tübingen, 1928, p. 385.
40. Reuel L. Howe, *Partners in Preaching*, p. 40.
41. Rudolf Bohren, *Predigtlehre*, p. 55.
42. Willem Berger, *Wat is er in godsnaam tijdens de preek gebeurd?* In: Praktische Theologie, nederlands tijdschrift voor pastorale wetenschappen, 3. Jg., 1976, p. 248.
43. Hans-Dieter Bastian, *Verfremdung und Verkündigung*. Gibt es eine theologische Informationstheorie? ThExNF 127, Munich, 1965, p. 58.
44. Hans-Eckehard Bahr, *Verkündigung als Information*. Zur öffentlichen Kommunikation in der demokratischen Gesellschaft (Konkretionen 1), Hamburg, 1968, pp. 96 ff.
45. Wolfgang Hammer, *Die Sprache der Verkündigung im Prisma moderner Literatur*. In: J. Roloff (ed.), Die Predigt als Kommunikation, Stuttgart, 1972, pp. 11 ff.

Chapter Three

1. See: Jürgen Moltmann, *Das Prinzip Hoffnung und die christliche Zuversicht*. Ein Gespräch mit Ernst Block. EvTh, 23. Jg., 1963, p. 537.
2. Jürgen Moltmann, *Theology of Hope*. New York, 1967, p. 16.
3. Cited in Kornelis Heiko Miskotte, *Om het levende Woord*, p. 305.
4. Ernst Lange, *Zur Theorie und Praxis der Predigtarbeit*. PrSt Beiheft 1, 1968, p. 31.
5. See the so-called "East Harlem model" in Clyde H. Reid, *The Empty Pul-*

pit, New York, 1967. The sermon text is discussed in various groups during the week preceding the sermon, and these discussions can be a source of ideas for the preacher.

6. Hans Adolf Oelker, *Der Hörer der Predigt.* MPTh, 53. Jg., 1964, pp. 465 ff.
7. Verfremdung und Verkündigung, p. 64.
8. Ernst Lerle, *Die Einleitung der Predigt.* Eine homiletische Untersuchung (Arbeiten zur Theologie I, 49). Stuttgart, 1972, p. 52.
9. Ernst Lange, *Zur Theorie und Praxis der Predigtarbeit.* PrSt Beiheft 1, 1968, pp. 26 ff.
10. Gerhard von Rad, *Old Testament Theology,* Vol. II. New York, 1965, p. 409.
11. Eric Berne, *Transactional Analysis in Psychotherapy.* New York, 1961, pp. 33 ff.
12. Kurt Marti, *Wie entsteht eine Predigt, Wie entsteht ein Gedicht?* Ein Vergleich mit dem Versuch einer Nutzanwendung. In: Wort und Gemeinde, Festschrift Eduard Thurneysen zum 80. Geburtstag, Zurich, 1968, p. 195.
13. Erich Berne, *Transactional Analysis in Psychotherapy,* p. 195.
14. Rudolf Bohren, *Predigtlehre,* p. 543.
15. Helmut Gollwitzer, *Zuspruch und Anspruch.* Neue Folge. Predigten aus den Jahren 1954-1968. Munich, 1968, p. 236.
16. Gerhard Kittel, *Theological Dictionary of the New Testament,* Vol. I, Grand Rapids, 1964, p. 218.
17. Reuel L. Howe, *Partners in Preaching,* p. 47.
18. Otto Haendler, *Die Predigt,* p. 214.
19. Helmuth Schreiner, *Die Verkündigung des Wortes.* Homiletik. Hamburg, 1949, p. 127.
20. Helmut Gollwitzer, *Forderungen der Freiheit.* Aufsätze und Reden zur politischen Ethik. Munich, 1964, p. 108.
21. Otto Haendler, *Die Predigt,* pp. 211 ff.
22. Rudolf Bohren, *Predigtlehre,* p. 235.
23. Manfred Josuttis, *Reden, Träume, Fragen.* Predigten aus der Zeit. Munich, 1974, pp. 158 ff.
24. Hans-Christoph Piper, *Predigtanalysen.* Kommunikation und Kommunikationsstörungen in der Predigt. Göttingen/Wien, 1976, pp. 158 ff.
25. Manfred Josuttis, *Gesetzlichkeit in der Predigt der Gegenwart* (Studien zur Praktischen Theologie 3), Munich, 1974, p. 30.
26. Ernst Lerle, *Grundriss der empirischen Homiletik,* p. 56.
27. Manfred Josuttis, *Gesetzlichkeit in der Predigt der Gegenwart,* p. 40.
28. Rudolf Bohren, *Predigtlehre,* p. 229.
29. Manfred Josuttis, *Gesetzlichkeit in der Predigt der Gegenwart,* pp. 99 ff.

30. Martin Kriener, *Aporien der politischen Predigt*, pp. 43 ff.
31. Frederick Perls, *Gestalt-Therapy in Action*, New York, 1969.

Chapter Four

1. Ernst Lange, *Zur Theorie und Praxis der Predigtarbeit*, p. 25.
2. Martin Buber, cited in Lorenz Wachinger, *Erinnern und Erzahlen*. Reden von Gott aus Erfahrung. (Spielraum 21). Munich, 1974, p. 134.
3. Lorenz Wachinger, ibid., p. 85.
4. Kornelis Heiko Miskotte, *Wenn die Götter schweigen*. Vom Sinn des Alten Testaments. Munich, 1963 (Amsterdam, 1956), pp. 69 ff.
5. Ernst Lange, *Zur Theorie und Praxis der Predigtarbeit*, p. 30.
6. Eberhard Jüngel, *Die Freude am Erzählen wiedergewinnen*. Geistliche Konzentration des kirchlichen Lebens. EvK, 9, Jg., 1976, pp. 97 ff.
7. Ernst Lerle, *Die Einleitung der Predigt*, pp. 53-60.
8. Martin Buber, cited in Johann Baptist Metz, *Kleine Apologie des Erzahlens*. Co, 9. Jg., 1973, p. 335.
9. Martin Kriener, *Aporien der politischen Predigt*, p. 36.
10. Gert Otto, *Predigt als Rede*. Über die Wechselwirkungen von Homiletik und Rhetorik (Urban Taschenbücher 628), Stuttgart, 1976, pp. 56 ff.
11. Gerhard von Rad, Old Testament Theology, Vol. II, pp. 327 ff.
12. Ibid., p. 324.
13. Otto Haendler, *Die Predigt*, p. 278.
14. Lorenz Wachinger, *Erinnern und Erzahlen*, p. 49.
15. Hannelore Frank, *Damals ist heute*. Biblische Geschichten fur unsere Zeit (Gütersloher Taschenbücher 96). Gütersloh, 1975, p. 81.
16. Ibid., p. 59.
17. Robert Leuenberger, *Berufung und Dienst*. Beitrag zu einer Theologie des evangelischen Pfarrerberufes. Zurich, 1966, p. 140.
18. Albert Schädelin, *Die rechte Predigt*, p. 62.
19. Manfred Josuttis, *Praxis des Evangeliums zwischen Politik und Religion*, p. 79.

Chapter Five

1. Fritz Rieman, *Die Persönlichkeit des Predigers aus tiefenpsychologischer Sicht*. In: R. Riess (ed.), Perspektiven der Pastoralpsychologie, Göttingen, 1974, p. 155.
2. Ibid., pp. 160 ff., 155.
3. Otto Haendler, *Die Predigt*, p. 238.
4. Richard Riess, *Zur pastoralpsychologischen Problematik des Predigers*. In: Praxis Ecclesiae. Festschrift Kurt Frör zum 65. Geburtstag, Munich, 1970, p. 313.

5. Fritz Rieman, *Die Persönlichkeit des Predigers aus tiefenpsychologischer Sicht,* pp. 163 ff.
6. Ibid., p. 158.
7. Ibid., p. 161.
8. Otto Haendler, *Die Predigt,* pp. 146 ff.
9. Manfred Josuttis, *Gesetzlichkeit in der Predigt der Gegenwart,* pp. 115 ff.
10. Gert Otto, *Predigt als Rede,* p. 58.
11. Cited by Otto Haendler, *Die Predigt,* p. 147.
12. Ernst Lerle, *Grundriss der empirischen Homiletik,* p. 76.
13. Helmut Thielicke, *Über die Angst des heutigen Theologiestudenten vor dem geistlichen Amt* (Sammlung gemeinverstandlicher Vorträge und Schriften aus dem Gebiet der Theologie und Religionsgeschichte 247). Tübingen, 1967, p. 22.
14. Reuel L. Howe, *Partners in Preaching,* pp. 92 ff.
15. Richard Riess, *Zur pastoralpsychologischen Problematik des Predigers,* pp. 314 ff.
16. Heidelberger Katechismus, *Frage und Antwort* 64.

DATE DUE

DEMCO 38-297